Dark Paradise

Edinburgh Critical Studies in Victorian Culture
Series Editor: Julian Wolfreys

Volumes available in the series:

In Lady Audley's Shadow: Mary Elizabeth Braddon and Victorian Literary Genres
Saverio Tomaiuolo

Blasted Literature: Victorian Political Fiction and the Shock of Modernism
Deaglán Ó Donghaile

William Morris and the Idea of Community: Romance, History and Propaganda, 1880–1914
Anna Vaninskaya

1895: Drama, Disaster and Disgrace in Late Victorian Britain
Nicholas Freeman

Determined Spirits: Eugenics, Heredity and Racial Regeneration in Anglo-American Spiritualist Writing, 1848–1930
Christine Ferguson

Dickens's London: Perception, Subjectivity and Phenomenal Urban Multiplicity
Julian Wolfreys

Re-Imagining the 'Dark Continent' in fin de siècle Literature
Robbie McLaughlan

Roomscape: Women Readers in the British Museum from George Eliot to Virginia Woolf
Susan David Bernstein

Women and the Railway, 1850–1915
Anna Despotopoulou

Walter Pater: Individualism and Aesthetic Philosophy
Kate Hext

London's Underground Spaces: Representing the Victorian City, 1840–1915
Haewon Hwang

Moving Images: Nineteenth-Century Reading and Screen Practices
Helen Groth

Jane Morris: The Burden of History
Wendy Parkins

Thomas Hardy's Legal Fictions
Trish Ferguson

Exploring Victorian Travel Literature: Disease, Race and Climate
Jessica Howell

Spirit Becomes Matter: The Brontës, George Eliot, Nietzsche
Henry Staten

Rudyard Kipling's Fiction: Mapping Psychic Spaces
Lizzy Welby

The Decadent Image: The Poetry of Wilde, Symons and Dowson
Kostas Boyiopoulos

British India and Victorian Literary Culture
Máire ní Fhlathúin

Anthony Trollope's Late Style: Victorian Liberalism and Literary Form
Frederik Van Dam

Dark Paradise: Pacific Islands in the Nineteenth-Century British Imagination
Jenn Fuller

Twentieth-Century Victorian: Arthur Conan Doyle and the Strand Magazine, 1891–1930
Jonathan Cranfield

The Lyric Poem and Aestheticism: Forms of Modernity
Marion Thain

Forthcoming volumes:

The Pre-Raphaelites and Orientalism
Eleonora Sasso

Her Father's Name: Gender, Theatricality and Spiritualism in Florence Marryat's Fiction
Tatiana Kontou

The Sculptural Body in Victorian Literature: Encrypted Sexualities
Patricia Pulham

Olive Schreiner and the Politics of Print Culture, 1883–1920
Clare Gill

Victorian eBook: Nineteenth-Century Literature and Electrical Technologies of Representation, 1875-1910
Verity Hunt

Dickens's Clowns: Charles Dickens, Joseph Grimaldi and the Pantomime of Life
Johnathan Buckmaster

Victorian Auto/Biography: Problems in Genre and Subject
Amber Regis

Gender, Technology and the New Woman
Lena Wånggren

Visit the Edinburgh Critical Studies in Victorian Culture web page at edinburghuniversitypress. com/series/ecve

Also Available:
Victoriographies – A Journal of Nineteenth-Century Writing, 1790–1914, edited by Julian Wolfreys
ISSN: 2044-2416
www.eupjournals.com/vic

Dark Paradise

Pacific Islands in the Nineteenth-Century British Imagination

Jenn Fuller

EDINBURGH
University Press

Edinburgh University Press is one of the leading university presses in the UK. We publish academic books and journals in our selected subject areas across the humanities and social sciences, combining cutting-edge scholarship with high editorial and production values to produce academic works of lasting importance. For more information visit our website: www.edinburghuniversitypress.com

Edinburgh University Press Ltd
The Tun – Holyrood Road
12(2f) Jackson's Entry
Edinburgh EH8 8PJ

First Published in hardback by Edinburgh University Press 2016

Typeset in 10.5/13 Sabon by
Servis Filmsetting Ltd, Stockport, Cheshire,
and printed and bound in Great Britain by
CPI Group (UK) Ltd, Croydon CR0 4YY

A CIP record for this book is available from the British Library

ISBN 978 1 4744 1384 8 (hardback)
ISBN 978 1 4744 2611 4 (paperback)
ISBN 978 1 4744 1385 5 (webready PDF)
ISBN 978 1 4744 1386 2 (epub)

Contents

Series Editor's Preface

'Victorian' is a term, at once indicative of a strongly determined concept and an often notoriously vague notion, emptied of all meaningful content by the many journalistic misconceptions that persist about the inhabitants and cultures of the British Isles and Victoria's Empire in the nineteenth century. As such, it has become a by-word for the assumption of various, often contradictory habits of thought, belief, behaviour and perceptions. Victorian studies and studies in nineteenth-century literature and culture have, from their institutional inception, questioned narrowness of presumption, pushed at the limits of the nominal definition, and have sought to question the very grounds on which the unreflective perception of the so-called Victorian has been built; and so they continue to do. Victorian and nineteenth-century studies of literature and culture maintain a breadth and diversity of interest, of focus and inquiry, in an interrogative and intellectually open-minded and challenging manner, which are equal to the exploration and inquisitiveness of its subjects. Many of the questions asked by scholars and researchers of the innumerable productions of nineteenth-century society actively put into suspension the clichés and stereotypes of 'Victorianism', whether the approach has been sustained by historical, scientific, philosophical, empirical, ideological or theoretical concerns; indeed, it would be incorrect to assume that each of these approaches to the idea of the Victorian has been, or has remained, in the main exclusive, sealed off from the interests and engagements of other approaches. A vital interdisciplinarity has been pursued and embraced, for the most part, even as there has been contest and debate amongst Victorianists, pursued with as much fervour as the affirmative exploration between different disciplines and differing epistemologies put to work in the service of reading the nineteenth century.

Edinburgh Critical Studies in Victorian Culture aims to take up both the debates and the inventive approaches and departures from convention that studies in the nineteenth century have witnessed for the last half century at least. Aiming to maintain a 'Victorian' (in the most positive sense of that motif) spirit of inquiry, the series' purpose is to continue and augment the cross-fertilisation of interdisciplinary approaches, and to offer, in addition, a number of timely and untimely revisions of Victorian literature, culture, history and identity. At the same time, the series will ask questions concerning what has been missed or improperly received, misread, or not read at all, in order to present a multi-faceted and heterogeneous kaleidoscope of representations. Drawing on the most provocative, thoughtful and original research, the series will seek to prod at the notion of the 'Victorian', and in so doing, principally through theoretically and epistemologically sophisticated close readings of the historicity of literature and culture in the nineteenth century, to offer the reader provocative insights into a world that is at once overly familiar, and irreducibly different, other and strange. Working from original sources, primary documents and recent inter-disciplinary theoretical models, Edinburgh Critical Studies in Victorian Culture seeks not simply to push at the boundaries of research in the nineteenth century, but also to inaugurate the persistent erasure and provisional, strategic redrawing of those borders.

Julian Wolfreys

Acknowledgements

My very warm thanks go to Dr Joseph Kestner for inspiring me to take this literary adventure – 'Tho' much is taken, much abides.' Dr Laura Stevens also has my praise for her advice, support and encouragement over the course of this project. I would also like to thank Dr Jennifer Airey for her help and patience as I fretted over the details of these chapters and her unflagging support from over two thousand miles away. I am grateful for the continual encouragement of my fellow colleagues, especially those who helped with advice, commentary or a listening ear to bring this book into being: David Chandler, Samantha Extance, Kristen Gravitte, Carl Nery, Lexi Stuckey, Melissa Antonucci, Karen Dutoi, Matthew Kochis, Michael Griffin and Katherine McGee. I send a special thanks to Jami Barnett who kept me motivated with her continual good cheer and our belief that this book would indeed be published someday. I am grateful to the librarians of McFarlin and Warner Libraries for their valuable assistance in gaining materials on the Pacific otherwise largely unavailable to me and for the warm friendship and support of Amy Beatty. Grateful acknowledgment is also made to several institutions for granting me the resources and support to finish this project, including The University of Tulsa for granting me a Bellwether Fellowship to create the idea which became this book, Warner University for giving this project a home during revisions and Idaho State University for supporting its final steps to publication. I also want to thank the *Victorians Institute Journal* for giving me permission to print a revised and extended version of my essay 'Of Queens and Cannibals: Visions of Leadership in R. M. Ballantyne's Pacific Works' in Chapter 2.

Closest to home, I am eternally grateful to my parents, David and Bonnie Chapman, who have believed in me even when I have doubted, and never failed to say just the right thing at the right moment. I also owe a great deal to my ginger girl, Lizzie – my profound thanks for your calm spirit in times of trouble and your silliness in times of anxiety. Finally, to my loving husband David I owe a debt I can never repay for listening to me process this information over dinner countless times without ever once falling asleep. This project would not be possible without all of you – it takes a village.

Introduction

Almost all Pacific histories, ethnographic studies and literary analyses begin by commenting that the Pacific is a very large ocean. To scholars unfamiliar with Pacific studies this seems a rather obvious observation. Why not begin by saying that the Pacific is a very wet ocean or a very blue ocean? As I conducted my own research on the islands, however, I began to understand how this seemingly obvious statement underpinned so many of the choices, both rhetorical and theoretical, that defined my work. The Pacific Ocean covers a total area of over 69 million square miles, almost one third of the earth's surface, touching multiple continents and containing a constantly changing number of islands with a highly mobile and diverse set of populations. As a result, scholars refer to the ocean's vastness by way of an apology: 'Please forgive what I cannot begin to cover; the peoples and places that my account sacrifices to present one study, one viewpoint, one glimpse into a vast and ever-changing area. The Pacific is a very large ocean.' There are so many Pacific stories to be told; I can only examine a microscopic portion of a vast network that still has many avenues that should and hopefully will be explored. By necessity, this book focuses on a very narrow vision of the Pacific as it attempts to trace the story of British literature produced in the long nineteenth century outside the colonial centres of Australia and New Zealand. By narrowing my project to focus only on the impressions of one country and time period, I unsurprisingly exclude many interesting and important perspectives that I hope future scholars will trace, and in defence of the choices I have made, I offer the following rationale: the Pacific is a very large ocean.

Despite the vast size of the Pacific, or perhaps because of it, the ocean has always been home to a unique breed of explorer. While there is a great deal of debate amongst anthropologists as to where and when the earliest travellers from the Asiatic mainland headed out into the vast ocean emptiness in search of new horizons, no one argues that such an undertaking was anything less than monumental. Settlement seems to have occurred in two phases, with the earliest explorers entering Sahul (an area which includes Australia and New Guinea) and the surrounding islands during the Pleistocene era anywhere from one hundred thousand to ten thousand years ago. A second wave of colonisation occurred in the late Holocene era between three and four thousand years ago, with people crossing the Solomon Islands and entering into the more remote islands of Oceania. These early Pacific peoples developed a surprising array of cultural, linguistic and racial differences as they adapted to the unique geographical considerations of individual islands leading to the variations, for example, between the dark-skinned hunter/gatherer natives of Australia and the lighter-skinned gardening natives of Tahiti.[1] The exact lineage and distribution of Pacific peoples is difficult to ascertain, largely because islanders continued to travel and interact with a variety of other islands and tribal peoples, creating a large network of exchange for goods, stories and relationships that lasted well into what historians have dubbed the 'contact period' with Europeans in the sixteenth century.

Until relatively recently in the timeline of Pacific history, Europeans left islanders largely undisturbed, as European and Asian trade was restricted mainly to the coast. Even after Magellan's crossing in 1521, the central islands of the Pacific were primarily ignored. Europeans sent out tentative explorations throughout the sixteenth and seventeenth centuries, but it was not until James Cook, Louis Antoine de Bougainville, William Bligh, William Dampier and Samuel Wallis (among others) mounted expeditions in the mid-eighteenth century that the smaller Pacific islands began to capture the European imagination.[2] The growing reading public devoured the journals of these explorers and their stories of 'savages' in paradise. Inspired by these narratives, missionaries and traders began their own forays into the islands and by '1780 there were few archipelagos of importance that had escaped discovery and identification. In essentials, the modern map had assumed its form.'[3]

In retrospect, the European invasion of the Pacific showcases both the unbridled power and hubris of the West during the age of imperial might and the developing empires' greatest and most profound fears. Beginning with the considerable efforts of the Portuguese and the Spanish, followed by those of the Netherlands, England and France, the Pacific became the proving ground for imperial naval power, offering a seemingly unending opportunity for colonial expansion. By the beginning of the nineteenth century, the great Western powers had laid claim to the most fertile and exploitable regions of the Pacific, the densely clustered and economically viable western islands. The Dutch, through the power of the East India

Company, would gain control of much of the Malay Archipelago, the Spanish would control the Philippines and much of Micronesia, while Britain would control Australia and New Zealand.[4] Although claims to the western islands were quickly and firmly established, the more spread out and less utilitarian eastern islands of the Pacific remained largely unclaimed by the official governments of the imperial powers.

While European powers continued to debate colonial possession of the Pacific islands, Britain largely remained aloof from island politics. The government was content to send scientific explorations, but was unwilling to settle local disputes even in the Australian colonies. As a result,

> until 1817 the Governors were left to their own devices in handling the island problem. The British Government, burdened by the Napoleonic Wars, and resenting the increase of responsibilities arising from the Australian colonies, remained almost indifferent to the mounting disorder in the South Pacific.[5]

Britain quickly found itself outpaced in the early trade boom of the nineteenth-century whaling industry as

> Cook's writings had attracted English and American whalers to the Pacific from the now-depleted whaling grounds of the Atlantic. Lasting from 1789 until the 1850s, whaling was the longest lived, largest, and most profitable of all Pacific commerce, especially in the boom years of the mid-thirties to the fifties. English whalers, who first operated out from Sidney and in Chilean waters, soon dropped out of the race.[6]

The British government never viewed the small islands of the Pacific as a viable colonial enterprise, and while

> naval commanders, especially the British, took possession in the name of their sovereign and raised their flags with considerable regularity over many islands the length and breadth of the Pacific . . . these precautionary ceremonies were never confirmed by their home governments. The British particularly were reluctant to take responsibility for distant territories of questionable use of productivity.[7]

Yet despite the official lack of interest of the British government, British authors continued to be fascinated by these 'unproductive' islands which, while limited in their commercial value, were potentially unlimited as sites for the imaginative re-envisioning of 'civilised' society.

The non-fictional accounts provided by explorers, missionaries, traders, scientists and the islanders themselves provided fuel for the growing market of adventure fiction for both children and adults throughout the nineteenth century. Islands played into a key portion of the British psyche as 'island discourses . . . represent the model cultural framework for the production of an idealised, sanitised account of European colonial history since their central impulse is to create a *tabula rasa* upon which they can erect their own story'.[8] Early and mid-nineteenth-century writers used Pacific islands specifically to contrast the idealised vision of the British coloniser (often portrayed as a 'boy hero') with the 'savagery' of the native islanders. As Roger Ebbatson and Ann Donahue argue, 'The South Pacific functioned . . . as a fictional construction upon which European repression, erotic fantasy and desire for domination was projected. But this was a paradise tainted, in the Eurocentric imagination, by the practice of cannibalism.'[9] Adventure fiction supported colonial and imperial actions in the Pacific Ocean by presenting the British as a noble 'civilising' force bringing religion and culture to the islands.

By the late nineteenth century, however, authors had begun to challenge the traditional imperial mindset that neatly separated the 'civilised' British islands from their 'savage' Pacific counterparts. The age of discovery had transformed into a politicised power struggle between European nations. Ernest Dodge explains,

> To complete Cook's work the governments of Great Britain, France, Russia, and the United States sent well-equipped scientific naval expeditions into the Pacific until as late as the 1870s. Gradually the purposes of the naval cruises changed. When it became evident that there were no more lands of consequence to discover, emphasis shifted to surveying and exploring lands already known.[10]

With island exploration largely complete, the logical next step was to bicker over possession and

> the last half of the nineteenth century almost exactly coincided with the partitioning of all the islands of the Pacific among the world powers. The progressive and continuing European impact, beginning with exploration and followed by missionaries, traders, and exploiters, culminated in some form or degree of European or American political control of every piece of South Pacific real estate, no matter how desolate or impoverished.[11]

With the veneer of genteel imperialism stripped away by growing trade clashes, British authors used the Pacific conflicts to remark on the general decline of 'civilised' British society.

Despite their fascinating history and importance in the construction of British identity throughout the nineteenth century, the smaller islands of the Pacific have not received the critical interest that the British colonies of Australia and New Zealand have garnered from scholars of nineteenth-century British literature.[12] While a few excellent literary studies of the region do exist – Rod Edmond's *Representing the*

South Pacific, Diane Loxley's *Problematic Shores: The Literature of Islands*, Neil Rennie's *Far-Fetched Facts: The Literature of Travel and the Idea of the South Seas* and Vanessa Smith's *Literary Culture of the Pacific* serve as notable examples – these studies focus on colonial experience in the Pacific through the lens of multiple nations and conflate multiple regions of the Pacific in order to provide either broad overviews of Pacific literature or to focus on a single concept, such as the role of the beachcomber. Such studies have greatly increased our knowledge of how Europeans viewed and interacted with the islands of the Pacific. The conflation of multiple European powers, however, exhibits a lack of specificity in the nuances of differing colonial policy between the various European nations and their respective areas of influence. The narrative of a Spanish plantation owner in the Philippines differs widely from that of an American whaler or, of more interest to this study, a British missionary or independent trader. Alternatively, critics gravitate towards single author studies, as is evident in the body of work contributed by Oliver Buckton, Ann Colley, Joseph Ellison, Robert Hillier and Roslyn Jolly on Robert Louis Stevenson's life and works during his residence in Samoa. Such studies provide an excellent focused look at the singular experiences of a specific British citizen in the Pacific, but they lack the scope and breadth to show the development of British attitudes towards the islands as a whole. Instead of focusing on a single concept or author, this book focuses on a single imperial power, tracing the changing attitudes and perceptions the British exhibited across the long nineteenth century in their literary depictions of these often neglected islands. Rather than dividing the 'colonisers' and the 'colonised' into two orderly groups to trace a larger theme of Pacific occupation, this study focuses on the geographic particulars of the British colonial experience.

By examining the British experience individually, I argue that a distinct narrative develops which shows the changing attitudes of Britain towards the Pacific and its larger position as a growing imperial power. British interactions with islands and islanders over the long nineteenth century challenged their assumptions about British identity and led to an increasing fear of physical and moral degeneration. I explore the evolution of South Pacific literature as it progresses from treating the islands first as heathen spaces full of 'savage' children waiting to be converted by missionaries to a haven for boyhood adventures and imperial conquest and finally to a dark hellish nightmare of regressive, degenerate adulthood.

While eighteenth-century island narratives concerned themselves with the discovery and possible exploitation of island resources, nineteenth-century narratives exhibited more interest in the islands as places for adventure, personal growth or spiritual introspection. Unlike with British holdings in Africa or India, trade in the South Pacific was a highly uncertain venture, attempted primarily by risk-takers or those in need of a second chance. It was members of the missionary societies, seeing the potential for mass conversions in the Pacific, who primarily 'settled' the islands. As the British expanded into the Pacific, however, they discovered that the islands of the South Seas could not and cannot be defined in singular terms: they are peaceful and hostile, familiar and foreign, individual and communal, populated and isolated. This ambiguity lent itself well to the emerging genre of nineteenth-century romantic adventure fiction. At the same time, the lack of a continued British presence in the islands increased tensions in the relationships between self and Other, personal and social identity. By exploring the history of trade and religion in the South Pacific, this book thus illuminates why and how British Pacific narratives shifted from a focus on exploration and critical inquiry towards an investigation of the fear of societal collapse.

I begin in Chapter 1 by analysing the works of the first British visitors to the Pacific, missionaries from the newly formed London Missionary Society (LMS). Missionaries argued that the islanders were not 'noble' savages and were in desperate need of a 'civilising' education. In order to gain financial support, missionaries constructed their accounts as both containing evidence of viable mission projects but also as providing new information about strange peoples and customs and their adventures in these new islands. The tension between the mission narrative and the adventure narrative also appears in fiction of the period, including William and Mary Godwin's English translation of Johann Wyss's *The Swiss Family Robinson*, a novel that depicts the Swiss family's negotiations between the obligation to God to settle the land and a dispassionate scientific interest in new species and experiences.

My second chapter explores the transition from the early religion-centred texts of the missionaries to a more secularised portrayal of the islands in adventure fiction. I begin by discussing the account of George Vason, an LMS missionary who 'went native' and lived amongst the islanders, as this account serves as a transition point between earlier fiction focused primarily on conversion narrative and mid-century fiction recording exciting experiences primarily for the enjoyment of the home audience. The emerging genre of 'boy's' fiction reflected this new focus on entertainment rather than moral edification, particularly in the works of Frederick Marryat and R. M. Ballantyne, which primarily act as imperial propaganda for the growing empire. Marryat deliberately rewrites *The Swiss Family Robinson* in his novel *Masterman Ready* both to offer a more 'authentic' representation of British trade and to showcase how boys could best serve the growing empire. R. M. Ballantyne's first Pacific novel, *The Coral Island*, also showcases boys as 'men of empire' but, through the character of Bloody Bill, warns against the dangerous implications of Pacific trade. In his later works, *Gascoyne, the Sandal-wood Trader* and *The Island Queen*, Ballantyne explores other alternatives for the future of the British presence in the Pacific, transforming pirates into productive traders and evaluating the effect of female leadership on the masculine tradition of Pacific fiction.

While 'boy's books' depicted the Pacific islands primarily as potential colonies, authors throughout the nineteenth century became increasingly interested in the islands as places for discovery as well. Intrigued by the descriptions of hitherto unknown species, Victorian naturalists joined Pacific journeys to study these new flora and fauna. My third chapter follows a young Charles Darwin and Thomas Henry Huxley as they board ships into the unknown and develop theories that would challenge the assumed boundaries between 'civilised' and 'savage' man. By examining their often overlooked travel narratives, *The Voyage of the Beagle* and *The Voyage of H.M.S. Rattlesnake* respectively, I argue we see a glimpse not only into growing theories on evolution and natural selection, but also early biological and anthropological observations that contemplated whether Pacific islanders were truly so different from British ones. While traders and missionaries painted an optimistic portrait of Pacific settlement, scientists began to undermine such assumptions and even posit that all men had the potential for savagery. These radical new ideas, spurred on by later works such as *Origin of the Species* and *The Descent of Man*, influenced novelists to use the Pacific islands as a testing ground for new theories of regressive evolution. Capitalising on the emerging genre of 'science fiction', H. G. Wells imagined the Pacific in *The Island of Doctor Moreau* not as an idyllic paradise but a horrific nightmare that reduced all islanders, whether British or native, into their most bestial forms.

Late nineteenth-century authors presented a growing vision that the British Empire was not inherently superior to, or even that different from, the Pacific islands. In my fourth chapter, I turn my focus to British settlers in the Pacific whose attempts to create ideal colonies reveal the weaknesses inherent in the British concept of themselves as the 'superior' civilising force. After Robert Louis Stevenson moved to the tiny island of Upolu in Samoa his interest in Pacific peoples and politics grew exponentially. In his *Vailima Letters* and *The Beach of Falesá*, Stevenson questions the right of the British to colonise or settle in the South Seas as part of a 'civilising mission'. By examining the effects of the invasive settler, explorer or trader on the island landscape, Stevenson linked the islanders and the islands, presenting the potential dangers of the 'disease' and violence of European invasion. I also examine Joseph Conrad's later Pacific works *Freya of the Seven Isles* and 'Because of the Dollars'. While Stevenson focused largely on the interactions between British and Pacific islanders, Conrad instead looked at how life in the Pacific impacted British individuals. I argue that Conrad's work reflects an increasingly dark vision of British settlement in the Pacific, one that depicts British men and women as weak and degenerate. In Conrad's fiction, men are corrupted by obsession with trade in the islands of the Malay Archipelago, while the women and islands they claim are helpless to prevent their downfall and quickly tainted by association, rendering all worthless.

My final chapter looks at the works of Pacific islanders that were published and circulated by the British press. While influenced and edited by the British, the stories of Lee Boo, Ta'unga and Queen Emma provide a small glimpse into how Pacific peoples viewed the British and how the British, in turn, conceived of islanders. Popularised through the mid-century by the children's book *The History of Prince Lee Boo*, Lee Boo's journey to England is originally conceived of as a way to teach children 'civilised' behaviour. Instead, Lee Boo subverts the categories of 'noble savage' and 'savage islander', proving instead a complex individual with the best interests of his home at heart. A missionary to New Caledonia, Ta'unga is one of the few translated Polynesian writers of the nineteenth century. His writings seek to balance the need to preserve his Polynesian heritage with the desire to convert the islanders to Christ. Finally the story of Queen Emma, as told through largely through the Australian press, shows an islander who resists traditional definitions. A Samoan-American woman, Emma created one of the largest and most powerful trading empires in New Guinea, and all the Western Pacific, defying cultural constructions of weak or subservient island women. Her fame rested largely on her business acumen and her ability to flout the social codes of nineteenth-century society and still prove immensely successful.

If the small islands of the Pacific had emerged in the British imagination at the beginning of the nineteenth century as potential colonies in a paradisial setting, by the end of the century they had transformed into dangerous and destructive spaces that reveal growing British fears of imperial and moral decay on the eve of World War I. While early missionaries and traders held out hope that the islands would quickly be converted to Christ and prove valuable commercial allies, such dreams were already being challenged by mid-century. As scientists began to undermine the theories of British cultural superiority and settlers began to see no easy way to navigate relationships between whites and islanders, the hopeful vision of a colonial paradise quickly faded into a much darker reality. As the islanders themselves showed, the Pacific defied easy definitions and instead proved a complicated challenge that redefined British identity in entirely new way.

Notes

1. For a more complete look at the prehistory of the Pacific islands, I turn to my colleagues in anthropology, archaeology and history. While an exhaustive list is far beyond the limits of this study, some representative examples of work in Pacific prehistory include Craib, 'Micronesian Prehistory'; Friedlaender, *Genes, Language, & Culture History in the Southwest Pacific*; Kirch, *Island Societies*; Kirch, 'Peopling of the Pacific; Kirch and Kahn, 'Advances in Polynesian Prehistory'; Kirch and Weisler, 'Archaeology in the Pacific Islands'; Lilley, *Archaeology of Oceania*; Matisoo-Smith et al., 'Origins and Dispersals of Pacific Peoples'; Nunn, *Climate, Environment, and Society in the Pacific during the Last Millennium*; Scarr, *A History of the Pacific Islands*; Thomas, 'The Precontact Period'.
2. Eighteenth-century scholars have produced a wide variety of monographs on the Pacific islands during the 'age of exploration'. See, for example, Aravamudan, *Tropicopolitans*; Bolyanatz, *Pacific Romanticism*; Guest, *Empire, Barbarism, and Civilization*; Howse, *The Background to Discovery*; Lamb, *Preserving the Self in the South Seas*; Lincoln, *Science and Exploration*; Nussbaum, *Torrid Zones*; Smith, *Intimate Strangers*; Wilson, *The Island Race*.
3. Beaglehole, *The Exploration of the Pacific*.
4. Writing a detailed history of the European conquest of the Pacific, even without acknowledging the history of the native islanders, has proven a daunting task for historians. Reviewers consider many attempts, such as Campbell's, Oliver's and Ward's too Eurocentric. While more modern histories, such as those by Howe, Thomas and Scarr have attempted to incorporate new theories and interpretations, these new histories also suffer from the challenges inherent in providing so many perspectives. See Campbell, *A History of the Pacific Islands*; Howe, *Where the Waves Fall*; Oliver, *The Pacific Islands*; Scarr, *A History of the Pacific Islands*; Thomas, *Islanders: The Pacific in the Age of Empire*; Ward, *British Policy in the South Pacific*.
5. Ward, *British Policy in the South Pacific*, 33.
6. Howe, *Where the Waves Fall*, 93.
7. Dodge, *Islands and Empires*.
8. Loxley, *Problematic Shores*, 102.
9. Ebbatson and Donahue, *An Imaginary England*, 141.
10. Dodge, *Islands and Empires*, 102–3.
11. Ibid., 183.
12. Discussions of Pacific islands are also largely absent from postcolonial theory, presumably because Britain was reluctant to officially colonise islands (though they often created 'protectorates' and undoubtedly

influenced the islands through imperial policies). Recent scholars have taken up Australia and New Zealand for postcolonial analysis and the rest of the Pacific is likely to produce productive readings as well. See Crane, *Myths of Wilderness in Contemporary Narratives*; Huggan, *Australian Literature*; Keown, *Pacific Islands Writing*; McCusker and Soares, *Islanded Identities*; Ravenscroft, *The Postcolonial Eye*.

Chapter 1

Moving Missions and Novel Settlements: Early British Pacific Propaganda (1796–1866)

Introduction

It was a strange little ship that sailed down the Thames on 10 August 1796. Instead of gruff shouts or a strain or two of a rough shanty, the passengers of the *Duff* sang hymns as they headed out to sea. A later account of the event by George Cousins[1] records a confused man-of-war asking, '"What ship is that?" "The *Duff*" "Whither bound?" "Otahetie." "What cargo?" "Missionaries and provisions." Missionaries and provisions! What could they be? Such a cargo had never been heard of before.'[2] While Cousins's account is a bit histrionic, the voyage of the *Duff* in many ways represented a landmark moment for the British. One of the first large-scale foreign missionary efforts,[3] the voyage featured men, women and children drawn largely from the working class and with little evangelical training. Their efforts primarily met with failure, as the missionaries were ill-equipped to deal with the people and political realities of Tahiti, Tonga and the Marquesas. Undaunted by these initial failures, however, the LMS persisted in its efforts, sending more and better trained missionaries to the small islands of the South Pacific. These outreaches eventually proved successful, both in converting islanders to Christianity and in enlarging the British presence in the Pacific. The historical reality of forays of the LMS missionaries would in turn shape the future of British adventure fiction. The excitement of finding and taming this Pacific paradise, brought to public attention by missionary narratives, would inspire novelists to create their own versions of the Pacific experience and shape the initial view of the Pacific islands for British readers.

Non-fictional narratives of the early Pacific were predominantly missionary accounts that sought to depict the British as helpful, productive Christians suffering for God in a frightening hostile environment, but fictional accounts of Pacific adventures that investigated similar themes were also beginning to gain in popularity. When William and Mary Godwin[4] published a translation of Johann Wyss's *Swiss Family Robinson* in 1814, the British public devoured the text.[5] The translation was widely adapted by British authors throughout the nineteenth century and became an example of the 'contact' literature Mary Louise Pratt identifies when she writes that Europe was constructing its identity 'from the outside in, out of materials infiltrated, donated, absorbed, appropriated, and imposed from contact zones all over the planet'.[6] Instead of viewing the story as a German text, the British adapted the story to support their imperial mission, eventually rewriting the novel to support British control over the original Swiss colony connecting to what Christopher Prendergast, drawing on Franco Moretti, has called the 'the "narrative markets" in the nineteenth century, an import/export trade carried out largely on the back of translations'.[7]

Wyss's novel draws strongly on the narrative of Robinson Crusoe when describing the lives and adventures of his castaways but moves the popular shipwreck story to the Pacific islands. Like the missionary narratives, *The Swiss Family Robinson* seeks to explain the proper way to engage with and develop these newly explored territories. Both the missionaries and the character of Father – otherwise unnamed – advocate for strong leadership, hard work and devotion to God, all of which will transform the landscape, and by extension the people, into productive servants of the empire and protect them from physical danger and moral vice. With its investment in the politics of New Guinea, however, *The Swiss Family Robinson* has a more vested interest than missionary accounts in 'settler' rhetoric which emphasises developing the islands as potential trading partners or even colonies. While missionaries primarily depicted the islands as sites for conversions, fictional accounts focused more on the economic possibilities of new island settlements. In this chapter, I argue that both the missionary narratives and the fictional story *The Swiss Family Robinson* created two distinct and often overlapping visions of the Pacific enterprises: one depicting travellers to the Pacific as noble adventurers, observing and recording exciting new experiences to benefit the social and moral development of island peoples, and the other as commercial agents funding missions and expanding productive trade interests in the Pacific. While different in their goals for the new islands, both missionaries and adventurers believed that these island paradises provided new and exciting possibilities for British settlement.

The Swiss Family Robinson: Early Pacific Fiction

The departure of the civilising missionaries at the turn of the century ignited the imagination authors of fictional stories as to the fate of these new forays into the unknown islands.[8] One of the earliest Pacific novels to capture the British imagination was written not by an Englishman, but by a Swiss pastor seeking to educate his sons. Two years after its 1812 publication in Zurich, Johann Wyss's *Der Schweizerische Robinson*[9] would be translated into English by philosophers William and Mary Godwin and become an overnight success. The novel would subsequently be liberally re-translated throughout the nineteenth century, with famous children's author William H. G. Kingston finally producing in 1889 the novel's most famous and enduring English adaptation.[10] Through its long and varied publication history, the novel slowly evolved from its original Swiss roots providing an exemplary model for the British narrative of Pacific expansion. Examining *The Swiss Family Robinson* as more than a pleasant novel for children thus reveals a growing British interest in the possibilities of colonial development in the Pacific islands.

While explorers such as Cook and Bougainville and Wallis had provoked popular interest in the islands of the Pacific, their narratives had not had an equal influence over official policy. As historian Ernest S. Dodge explains,

> Following the spectacular voyages and discoveries of Cook there was an opportunity to make the entire Pacific British. Britain did not avail herself of it. There was no gold, no commercial value ... British governmental policy toward the islands was nonexistent and the attitude of Parliament and officials alike almost uniformly one of indifference.[11]

Due to the British government's non-committal attitude toward Pacific expansion, the smaller islands of the Pacific were left open to independent missionaries and imperial explorers. The preface to the 1816 edition of *The Swiss Family Robinson* makes the conflict between these two dominant groups in the Pacific, missionary and explorer, abundantly clear. Father is a pastor or clergyman who, after misfortunes, sailed with his family to England,

> where he accepted an appointment of missionary to Otaheite [Tahiti]; not that he had any desire to take up his abode in that island, but that he had conceived the plan of passing from thence to Port Jackson [Australia], and domiciliating himself there as a free settler.[12]

He is quite literally caught between two worlds, the missionary project currently happening in Tahiti and the colonising efforts of the early

British settlements in Australia. Shipwrecking its castaways before they reach either island, *The Swiss Family Robinson* is therefore able to investigate Father's motivations as both founder of a religious family and as the keeper/cataloguer of a vast uncharted island.

The shipwreck maroons the family not in the previously explored islands of Tahiti or Australia but off the coast of the mysterious island of New Guinea. In 1816, the east coast of New Guinea was still largely unexplored, and while several explorers had sailed past the large island, few had ventured beyond its beaches. Even the great Pacific explorer Captain Cook was attacked by natives when he attempted to approach the island from the east, and he quickly abandoned any scheme of adventuring further inland.[13] John Seeyle has noted the importance of the map accompanying the 1816 edition of the novel, which displays only half of an island with unexplored land stretching eastward. While Seeyle argues that this map shows that the 'island' in fact functions more as a peninsula,[14] more likely such unexplored land is not an ideological choice but a simple fact of geography. While British Lieutenant and trader John Hayes did establish one private settlement at Dorei Bay in 1793, a lack of governmental assistance, coupled with the wars between the British and the Dutch, ruined the fledgling settlement's chances and left the viability of New Guinea as a colonial prospect open to debate.[15] Throughout its early history, then, New Guinea retained an aura of mystery and danger well suited to Wyss's tale and one which resonated with a British audience interested in colonial expansion. While the family in *The Swiss Family Robinson* never faces any serious threat to its health in this early edition, the fear of savages and dangerous animals is never far from each character's mind. Wyss's narrative is the first to explore the fictional possibilities of a flourishing settlement in New Guinea, yet while it resonated with expanding Pacific interests, the novel was also interested in providing a moral education as well as a colonial prospect.

The Island as Laboratory: Education and Civilisation

The Swiss Family Robinson explicitly states its intention to serve as an educational text for children, explaining in detail how to civilise a savage land. The first line of the preface indicates that the novel functions both morally and scientifically as an instructional guide for children. Father is an expert on native species, and 'the island [becomes] a metaphor for the classroom or the learning laboratory, a tableau vivant in which, like Adam in the Garden of Eden, the human beings have a lot of practice in taxonomy'.[16] Like Adam, Father spends a great deal of time cataloguing the native species that he might instruct his sons Fritz, Jack, Francis and Ernest. Upon seeing a bird, for example, Father asks his sons to observe each of its characteristics and match the description to one in a natural history book. Father explains,

> You now then perceive, my son, of what use it is to read, and to extend our knowledge, particularly on subjects of natural history and the productions of nature in general; by this study and knowledge, we are enabled to recognise at the moment, the objects which chance throws in our way, whether we have seen them before or not.[17]

The text argues both that adults should venerate and explore science themselves and that teaching children to do so is a valuable, worthy occupation. It is only by evaluating and understanding the flora and fauna around them that the children (under the guidance of their father) are able safely to transform the native environment into a flourishing settlement.

While *The Swiss Family Robinson* is concerned with the proper education of children, these educational passages are provided as much for the benefit for the reading audience as for the fictional sons. On one hand, the mythical New Guinea of the text is populated with an impressive array of newly discovered species. On the island, the family encounters not only animals native to other parts of the Pacific (usually Australia), but also a margary, a porcupine, flamingos, penguins, jackals and buffalos, none of which actually inhabit New Guinea. While the inclusion of such animals enlivens the text and contributes to the exoticism of the island, such descriptions also educate the curious domestic reader about foreign animals. The 1816 text included multiple explanatory notes to supplement Father's extensive knowledge of plants, minerals and creatures. When the family discovers the flamingos, for instance, the text includes a lengthy citation in a footnote attributed to the *Nouveau Dictionnarie d'Histoire Naturelle* describing the bird's attributes, behaviours, and habitats.[18] Thus the purpose of Wyss's text is twofold: to develop and explain theories of children's education and to educate the growing reading public about the exotic and exciting flora and fauna rapidly being discovered, especially in the Pacific.

Father's descriptions also serve another purpose: to reveal the fertility of the Pacific and propose that the unknown or unexplored islands may be desirable as possible settlements. In 1816, Britain had yet to define fully its colonial policy toward the Pacific, and the overarching attitude towards the islands was one of curiosity and potential, an interest fuelled by narratives like *The Swiss Family*. The sheer abundance of creatures is remarkable; as literary critic J. Hillis Miller has rightly observed, 'Wyss's

"New Switzerland" is an Edenic world of profusion, of plenitude. It is a world swarming with things to be shot, tamed, or eaten, or farmed and then eaten, if you are clever enough to know how to do so.'[19] The family's ability to utilise the profusion Miller aptly describes shows its superiority to the creatures of the island, and its ability to control and profit from these creatures represents inherently an act of control. The text thus functions as a narrative of civilisation, in which the island space teems with goods waiting to be consumed or appropriated by those with the skills to control them.

The need to 'civilise' the island begins the moment the castaways land upon the deserted beach. The Swiss family has the good fortune to be shipwrecked with every imaginable shipboard item, from munitions and fishing rods to saws, hammers and hatchets. The family members have many of the same civilising impulses as early missionaries, such as the desire to build a house. House-building would develop as a staple of missionary fiction, becoming almost synonymous with the progression from savagery to civilisation. Unsurprisingly, then, the family finds itself building not one dwelling, but two. The family's famous tree house is inspired more by the beauty of the landscape than by the need for safety. Father remarks,

> I felt I could never tire of beholding and admiring this enchanting spot; it occurred to me, that if we could but contrive a kind of tent that could be fixed in one of the trees, we might safely come and make our abode here.[20]

The family focuses on the civilising benefits of dwellings, on the ways in which having a comfortable, secure and well-decorated dwelling place adds to the sense of comfort and ease necessary for a truly domesticated settlement.

While house-building is one of the earliest signs of the family's domestication, it is quick to find new uses for all of the island's products, especially when it comes to procuring various household goods. Father and his sons are constantly explaining the ways in which mysterious or unknown island products can be re-purposed and transformed into useful everyday items. Father is quick to note, for instance, that they can carve gourds into 'various utensils . . . plates, dishes, basons, flasks'.[21] While such items are helpful, they are unnecessary except insofar as they help maintain a sense of civilisation and decorum. The island teems with these sorts of luxury items, allowing the family to create everything from a suit of porcupine mail for their dogs, to beeswax candles, a tortoise shell washtub and coconut liqueur. It is *The Swiss Family Robinson* which first provides a lengthy description of coconuts, their various uses, and their convenience as both a food and a beverage, all of which later become a staple of Pacific fiction and non-fiction alike. The members of the Swiss family find both necessities and luxuries simply by exploring the island and employing imagination. The family's ability to domesticate its environment also extends to its interactions with the various creatures on the island. During their stay, the family captures and quickly tames a monkey, a flamingo, a bustard, a parrot, a buffalo, a falcon, a jackal and an onagra or wild ass. While a few of the animals, such as the monkey and the parrot, serve as entertainment, most are employed in assisting the family's efforts at hunting and gathering. The family members are indefatigable civilisers, able to tame the birds of the air and the beasts of the land, as well as carve a home out of raw material and stock it with every imaginable convenience, creating the indelible fantasy for the domestic reader of the unconquerable coloniser.

'The Promised Land': The Island as Conduit to God

While the novel positions the family members as incredible survivors, it is quick to remind the reading audience that the family has been granted the gifts of a lively menagerie and continually expanding settlement only so long as they remain stewards of the larger kingdom of God, connecting the text to concerns which appear in works by early missionaries. Father's pastoral background corresponds directly with the family's growing need to civilise the wilderness. *The Swiss Family Robinson* positions Father as the voice of authority, yet it is only through his sons' occasional rebellions and missteps that he is able to illustrate fully the appropriate relationship between Father and his sons, and by extension, between God and his children. By enabling an unquestionable Father to correct the doubts and worries of his sons, the novel emphasises that hard work and obedience to will of the Father – both earthly and divine – rather than individual discovery and introspection produce a successful settlement.

The religious underpinnings of *The Swiss Family Robinson* are almost inseparable from the focus on work and improvement. Upon first landing on the island, Father celebrates the providence of the family's escape while insisting on the need for a great deal of work. He remarks, 'My dear ones, we must now trust to our own exertions. Let us be willing to help ourselves, and we shall obtain support from Heaven. Let us never forget this useful maxim, and let each labour according to his strength.'[22] Later he adds, 'We, now, my best beloved, with the assistance of heaven, must enter upon the work of our deliverance.'[23] The family does not develop the island because it is exceptionally harsh or hostile, but because doing so is God's commandment and because work is essential to the family's moral, not just physical, salvation.

Unsurprisingly then, the family appropriates Biblical terminology to explain and understand its work on the island. As Father explains to his sons:

> My dear children, we are here in this desert island, in just such a situation as that of our first parents when they were driven out of the garden of Eden; it was still in their power to enjoy happiness in the fertile land in which God permitted them to live; and this happiness was to proceed from their obedience, from the work of their hands, and the sweat of their brow.[24]

The family envisions its island as a 'fertile land' that needs the civilising influence of a paternal eye and unquestioning obedience to the Heavenly 'Father' to develop into a productive settlement. The family names one section of the island 'The Promised Land', indicating the island's function as a place of promise and testing, and Father warns his sons that their only hope of dwelling in peace and prosperity is to follow his commandments and the commandments of the heavenly Father.[25] During the family's first Sabbath on the island, Father instructs his sons with a lengthy parable. He speaks of a Great King who maintained

> an uninhabited island of considerable extent; it was his wish to people and cultivate this island, for all within it was a kind of chaos; he destined it to be for some years the abode of such future citizens as he intended to receive finally into his residence, to which only such of his subjects were admitted, as had rendered themselves worthy by their conduct. This island was called Earthly Abode; he who should have passed some time in it, and by his virtues, his application to labour, and the cultivation of the land, should have rendered himself worthy of reward, was afterwards to be received into the Heavenly City, and made one of its happy inhabitants.[26]

With this parable, he explains the religious reasoning behind his expectations for his family. For Father, the island represents a microcosm of the Protestant experience, in which hard work and virtuous living could please God and thus secure one's place in heaven. Of course, underpinning this sermon is also a rather clear social imperative that the 'uninhabited' islands of the Pacific need only citizens of God to transform them into cultivated lands worthy of the Great King. This message was especially salient to the British reading public which, unlike the original Swiss audience, was confronting the possibility of continued expansion in the Pacific, from the colonial efforts in Australia and New Zealand to the LMS's labours in Polynesia.[27] Thus the parable (and the overall story) urges the parent country not just to view the islands as potential colonies or settlements but also to recognise that such islands serve as educational resources and moral testing grounds. This language balancing a 'settler' rhetoric with a 'civilising' mission would drive much of the exploration and early settlement of the British Pacific.

The boys quickly learn Father's lessons and yearn to improve their new home. On the morning of the first Sabbath, the sons actually beg, 'Let us go to work again to-day: What is there to do? What will you give each of us to do?'[28] Although the Sabbath is meant to be a day of rest, Father quickly creates projects for his energetic sons. There are houses to be built and animals to be tamed; a continual supply of work is necessary just to maintain the community. The family spends time not just in exploration and education, but also in basic maintenance, checking on livestock and hunting for food. None of these activities seems particularly challenging, but the family sees each as equally rewarding.[29] Thus the Swiss family members view work not just as a necessity for survival (though it is), but as a communal practice that unites them with each other and with God.

Law and Order: Controlling the Island

While *The Swiss Family Robinson* seems to embrace an idyllic view of the perfect family living in communal harmony, it is abundantly clear that the unquestioned and unchallenged acceptance of Father's pronouncements makes this happiness possible. Father's authority is absolute, and he requires perfect obedience to ensure that the settlement runs smoothly. It is perhaps unsurprising that the text's firm stand on leadership and patriarchy resonated with the British reading public considering Britain's uncertain involvement in the Pacific which depended largely on the prowess of the growing English navy. Victorians linked British military might with a patriarchal hierarchy of authority as well as concepts of duty and honour in the service of the king or queen or their appointed leaders. An unquestionable authority is a hallmark, for example, of Cook's *Journals*; to protect his expedition from undue violence Cook often asserts his influence both over his crew and over the various islanders he encounters.[30] The question of who would eventually become the unquestioned authority of the island territories – the home government, the settlers, the missionaries or the traders – would occasion a great deal of debate both at home and in the Pacific.[31] As critic Diana Loxley points out,

> Central to the *Swiss Family Robinson* . . . is the question of authority, or of the establishment of a colonial law and order, and if there is shown to be one

supreme duty of governors towards the governed, it is to make sure that they are *governable*.[32]

While the original text is concerned with the running of one specific island, the popularity of the English translation of the novel reflects growing British interest in the governability of all the newly discovered island territories.

The Swiss family's Pacific island cannot therefore be fully separated from the British audience, also living on an island, for whom the Godwins' translation was intended. The novel suggests that if Father can govern his sons on an uncivilised island full of distractions, then surely by following his lead via hard work and communal living, the British can apply his lessons and produce civilised children on their own island. The family's continued successes reinforce Father's authority. As Loxley argues,

> The overwhelming image of male firmness is governed by his constantly administering to his sons the educational, moral and religious responsibilities of fatherhood in an historical context in which the family is exalted as the ideal and natural unit. It is within this context that the distinctions between public and private, home and work are acted out even against the fearsome strangeness of an alien territory which properly separates the family unit from the real material conditions, the economic and political environment of European capitalism, under which it would normally thrive and for which it was constructed.[33]

While Wyss's work showcases the ways in which proper male authority produces civilisation out of savagery, clearly the secondary lesson for the British islanders is that a similar system would be easy to implement at home. The education of children follows the same basic principles whether at home or abroad.

With all of this productivity both of land and family, it seems that the narrative has created the perfect settlement, in which work and nature combine to produce a comfortable, civilised living for a British citizen in the Pacific. Of course, much of this idyllic progress is made possible by the fact that the family faces no threat to its island home; creatures are usually non-hostile or tamable,[34] and there are no inhabitants either on their island or close enough to visit, a noteworthy omission.[35] The family members in *The Swiss Family Robinson* themselves are very aware of the possibility of invasion, however, even in their idyllic state. Upon first surveying the island, Father praises the Divine Being that they 'encountered no venomous or ferocious animals; and as far as our sight could yet reach, we were not threatened by the approach of savages'.[36] Despite visual confirmation that their island (or at least the part they inhabit) is free of savages, the fear of invasion lingers in their minds.

Ernest is thrilled with Father's idea that they make a barrier of thorns, stating,

> Ah, papa, do let us make such a hedge round our tree; we shall then have no further occasion to light fires to preserve us from wild beasts, or even from the savages, who from one day to another may arrive in their canoes, as they did on Robinson Crusoe's Island.[37]

Ernest's allusion to Crusoe is not just an authorial nod to a source of inspiration; it also serves to remind the readership about the most unpredictable aspect of savages: their mobility.

Despite the fear of invasion, the family is able to spend most of its time on the island happily occupied. In fact, the only time the Swiss family is forced to confront its fears is upon hearing unusual sounds. On one occasion, the men hear a sound which reminds Father 'of music played by savages' but which turns out to be only a bird striking its wings against a tree trunk.[38] On another, the men hear 'at a distance two strange peculiar kinds of voices, which resembled the howlings of wild beasts, mixed with the hissings and sounds of some creature at its last gasp'.[39] Each of the sons has a different theory as to what has caused the unusual sounds. Jack hopes that they are made by lions so he may see one of the majestic beasts, Fritz presumes jackals, Ernest guesses hyenas and young Francis believes 'they are savages come to eat their prisoners on our island; I wish we could save them, and get a good *Man Friday* as Robinson Crusoe did'.[40] The sons' interpretations present a glimpse into the predominant thinking about savages in the British worldview. As the sons implicitly reveal, the music or language of savages is easily confused with that of ferocious beasts, and if the savages are to leave their homes, it must surely be to cannibalise prisoners. Father does not contradict these fears and assumptions directly; instead he tells his boys, 'Let us not yield to fear or imagination; we are in safety here.'[41] While the text draws its fears of natives from the emphasis on cannibalism in the Crusoe story, it argues that fear should be tempered by investigation and proof. Father's rational guidance proves yet again to be sound as the family discovers that the noise was only the brays of Grizzle the donkey.

The erasure of a native presence on the family's island serves to illuminate discourses on and fears of savages and savagery. By excising natives and native culture, *The Swiss Family Robinson* constructs an island that cannot challenge the civilising authority of the Swiss family. Diane Loxley explains:

> What is effaced is precisely the significance of the history and culture of the territory's fictionally removed original inhabitants. What is maintained,

perhaps more crucially, is a subversion of the terrifying image of a European 'imitation' of non-European civilisation. The island is finally safely sterilised from contamination by a potentially more effective counter-culture, is made, in the end—as all these fictional islands inevitably are—to resemble home, with all the comforting effects of European luxury and sophistication.[42]

By erasing the 'original inhabitants', Father and his family become free to mould the island in their own images without any resistance or hesitation from hostile natives or from the British government. This erasure also allowed British readers to maintain the colonial fantasy of productive imperial commerce without focusing on its morally repugnant aspects, such as the recently closed Atlantic slave trade.[43] By the end of the text, it is clear that despite differences in scenery, the island resembles Britain in all ways that matter, from religious conviction to a properly outfitted domicile.

Uncertain Endings: The Fate of the Swiss Family Robinson

The Swiss Family Robinson concludes with the family comfortably settled on its island home with only a wistful hope of returning to its parent country. While the story is unquestionably episodic, the end seems surprisingly sudden, as if the narrative could have continued indefinitely. Father ends his narrative by describing the luxury of both the family's house and its newly built chapel. He seems completely contented in his self-created settlement, noting, 'We passed our days in a course of industry, innocent pleasures, and reciprocal affection.'[44] Still, despite their gratitude and contentment the family's fate seems uncertain, as Father is hopeful that he will once again meet with the outside world. He 'trust[s] in the same goodness for restoring us once more to the society of our fellow-men, or for bestowing upon us the means of founding in this desert a happy and flourishing colony of human beings'.[45] Father proves an anomaly in shipwreck fiction where victims usually return home.[46]

As Wyss's novel ends on an uncertain note, it fell to the Godwins' addendum, an original postscript, to reveal the fate of our lonely settlers. In Wyss's version, the introduction explains that the story was only 'found' through the happy accident of the Swiss Counsellor Horner accidently landing on an uncharted island near the coast of New Guinea and recovering the journal from the family. The Godwins, however, seemed unsatisfied with this version of events and attached a postscript to the text, transforming both the vessel and its crew from Russians into Englishmen (the discrepancy between the added postscript and Wyss's introduction apparently did not bother the Godwins).[47] While Wyss's introduction does not indicate the fate of the Swiss family, the Godwins' postscript explains that a terrible tempest prevented the ship from returning to the island the evening of the discovery, and the Captain was forced to put to sea, keeping him from rescuing and returning the family to Europe. As editor John Seeyle notes, after 1824 the Godwins' postscript, with its English crew as saviours, would replace Wyss's original introduction until an English translation of the 1848 French sequel was published by the Baroness de Montolieu.[48] The Godwins' early translation thus gestures to the uncertainty of the fate of British exploration in the Pacific. While the Godwins seem optimistic that these islands are waiting to serve as new miniature settlements, it is equally possible that such a project is too uncontrollable and destined to be lost. After all, there are no women on the island besides Mother. Without direct intervention, or a very lucky shipwreck, the colony cannot survive and pass on its lessons to another generation. Thus the Godwins' ending serves both as an instruction manual on how to create an island civilisation and as a subtle warning against the dangers of leaving such societies unsupported. *The Swiss Family Robinson* raised new questions as to the fate of the Pacific settlements when the missionaries and adventurers returned home.

The Story Continued:
William Kingston's Translation and its Legacy

While the Godwins' family may have been left marooned on the island with its fate uncertain, the fate of the novel was far clearer. Like its predecessor *Robinson Crusoe*, *The Swiss Family Robinson* was continually retranslated, reproduced, adapted and transformed throughout its long history. According to Martin Green's book *The Robinson Crusoe Story*, approximately three hundred English editions of *The Swiss Family Robinson* were released throughout the nineteenth and twentieth centuries.[49] However, despite the wide variety of editions, by far the most lasting, and the most likely to be encountered today, was William H. G. Kingston's translation of 1889. Kingston's later edition contains several significant variations from the Godwins' earlier edition, most notably at the end of the text, and these changes reveal not only the evolution of British thought about New Guinea, but also the changing philosophy towards wider Pacific expansion.

Such changes are apparent from the beginning of the text. Both Wyss's Preface and Introduction are omitted in Kingston's edition of *The Swiss*

Family Robinson, transforming an Enlightenment treatise on the proper education of children into an adventure story championing the boys and men of the British Empire. By eliminating the Preface, Kingston's translation loses the history of the Swiss family and their motivations. Rather than telling the story of a Swiss pastor dreaming of establishing a new settlement, the novel champions a group of valiant adventurers determined to survive for the glory of God and country. These shifts, while subtle, reflect the impulse to remove the 'distracting' elements of the story, those which seem outdated or outmoded.

The more significant changes in Kingston's translation occur in the additional chapters appended to the end of the novel, including the Swiss family's new fate. The introduction in the final chapters of the character of Miss Jenny Montrose, 'the daughter of a British officer who had served for many years in India, where she herself was born' is perhaps the most shocking change.[50] Like the Swiss family, Jenny is the victim of a shipwreck forced to survive alone in the wilds of the island. Jenny's influence begins transforming the family's identity from Swiss to English. It is Jenny who teaches the family to speak English through the long winter, and 'amongst us the usual feeling of weariness and discontent never appeared; the English language was quickly acquired by all hands, Fritz, in particular, speaking it so well that Jenny declared she could scarcely believe he was not an Englishman'.[51] Jenny does not only bring the English language to the Swiss family; she is also responsible for its transformation from a lonely Swiss outpost to a possible English colony.

With the coming of the spring, an English 'brig-of-war' visits the isolated island searching for the lost Jenny. Unlike in the Godwins' translation where the family is left marooned, Kingston allows the family an opportunity to leave New Switzerland and return to Europe. While Mother and Father choose to stay on the island, Fritz and Franz decide to return with the captain, Fritz to remain with Jenny and Franz to attend school. Ernest remains behind to continue studying the island's scientific phenomena and Jack as well, who wants to be a perpetual adventurer. While the Godwins' translation shows the boys in many ways as very similar, by the time of Kingston's they have evolved into individual specimens of the British boyhood and masculinity essential to adventure fiction, with Ernest as the scientist, Jack the explorer, Fritz the dashing ladies' man and Franz the curious scholar.

The family's future is not the only thing to change at the end Kingston's translation, so is the 'ownership' of the island. While the family still refers to the island as New Switzerland, Mother is quick to tell her sons that they must endeavour to send out emigrants of a good class to join us, and form a prosperous colony, adding . . . the island ought to continue to bear the name of our native country, even if inhabited in future time by colonists from England, as well as from Switzerland.[52]

Father is even more convinced of the superiority of the English sailors, soon after Mother's speech, 'consulting with Captain Littlestone on the subject of placing the island under the protection of Great Britain'.[53] While the novel ends with an homage to New Switzerland, Kingston has clearly transferred all but symbolic control of the island to the British state.

While Kingston added these nationalising impulses in part to play to his British audience, they also reflect the changing policies towards New Guinea and the rest of the Pacific. In the 1870s and 80s, gold was discovered in New Guinea adding to its already rich supply of trade goods like *bêach-de-mer* and pearl. Both the west and east coasts of the island proved exceedingly useful as stop-over points for traders. Thus, while Britain had increased its presence in the Pacific throughout the 1870s, it would officially claim southeast New Guinea as a colony in 1888.[54] Despite diplomatic arrangements, the borders of British New Guinea were still being contested by Germany, while western New Guinea was still controlled by the Dutch. Needless to say, Kingston's translation unsurprisingly champions Britain's claims to New Guinea, and by extension all profitable islands of the Pacific.

Long considered only an amusing tale for children, *The Swiss Family Robinson* provides an exceptional glance over its long history at the construction of British identity in the Pacific. The Godwins' early success with their 1814 translation shows the burgeoning interest of the British reading public in the Pacific as a wild, seemingly unexplored place for adventure and discovery. The Godwins' family stands in for all possible English colonial ventures in the Pacific, where obedience to a righteous authority produces a model of civilisation. The novel shows New Guinea, and by extension other Pacific islands, as paradises full of viable products that only need the hand of a colonial presence to tame and civilise them. Kingston's 1889 translation, by contrast, shows the evolution of colonial thought as Britain established greater control over its Pacific holdings. This newer translation affirmed the unquestioned belief in British right at the end of the nineteenth century as supreme ruler of all current and potential imperial holdings, turning an obscure philosophical German novel into an astonishingly popular and power piece of British imperial propaganda.

John Williams and John Campbell: Early Experiences of the London Missionary Society

While *The Swiss Family Robinson* remained the quintessential fictional narrative of the Pacific throughout the early nineteenth century, a tale revived in many translations and variations throughout the century, the curious reading public also sought out and devoured non-fictional travel writings produced by missionaries. In many ways, missionary accounts echo the themes and concerns represented by the *Swiss Family*'s Father. The first missionaries who journeyed to Polynesia on the *Duff* in 1796 encountered far greater hardships than those faced by Father and his family.[55] For example, missionaries reported thievery and were often threatened by the very real possibility of attack. Unprepared for such a reception, more than half of the missionaries abandoned the project in March 1798, when a passing ship offered them passage to Sydney. While the remaining missionaries enjoyed limited success, building a chapel and several schools, everything changed when the chief of Tahiti, Pomare, declared war on his rival tribes in 1808. Caught between the warring factions, several missionaries fled while others, upon Pomare's defeat, either fled to Eimeo and escaped or were killed by the natives.

Despite these misfortunes, the LMS persisted in its efforts to convert the peoples of Polynesia, sending a new group of missionaries back to Tahiti in 1812.While earlier attempts at Christianising the natives had ended in failure, this second attempt proved more fruitful. The missionaries successfully converted Pomare, rebuilt their schools and chapel, worked on 'improving' native living conditions, and translated the native language into English. By the time of missionary John Williams's visit in 1817,[56] the missions in Tahiti were growing in both strength and support. Williams's account of his trip to the islands, *A Narrative of Missionary Enterprises in the South Sea Islands*,[57] was one of the first and most widely read of the published missionary narratives. Williams's text functioned primarily as propaganda, working to raise money and support for missionary efforts; as Rod Edmond summarises, 'Williams saw the capture and recovery of lost souls as a commercial enterprise.'[58] However, it also functioned as a rather interesting piece of travel writing as well, as Williams's full title, *Remarks upon the Natural History of the Islands, Origin, Languages, Traditions, and Usages of the Inhabitants*, suggests. Implicit in the full title is Williams's desire to build a 'civilised' race of islanders even as he seeks to explain and explore the natural state of the islands and their peoples.

Williams was clearly unnerved by the many depictions of violence in Cook's *Journals*[59] and unsure of the reception his voyage will find among the natives. The British had decided to focus on the milder and paler-skinned natives of the eastern islands as prime candidates for conversion rather than the darker-skinned peoples of the western islands, considered overtly hostile.[60] As he explains, the missionaries' landing

> will, no doubt, be attended with much danger, as some of the inhabitants are cannibals of the worst character; others of ferocious habits and cruel practices, using poisoned arrows, and poisoning the very food they bring to sell, and even the water which is taken from their shores; whilst others are mild in their manner, and kind in their treatment of strangers. The adventurous trader, however, braves all these dangers: and shall the devoted Missionary of the Cross, whose object infinitely surpasses in importance that of the merchant, and who professes to be influenced by motives of a higher order, be afraid to face them?[61]

While Williams cannot help but be fearful having read of Cook's dangerous interactions with cannibals, his narrative shows that he sees this hostility as a sign of savagery, a correctable vice brought on by the lack of civilisation and 'proper' religion. Unlike Cook, who merely records these incidents, Williams feels a need to right this savagery, presenting himself as a settler who will transform the people through religion and 'civilisation'.

Williams's plea for righteous missionaries to brave the dangers of heathen islanders also addresses the other primary Western influence on Pacific natives, the equally 'savage' traders. From the mid-1700s to the 1830s, the East India Company maintained a trade monopoly over much of the Pacific. Historian John M. Ward explains that

> legally, the commerce of the South Pacific could be developed only as the requirements of the penal colony in New South Wales necessitated and as the Company, whose main interest was the protection of its inner citadel, the Chinese market, chose to permit.[62]

Unwilling to challenge the powerful company, the British government limited its direct trade interests in the Pacific to its colonies in Australia and New Zealand. Thus private merchants operating with limited governmental control conducted the vast majority of trade in the eastern regions of the Pacific. According to K. R. Howe's history of the South Seas, the writings of Cook

> had attracted English and American whalers to the Pacific from the now-depleted whaling grounds of the Atlantic. Lasting from 1789 until the 1850s, whaling was the longest lived, largest, and most profitable of all Pacific commerce, especially in the boom years of the mid-thirties to the fifties.[63]

Early whalers used the Polynesian islands as refuelling stations, exerting a less than righteous influence upon the native peoples. Missionaries like

Williams thus worked hard to combat the power of these traders and turn the natives toward God and more 'civilised' culture.

Although Williams is opposed to traders, he does recognise the importance of trade as he believed that presenting the islands as valuable to the trade economy might encourage support for his project from the government and investors. Williams argues that in order for the islands to contribute to the British economy, they must not only be self-sustaining but also produce useful goods. As is the case with the Swiss family, local missionaries spent a great deal of time cultivating the land for both native and imported products. Williams champions this work, noting, 'In reference to the islands generally, it may be observed, that the blessings conveyed to them by Christianity have not been simply of a spiritual character; but that civilization and commerce have invariably followed in her train', specifically in the case of the 'arts, the animals, and the vegetable productions.'[64] Like in *The Swiss Family Robinson*, Williams presents the islands as almost unending storehouses of products that would benefit Britain. He explains:

> I firmly believe that, in a few years, cargoes of coffee, as well as of arrow-root, cocoa-nut oil, and sugar will be shipped by our converts at the Missionary stations in the South Sea Islands. Ought not a great and mighty nation like England, with the generosity which is allied to true greatness, to put forth her hand, and help her infant offspring, who has been raised from barbarism, and brought into national existence, by the benevolent efforts of her own subjects.[65]

For Williams, the missionary works to save the souls of the natives, but also helps to expand the nation of England, aiding in its great mission to convert islanders into productive citizens of empire.

Despite clear indications that Williams thinks of himself in some sense as an agent of empire, he is quick to point out that he has no official governmental authority. Williams states,

> And here, in answer to the charge that the Missionaries in the South Seas have assumed even regal authority, I may observe, that no Missionary in the Pacific ever possessed any such authority; that his influence is entirely of a moral character.[66]

Despite being aware of their lack of position as sanctioned agents of the government, at least early in the project, many missionaries still believed they were extending the ideas and customs of the empire abroad. Neil Gunson notes,

> The very early missionaries and directors possibly saw the 'South Sea Mission' as an extension of the British *imperium*. Dr Haweis [an outspoken

founder of the LMS], at least, informed Henry Dundas, the Home Secretary, that the missionaries represented 'an English incipient Colony, and ever Benefit resulting from Civilization we hope to introduce must ultimately terminate in Britain'.[67]

Even though the British government generally ignored the Polynesian islands,

> missionaries generally behaved as if colonial status was imminent or even already in place – indeed, in many places, they introduced the signs and institutions of a colony regardless of the intentions of the imperial nation. In some ways, missionaries operated as founding settlers of a potential Pacific colony.[68]

Thus missionaries like Williams found themselves in the interesting predicament of presenting themselves as colonisers while lacking the support and protection of their parent country. As later missionaries came to realise that the ambitious plans to transform the small islands into miniature colonies were doomed to failure, largely because of the lack of success in producing trade goods on a large scale, they turned their attention away from the idea of colonial enterprise and focused instead on the civilising aspects of their missions.

Earlier depictions of the islands, such as Denis Diderot's popular *Supplement to Bougainville's 'Voyage'*, argued that the islands followed the 'law of nature' and thus their peoples were perfect stand-ins for the noble savage in the eighteenth-century imagination.[69] While initially challenged by Cook's writing, this peaceful ideal was finally shattered by the end of the century. While contemporary audiences found the narrative of John Williams with its descriptions of exotic places and peoples inherently intriguing, a great deal of its popularity accrued after Williams's 1839 murder in Melanesia. This murder, combined with that of Cook in 1779 and the mutiny on the *HMS Bounty* in 1789, created a sense of menace around the Pacific islands. Far from the paradise depicted by Enlightenment authors, the reality that the Pacific islands were dangerous and unpredictable began to develop in the nation's consciousness. According to Sivasundaram,

> The religious public already thought of the islands in Edenic terms, and so an event as momentous as the death of a missionary hero produced questions about the status of the landscape and the sinfulness of the islanders. Brutal acts such as the murder of a messenger of the gospel would have no place in heaven where nature would be perfect.[70]

Nineteenth-century missionary narratives began to alter British thought; rather than simply viewing Polynesia as an idyllic colonial prospect, dedicated men and women needed to bring civilisation to the hostile heathens of the islands and welcome them into the fold of Christ. Missionaries would increasingly link this project with the potential for great but perilous adventure.

Although Williams first journeyed to the Pacific in 1817, he continued to live and travel there until his death in 1839. In the late 1830s, he published the first and only major narrative of his adventures. While reports from the Pacific missionaries appeared in the papers of the LMS, the bound volumes only began appearing in the late 1830s and 1840s after the marked success of Williams's account. By capitalising on the martyring of Williams, LMS missionaries hoped to garner further support for their lengthy and dangerous efforts. John Campbell,[71] primarily known for his missionary work in Africa, published in 1840 just such a 'companion' to the works of John Williams. Throughout his account, Campbell works to establish a view of missionaries as peaceful and friendly to the islanders. In his introduction, he notes that unlike other British imperial missions,

> in Polynesia . . . conquest and thralldom were not the first step to illumination and conversion! The soldier and the Missionary were not mess-mates! Gunpowder and the gospels were not carried in the same packet! The alternative of proselytism was not the gibbet![72]

Campbell sets the missionaries apart not only from savage violence, but also from the colonial projects in Australia and New Zealand. In the Pacific, missionaries were defined by their ability to civilise the natives without resorting to force of arms. This focus on pacifism, while theologically motivated, also had very real historical underpinnings as well. Having established its colonies in Australia and New Zealand, Britain remained firm in its refusal to commit itself to any further colonial activity in the Pacific. According to historian Ernest S. Dodge:

> By right of discovery in the third quarter of the eighteenth century the British could have claimed more islands in the Pacific than any other power. Following the spectacular voyages and discoveries of Cook there was an opportunity to make the entire Pacific British. Britain did not avail herself of it. There was no gold, no commercial value—only natives. The English Protestant missionaries could have further solidified British claims had they been made, but raising the Union Jack over an island meant little to the home government. British governmental policy toward the islands was nonexistent and the attitude of Parliament and officials alike almost uniformly one of indifference.[73]

Without the support of the British government or its powerful navy, missionaries were essentially marooned on these uncharted islands, left to their own devices to carve out a new civilisation. Rather than serving as an impediment, however, this solitude actually aided the missionaries' goals by removing any problematic influences from the natives. Missionaries began to embrace an idea of themselves as heroic adventurers working to bring native peoples to Christ in the face of harsh conditions and adversity.

As Campbell's narrative shows, the missionaries embraced their solitude in a way very similar to the fictional character of Father in *The Swiss Family Robinson*, and actually tried to avoid outside influences on the natives, either from wandering traders or missionaries of other faiths. Increasingly, missionaries relied on isolation to assist their work to effect change. According to Jane Samson, missionaries began to treat other whites,

> whether the sporadic spawning of beachcombing settlements or the planned settlement of traders and entrepreneurs, [as] an evil to be avoided, an inimical influence in the shaping of a Christian society. Whereas, over previous centuries, missionaries had taken for granted the protection and continued presence of the imperial authority, the missionaries of the Pacific discovered a new freedom in asserting the rights of indigenous governments against the representatives of the imperial powers.[74]

Isolated with the natives, missionaries found a greater need to understand them, their ways and habits, in order to glean the necessary information for successful conversion. While critics such as Peter J. Kitson and Tim Fulford have argued of Tahiti that 'missionaries were not the enlightened natural philosophers like those who sailed with Cook, but instead determined servants of their Lord who had little ethnological respect for the cultures of others', many missionaries were in fact deeply concerned with recording and understanding the actions and customs of the native islanders.[75] Many missionary narratives, including Campbell's, act as early anthropological or historical surveys of the various islands. In one sense, missionaries included this information for the same reason Cook did, to inform a curious reading public. These facts also took on new life, however:

> when the Evangelical missionary investigated the mythology, traditions and customs of the islanders his aim was twofold. He sought to learn more about the peoples amongst whom he was living, mainly so that he would be better equipped to overthrow 'the system of false gods'. He also hoped that his work would add to man's knowledge of the world.[76]

The missionaries acted as impartial scientific observers to suit their unique purposes, applying the interest in recording natural history and behaviours to their Evangelical mission.

Missionaries also began transforming the 'settler' narrative, the isolated family whose spiritual piety transforms the natives and the land into a productive colony, to suit their changing mindset. Settlements based only on the production or transportation of goods and their propagators quickly became the enemies of missionary discourse. Campbell's description of a Swedish captain who settled in Tahiti and resembles the island 'savage' far more than the 'English gentleman', is a typical example of such discourse:

> His tastes and habits were those of a man by birth a savage. The indolent life which he had led at Otaheite, the facility with which all his sensual appetites had there been gratified, the aversion which he felt to honest industry, and the necessity of labour in the event of returning to Europe, these conditions constrained him to prefer the society of savages, combined with all its attendant privations. Perhaps, too, he felt what all men feel, a pleasure in superiority— and such a feeling is always easily and abundantly gratified among hordes of naked men.[77]

Instead of championing the idea of superiority towards and subjugation of native peoples, Campbell and other missionaries instead focus on the importance of proper settlement, of labouring to control the land and civilise the people, much like Father in *The Swiss Family Robinson*.

William Ellis: A New Perspective

While John Williams's and John Campbell's narratives are primarily concerned with laying out the importance of the missionary enterprise and separating it from other British interests or colonial concerns, fellow missionary William Ellis's narrative extended beyond the boundaries of the traditional conversion story.[78] In 1833, William Ellis offered a different but equally influential perspective on the early missions by publishing his work, *Polynesian Researches*.[79] Spanning two volumes, Ellis's work is memorable for its emphasis not on the conversion of individual islands or tribes which makes up the majority of Williams's text, but on recording in great detail the workings of the mission along with the detailed lives and customs of the islanders. As in *The Swiss Family Robinson*, Ellis's stories consist mostly of episodic relations of individual events or encounters related for the education of a mostly ignorant reading public. Ellis emphasises interesting cultural discoveries, not just native conversions, and justifies this interest by connecting it back to the missionaries' goal of civilising the islanders.

In his introduction, Ellis quickly acknowledges his debt to Captain Cook and other explorers:

the descriptions already given to the public, of the loveliness of their general appearance, and the peculiar character and engaging manners of their Inhabitants, have excited a strong desire to obtain additional information relative to the varied natural phenomena of the Islands themselves; the early history; the moral, intellectual and physical character of the people, and the nature of their ancient institutions.[80]

Ellis's interest was genuine; Neil Gunson explains,

The missionaries were conscious of the interest value of Polynesian history and culture. They recorded it merely to add to the sum of human knowledge and they did good work in this field, but in art this material had to serve some higher end.[81]

Like Cook, Ellis portrays himself as a scientific observer, but unlike Cook, whose scientific explorations were funded by the Royal Society and the Royal Navy, Ellis has to justify his scientific information to a mission-orientated readership. Thus Ellis declares native religion and culture the antitheses of progress. He explains, 'whether invested with the gorgeous trappings of a cumbrous and imposing superstition, or appearing in the naked and repulsive deformity of rude idolatry, [polytheism] is alike unfriendly to intellectual improvement, moral purity, individual happiness, social order, and national prosperity'.[82] In opposition to the 'savagery' which Ellis records in great detail, he also reports the 'results of the Missionary enterprise, which, during the last thirty years, has, under the Divine blessing, transformed the barbarous, cruel, indolent, and idolatrous inhabitants of Tahiti, and the neighbouring Islands, into a comparatively civilized, humane, industrious, and Christian people'.[83] By comparing what he sees as natives' prior savagery with their current civility, Ellis produces a detailed and thorough study focused primarily on the customs and culture of the people, not just their conversions.

In the opening chapters of his narrative, Ellis's text establishes both the natives' potential for savagery and the importance of the missionaries' influence to prevent hostile actions. In a memorable episode, a group of natives in Rapa[84] storm the ship and carry off anything they believe to be of use. Ellis fears for his four-month-old daughter and worries,

Had the child been on deck, and had my attention been for a moment diverted, even though I had been standing by the side of the nurse, there is every reason to believe that the motives which induced them to seize the boys on the deck, and even the dog in his kennel, would have prompted them to have grasped the child in her nurse's lap or arms, and to have leaped with her into the sea before we could have been aware of their design.[85]

Despite the danger he faced, Ellis uses this adventure to proclaim the importance of the missionary efforts which had recently expanded from Tahiti to Rapa. As Ellis explains,

> To reclaim the inhabitants from error and superstition, to impart to them the truths of revelation, to improve their present condition, and direct them to future blessedness, were the ends at which they [the missionaries] aimed; and here they commenced those labours which some of them have continued unto the present time.[86]

Ellis's narrative differs from Williams's more traditional conversion narrative because he provides and emphasises scenes of attack and escape that rival the excitement of early adventure fiction. By integrating such scenes into the Evangelical project and its goals, Ellis accentuates the precarious situation of South Seas missionaries and the need for further support to prevent acts of violence.

Upon reaching the islands, Ellis, like the explorers before him, finds himself overwhelmed by the paradise he encounters. Ellis explains,

> The effect of the scenery through which I have passed, and the unbroken stillness which has pervaded the whole, that imagination, unrestrained, might easily have induced the delusion, that we were walking on enchanted ground, or passing over fairy lands. It has at such seasons appeared as if we had been carried back to the primitive ages of the world.[87]

While Ellis maintains the feeling of enchantment which pervades earlier descriptions of the island, he also points out that this paradise is highly primitive and mystical, in need of the guiding hand of a superior culture. The focus on the island's beauty was especially salient in the Pacific where the British feared that physical beauty was intimately connected with moral lassitude. As Patrick Brantlinger has argued, 'In Haweis's estimation, the main danger facing missionaries in Polynesia would be sexual temptation rather than violence.'[88] For Hawais and Ellis, the Pacific islands were postlapsarian Edens full of mythic beauty hiding deadly temptation.

Like the Swiss family, Ellis is surprised by the sheer profusion of growth on the islands:

> The islands are certainly well stocked with all that the natives need for subsistence, in greater abundance than is, perhaps, to be found in any other part of the world, and, with a very small degree of care and industry, the inhabitants may, at all seasons, secure whatever is necessary to their comfortable maintenance.[89]

It is precisely this abundance, however, which greatly concerns him. The islands do seem to be a paradise where 'man seemed to live only for enjoyment, and appeared to have been placed in circumstances, where every desire was satisfied, and where it might be imagined that even the apprehension of want was a thing unknown'.[90] Ellis, however, sees this satisfaction as the islanders' primary downfall. He relates:

> All classes were alike insensible to the gratification arising from mental improvement, and ignorant of all the enjoyments of social and domestic life, the comforts of home, and the refinements and conveniences which arts and labour add to the bestowments of Providence . . . Their wants were few, and their desires limited to the means of mere animal existence and enjoyment; these were supplied without much anxiety or effort, and possessing these, they were satisfied.[91]

The islanders are the ideological opposite of the 'godly mechanics' and their Puritan work-ethic which treated labour as an essential conduit to God. Ellis clearly believes that idle hands are the devil's workshop and explains that the islanders' indolence

> was the parent of many of their crimes, infant-murder not excepted, and was also a perpetual source of much of their misery. The warmth of the climate, the spontaneous abundance with which the earth and the sea furnished, not merely the necessaries of life, but what was to the inhabitants the means of luxurious indulgence, had, no doubt, strengthened their natural love of ease, and nurtured those habits of excessive indolence in which they passed the greater portion of their lives.[92]

One of the missionaries' most challenging tasks in the Pacific was to turn this 'natural indolence', fostered in the British imagination by accounts like those of Cook and Bougainville, into productive Christian labour, mirroring, likely without knowing it, the actions of Wyss's Father.

To combat 'indolence', missionaries focused on two projects: the building of houses and gardens, both seen as essential steps in the movement towards a more civilised society. Ellis is quick to explain that

> although all were capable of building good native houses, and many erected comfortable dwellings, yet great numbers, from indolence or want of tools, reared only temporary and wretched huts, as unsightly in the midst of the beautiful landscape, as they were unwholesome and comfortless to their abject inhabitants.[93]

The missionaries, with their specific skill sets, encouraged the islanders to adopt the more English idea of a proper dwelling.[94] As is the case for the Swiss family, proper habitation is a top priority for the establishment of a workable settlement. Ellis notes that the missionaries

> recommended each family to build distinct and comfortable cottages for themselves, and the chiefs to partition bed-rooms in their present dwellings, in which they must reside while building others; even in these we recommended them to reduce the number of their inmates, and to erect distinct sleeping rooms for those they retained.[95]

While houses remain a stalwart gauge of the progress of a people, Pacific missionaries also emphasised the importance of gardens. While the aboriginal peoples of Australia were primarily hunter-gatherers, the peoples of Polynesia did engage in gardening, primarily growing breadfruit, pandanus (a fruit bearing tree), taro (an edible tuber) and arrowroot.[96] Ellis recognises the role that these gardens played in Polynesian society, explaining,

> A garden is a valuable acquisition in this part of the world; and, next to our dwellings, we regarded it as an important part of our domestic establishment. As soon as the sites of our houses were fixed, we employed natives to enclose a piece of ground adjoining them.[97]

Sujit Sivasundaram explains that while the island had its share of available goods,

> with Christianisation the population would grow and spread over all the vast wilderness of nature, improving, experimenting and making nature even more productive. Nature would no longer produce fruits and food which would be interred in the ground; the environment would support an industrious Christian population.[98]

While the islanders did garden to support their personal needs, they did not utilise a European system of agriculture that followed seasonal patterns or produced a wide variety of crops. Following in a long tradition begun in the seventeenth century, then, the missionaries began to emphasise the need to expand agriculture efforts in the islands, both in production and variety. As Ellis records,

> Anxious to increase the resources of the islands, those who had arrived in the Royal Admiral had brought with them a variety of useful seeds, with plants of the vine, fig, and the peach-tree, from Port Jackson, which were planted in the Mission garden. Many of the seeds grew, and the vegetables produced added a pleasing variety to the indigenous productions of the country.[99]

While large-scale European-style plantations were never particularly viable on the smaller islands of the Pacific, gardens became an important crossover point for the missionary project as they worked to adapt traditional practices to their ideas of British culture.

The emphasis on agricultural development was not, however, limited merely to the mission garden. Settlers and missionaries alike examined the possibility of developing Western style agriculture in the Pacific. Ellis is very aware of the limited commercial realities of Tahiti and similar islands, noting:

> None of the spontaneous productions of the islands were available for the purposes of barter or exportation. The sandal-wood of the Sandwich Islands,

and the pine-timber of New Zealand, produced without effort on the part of the inhabitants, being valuable commodities, and given in exchange for the articles conveyed by foreign vessels to their shores, afforded great inducements to commercial adventure, and furnished the natives of those countries with facilities for increasing their resources and their comforts, of which the Tahitians were destitute. Whatever articles of export they could ever expect to furnish, must be the product of their own industry.[100]

While Ellis and the missionaries would establish a moderately successful textile trade, the islands would never rival any major colony for exports. Thus one of the greatest challenges for the settlers of the Pacific was to justify British support for islands which could not produce a large quantity of useful goods. The coconut and breadfruit are the only native goods that Ellis spends a great deal of time describing and promoting. Ellis explains,

> It is impossible to contemplate either the bread-fruit or cocoa-nut tree, in their giant and spontaneous growth, their majestic appearance, the value and abundance of their fruit, and the varied purposes to which they are subservient, without admiring the wisdom and benevolence of the Creator, and his distinguishing kindness towards the inhabitants of these interesting islands.[101]

Coconuts became the symbol of human resourcefulness amidst a seemingly barren landscape and featured prominently in adventure fiction as well. For those clever enough to know how to use it, the coconut tree provided food, drink, building materials and, later in the century, a valuable trade good, copra. While the British government dismissed the small islands of Polynesia as poor investments, missionaries and private traders saw them as places of opportunity.

Ellis's account also features another common adventure staple of both Pacific fiction and non-fiction: the shark attack. Shark attacks remained a constant fear and occasionally a reality for the missionaries and natives of the Pacific. Ellis's primary encounter with a shark occurs when he is

> in a boat on a voyage to Borabora . . . a ravenous shark approaching the boat, seized the blade of one of the oars, and being detached from that, darted at the keel of the boat, which he attempted to bite . . . We were climbing up on the seats out of his way, but the natives, giving him two or three blows on the nose with a small wooden mallet, quieted him, and then cut off his head.[102]

While Ellis's account could be considered melodramatic, he later points out the realities of such attacks for the islanders. As he records:

> Many of their relatives or countrymen had been devoured by sharks; a limb or large portion of the fleshy part of the body of others, had been destroyed by these savage fish. A constant attendant on these meetings at Afareaitu[103]

had, while we resided there, one side of his face torn off, and eaten by one. The sharks, that had eaten men, were perhaps afterwards caught, and became food for the natives, who might themselves be devoured by other sharks.[104]

Ellis also points out the importance of sharks to Polynesian religion, noting,

> Tuaraatai and Ruahatu, however, appear to have been the principal marine deities . . . They were generally called akua mao, or shark gods; not that the shark was itself the god, but the natives supposed the marine gods employed the sharks as agents of their vengeance, in punishing transgressors.[105]

For Ellis, the shark, like the coconut, is essential as a staple of both Pacific culture and religion. If coconuts represent the potential worth of island goods, the shark serves as a reminder that such possibilities come at a high price, the threat of stealthy and unseen danger.

Ellis also connects shark attacks with what the British presented as one of the most prevalent Pacific vices, cannibalism.[106] According to Ellis,

> Cannibalism, though some deny its having been practiced among themselves, is supposed to have existed in one of the islands at least, and is known, and universally acknowledged to prevail among those by which they are surrounded . . . The men who had eaten their fellow-men, might, and perhaps often were, (as many of the cannibals inhabit the low coralline islands, and live by fishing,) eaten by sharks, which would sometimes be caught and eaten by the inhabitants of distant islands.[107]

These sorts of convoluted explanations add to the confusing belief that while there were certainly cannibals on the islands (at least according to generally held knowledge) descriptions of the practice were almost always gleaned from second-hand sources and included to emphasise the savagery of the natives. Ellis takes his account from an interview with a converted priest. His lengthy description includes the following:

> He [the victim] was usually murdered on the spot—his body placed in a long basket of cocoa-nut leaves, and carried to the temple. Here it was offered, not by consuming it with fire, but by placing it before the idol. The priest, in dedicating it, took out one of the eyes, placed it on a plantain leaf, and handed it to the king, who raised it to his mouth as if desirous to eat it, but passed it to one of the priests or attendants, stationed near him for the purpose of receiving it . . . when the ceremony was over, the body was wrapped in the basket of cocoa-nut leaves, and frequently deposited on the branches of an adjacent tree, After remaining a considerable time, it was taken down, and the bones buried beneath the rude pavement of the marae.[108]

As is the case with many Western depictions of cannibalism, it is difficult to discern the difference between real cultural practice in the

Polynesian islands and morbid or fantastic stories.[109] Either way, Ellis's depictions of fascinating and unusual cultural practices would become stock motifs in both the non-fiction and the fiction of the South Seas, contributing the idea that the islands were a threatening place for the unprepared.

While Ellis cannot help but be intrigued by the 'savagery' he sees around him, his narrative concludes with the firm establishment of the missionary settlements as civilised outposts where savage traditions have been abandoned for a new set of religious beliefs. Ellis notes the new social relationships that substituted indolence for activity and divided men and women into more 'appropriate' gender spheres:

> In former times the men were often cruel in their treatment of the women, and considered them as their slaves; but the husbands now treat their wives with respect, and often cherish for them the most sincere affection. The female character is elevated in society; the husbands perform the labours of the plantation or the fishery, recognizing it as their duty to provide the means of subsistence for the family; while the preparation of their food, (especially where the European mode of living has been adopted by them,) together with the attention to the children, and the making of clothing, native or foreign, for themselves and the other members of the family, is now considered the proper department of the females.[110]

According to Ellis, the men are finally acting like men, providing for their families through the sweat of their brow, while women act like women, caring for household needs. As the natives have now discovered the joys of productive labour, the small settlement has unsurprisingly grown as well. Ellis reports,

> Instead of a few rustic huts, a fine town, two miles in length, now spread itself along the margin of the bay . . . nearly four hundred white, plastered, native cottages appeared, some on the margin of the sea, others enclosed in neat and well-cultivated gardens . . . prominent above the rest was seen their spacious chapel.[111]

Of course, Ellis's deft positioning of the chapel hovering over the newly developed city is far from accidental. Despite situating himself primarily as a reporter of culture and custom, Ellis is still aware of the need to justify his project to a very mission-conscience audience. Thus his narrative ends by connecting religion with social progress:

> The same individuals, who on the former occasion had appeared uncivilized and almost unclothed islanders, now stood in crowds upon the beach, arrayed in decent apparel . . . while, beyond the settlement their plantations and their gardens adorned the mountain's side. These were but indications of a greater change among the people. All were professing Christians.[112]

Ellis attempts to balance himself between the 'explorer' and the 'settler' narratives, wanting to report disinterestedly the exciting and exotic peoples he discovers, but also aware of the need both to explain and to justify the civilising project of creating houses and gardens that funded the journey in the first place. Ellis achieved great success and popularity. Rod Edmond notes, 'Ellis' text did much to revise the widely held view of missionaries as ignorant and narrow-minded, and became probably the most important source of information about Polynesian cultures in the first half of the nineteenth century.'[113] While Ellis's goal may have been to argue for native progress, he also did much to illustrate the progress both of missionary ideology and its goals.

Civilising the Islands: The Narrative of Reverend Aaron Buzzacott

Ellis was not alone in transforming the missionary narrative from simply presenting a litany of successful conversions to envisioning the missionaries as adventurers taming a hostile land in order to garner continued funding. Reverend Aaron Buzzacott's narrative of his time as a missionary in Rarotonga and other Polynesian islands from 1828 to 1857 provides a glimpse both into missionaries' views of the island itself and into their various attempts to create civilisation out of untamed wilderness.[114] Published in 1866 after Buzzacott's death, the narrative shows the increasing trend among such narratives to describe more of the day to day life of the missionaries, their adventures as it were, rather than simply provide a litany of island chiefs converting to the faith. Buzzacott's introduction presents the missionaries among all the travellers in the Pacific the most able to record the true history of the islands. Unlike early missionary narratives, which focus on the missionaries' primary goal of saving souls, Buzzacott broadens the definition of missionary usefulness. He explains:

> The missionary combines characteristics not often found in combination. He is necessarily a traveller, and often in remote and unfamiliar countries; of which he is sometimes the discoverer and explorer. He is, moreover, a resident, and has peculiar opportunities for becoming acquainted with things which the mere traveller either sees cursorily or does not see at all. Missionaries, therefore, have contributed very largely to our knowledge of new countries and races of men, and to various departments of science.[115]

These later mission narratives argued that mission histories provide a wider view of the world to a curious audience.

That later missionaries emphasise the 'explorer' narrative does not mean, however, that they have completely lost the 'settler' narrative's interest in commercial possibility. Buzzacott argues that the missionaries' civilising project will as a pleasant side effect increase trade:

Commerce, again, is as deeply interested in the discoveries, achievements, and information of the missionary, as science. When a people is thus redeemed from savagery, and introduced into the community of civilized nations, new fields of produce and new markets for manufactures are opened. It would be difficult to estimate the commercial value of modern missions.[116]

Thus Buzzacott frames the missionary as an explorer by intention, as uniquely positioned to report on new cultures and educate a curious populace, and a trader by happy accident, bringing new commercial opportunities by civilising native peoples. While the missionaries' primary goal is salvation, commerce and discovery will follow by default.

With the deaths of Cook and Williams hovering in the collective memories of the nation, Buzzacott unsurprisingly depicts Polynesia as both a beautiful paradise and a home of moral depravity. He describes Rarotonga as

the very ideal of beauty and loveliness—a home for the great and good. Alas! it was the dwelling of cruel errors and lust and sin. Can this paradise be regained for its rightful Lord; be won to the love of the cross, and to the crown of Prince Emmanuel?[117]

While the land itself is good and wholesome and productive, it has been handed over to the fallen race that has corrupted it. Thus the missionaries' duty is the same as that of the Swiss family, to civilise the land (and its people) in order to create a productive Christian society that will (inadvertently, of course) serve in future as a viable commercial interest. Buzzacott's focus is always on both the people and the land, arguing that only by converting the former can they have true access to the latter.

The island paradise is not as perfect as it first appears, and Buzzacott relates several adventures during his journeys. One of the more memorable events involves a hurricane which decimated the mission settlement at Rarotonga. Buzzacott notes the horrifying consequences of such natural disasters:

For culture and beauty the island had been a garden of Eden. Provisions had been most abundant. In three short hours, the whole land had become one vast wreck; houses not only demolished, but their very sites buried deep beneath sand and masses of coral blocks.[118]

Later he continues in his description of the totality of the devastation: 'The next morning presented to our view a scene of desolation most heart-rending. The island looks like a wreck. A few headless cocoa-nut trees are the only conspicuous objects in the universal waste.'[119] The total eradication of the houses down to their foundations epitomises nature's destruction of civilisation. Missionaries like Buzzacott and Ellis emphasised these disasters both to show the inspiring spirit of the missionaries in the face of adversity and to remind readers of the continued need to support mission efforts.

As in *The Swiss Family Robinson*, missionaries viewed the building of houses as a triumph of civilisation over the primitive dwellings of the natives, an outward sign of inward conversion. The buildings, especially the houses and the chapel, also represent a landscape deliberately constructed to remind travellers of the home they left. Critic Sujit Sivasundaram explains,

> The landscape of the South Pacific had to be clothed in specific colours to visualize conversion. If a chapel stood in the foreground of majestic mountains, radiating light to the sea at night, then the message was clear. That island resembled Britain and had embraced the robes of Christianity.[120]

Buzzacott explains that the building of houses and the longing for civilisation are only brought about by a conversion to the faith. As he notes, 'It took a considerable time to induce the natives to build separate houses, and it was not until the gospel had quickened their moral natures that they were able to understand and to long for the comforts of a home.'[121]

Natural disasters were not the only threat Buzzacott faced within the early missionary settlements. As in other missionary accounts, Buzzacott explains the dangers brought by traders who were quick to take advantage of the newly pacified and civilised natives. Despite attempts to prevent them, 'American whale ships began to call at the island for supplies, and as they found a cheap and ample market, they came in great numbers.'[122] The islanders quickly figured out that the vagrant beachcombers[123] were useful in attracting ships to land. Buzzacott records that he found

> many of the Samoan chiefs with white men in their train—American and English sailors, who had run away from whaling ships, touching at the islands for provisions. The chiefs found these men useful in promoting their trade with ships, for captains would frequently be induced to land where a white man resided.[124]

Buzzacott, like his predecessors, cast these men as villains and impediments to the mission of salvation. Despite these continual challenges, however, Buzzacott's narrative is on the whole hopeful and positive, championing the missionary cause and subtly asking for support. In Buzzacott's narrative, the Christianisation of the island goes hand in hand with its moral and physical improvement. Buzzacott notes, 'In 1857, the fly pest had long since disappeared with the indisposition to thorough cleansing, while soap had come into constant use.'[125] Soap, the ubiquitous British symbol of progress for imperial adventure narratives of the latter half of the nineteenth century, had finally appeared in missionary narratives, and with it, civilisation.

The missionaries and novelists of the early nineteenth century painted a new vibrant image of a developing world. The Pacific was structured as a place in-between: in-between savagery and civilisation, idolatry and Christianity, exploration and settlement. Out of the Godwins' early translation of *The Swiss Family Robinson* and the various missionary accounts of the LMS, the islands of the Pacific gained a hold on the imagination of the British people as spaces of great promise but also great danger. As the novel gained popularity throughout the early nineteenth century, the stage was set for a new vision of the Pacific as the islands made their way into the rapidly growing genre of adventure fiction. Authors like Fredrick Marryat and R. M. Ballantyne would transform the religious narratives of the missionaries into thrilling escapades aimed at educating boys in the appropriate way to serve the growing British Empire.

Notes

1. In the 1890s Cousins was the Editorial Secretary and Assistant Foreign Secretary of the LMS. He wrote multiple accounts of the LMS's efforts in the islands of the Pacific.
2. Cousins, *The Story of the South Seas.*
3. As Cousins points out in his account, the South Seas were not chosen arbitrarily. As he explains, 'Why choose a small island [Tahiti] when large continents were without the light? Partly because those larger islands were closed against them; partly because the voyages of Captain Wallis, Captain Cook, and others, had aroused much interest in "Otahiti" and "other islands" of the South Ocean . . . India, Japan, China, Africa, were not yet open to the servants of Christ, but the islands were open.' Ibid., 2–3. While Britain had sent missionaries to the Indians of the American colonies in the eighteenth century, these efforts were enacted on a smaller scale than the LMS's projects and had more success in establishing mission rhetoric than long-term conversions. For more on early British missions in America see Stevens, *The Poor Indians*; Wyss, *Writing Indians.*
4. While it seems likely that Mary provided the translation while William produced and edited the manuscript, it is difficult to discern the exact

details and thus I will be crediting both Godwins with producing the translation.

5. From its inception, *The Swiss Family Robinson* has had a complicated publication history. While the original story was conceived by Johann Wyss, it was his son Johann Rudolph who transformed the manuscript fragments into a novel format (possibly with his father's help) and published his father's novel under the title *Der Schweizerische Robinson* in 1812 in Zurich. The Godwins translated and released the first volume in 1814, but due to delays in receiving a German copy of the second volume, they did not release the second volume until 1816. The Godwin translation of 1816 drew on the collaboration between Johann Wyss and Johann Rudolph to produce the text that the British would embrace until new translations began emerging in 1848. For more, see Seeyle, 'Introduction'.

6. Pratt, *Imperial Eyes*, 134.

7. Prendergast, 'The World Republic of Letters', 7.

8. While the British missionaries left before the publication of *The Swiss Family Robinson*, their writings were not in wide circulation until after the novel was released.

9. Wyss's original manuscript was also occasionally called *Charakteristik meiner Kinder in einer Robinsonade* (Characteristics of my Children in a Robinsonade) as well *Der Schweizerische Robinson* (The Swiss Robinson) so it is not surprising that the English translation muddled through a few variations of the title before settling into the well-known *The Swiss Family Robinson*.

10. Kingston's translation drew on changes added by an 1824 French translation by Madame de Montolieu as well as a continuation of the story written by Johann Wyss's son Johann Rudolph Wyss. For more on the story's rich translation history, see Martin Green's 'Der Schweizerische Robinson' in *The Robinson Crusoe Story*. My focus in this chapter is on the reception of the text by a British audience in a British context so while the original story was written in German by Wyss, I will be quoting from the most popular English translation available in Britain.

11. Dodge, *Islands and Empires*, 169.

12. Wyss, *The Swiss Family Robinson*, 7. The 1816 introduction explains that Father chooses to travel to the Pacific after having 'lost his fortune in the Revolution of 1798', connecting the story to Switzerland's role in the French Revolution. Later editions, like Kingston's, dropped the introduction, effectively erasing the original political context for Father's shipwreck.

13. Captain Cook landed in New Guinea on 3 September 1770. His nervousness and that of his crew is recorded in Cook, *The Journals*. See page 174.

14. Seeyle also argues that the zoning of the island into two regions by Baroness Montolieu, a Frenchwoman who after the Godwins produced an extended translation of *The Swiss Family Robinson* in French, echoes the 1790 map of North America. For more on Seeyle's interpretation of the map, see his 'Introduction', page 7.

15. Moore, *New Guinea: Crossing Boundaries and History*, 2.

16. Hannabuss, 'Islands as Metaphors', 73.

17. Wyss, *The Swiss Family Robinson*, 66.

18. Ibid., 138–9.
19. Miller, 'Reading "The Swiss Family Robinson" as Virtual Reality', 87.
20. Wyss, *The Swiss Family Robinson*, 103.
21. Ibid., 46.
22. Ibid., 15.
23. Ibid., 22.
24. Ibid., 90–1.
25. Ibid., 111, 90–1.
26. Ibid., 158.
27. After Cook's journals began to be published and circulated in the 1780s and 90s, Britain became increasingly intrigued by the newly discovered islands of the Pacific and began lively debates as to the nation's role in claiming, 'civilising', or settling the islands. Sujit Sivasundaram explains, 'In London, the published narratives of travel were received in a climate of acclaim and controversy. After the journal of the first voyage was published, not a day passed without letters appearing in the press about its contents.' Sivasundaram, *Nature and the Godly Empire*, 1.
28. Wyss, *The Swiss Family Robinson*, 155. The Calvinist background of Swiss Protestantism intimately connected work with salvation (as it was only through work that the elect revealed their chosen status). British Victorians viewed work as an essential tenant of masculine behaviour, connecting physical labour with manly achievement. Thus, Victorians were able to easily translate Father's Calvinist conception of work as salvation into what Carlyle would famously claim as the 'Gospel of Work' in the nineteenth century. See Sussman, *Masculine Identities*, 84–7.
29. For example, Father decides to employ the family in building and securing an orchard. As he explains, 'We employed six whole weeks in effecting what for the present it was possible to effect, of these laborious arrangements; but the continual exercise of mind and body they imposed, visibly contributed to the physical and moral health of the boys, and to the support of cheerfulness and serenity in ourselves.' Wyss, *The Swiss Family Robinson*, 303.
30. Evidence of Cook's unquestioned authority permeates the accounts of all three voyages, but for a token example, see 18 August 1773 where Cook is exchanging gifts with an island chief in Tahiti. After giving out 'presents', Cook notes, 'at last he [a native] was caught takeing things which did not belong to him and handing them out of the quarter Gallery, many complaints of the like kind were made to me against those on deck which induced me to turn them all out of the Ship'. Cook, *The Journals*, 283. For good measure, Cook 'fired two Musquet balls over his [the native's] head' and eventually fired the ship's guns to keep the natives from the ship. Neither Cook's crew nor the natives protest, and 'in a few hours after the People were as well reconciled as if nothing had happen'd'. Ibid.
31. Fearing French control of the Malay Archipelago during the Napoleonic Wars, Britain began expanding its control over Dutch possessions in the Pacific, most notably by seizing control of Java in 1811. Under the control of Stamford Raffles, the British expanded their trade interests through the profitable western islands. Influenced by European politics, the British would return control to the Dutch in 1815. While the British were willing

to intervene in the politics of the highly contested, and highly profitable, islands of the Malay Archipelago, they showed far less interest in the smaller islands of Polynesia so popular with shipwreck narratives. For more, see Webster, *Gentleman Capitalists*.

32. Loxley, *Problematic Shores*, 106.
33. Ibid., 90.
34. One memorable exception to this rule is the shark that attacks Fritz. While he quickly dispatches the animal, the connection between shipwrecks and shark attacks would remain a seemingly indelible part of Pacific fiction and non-fiction.
35. By removing any inhabitants, Wyss effectively renders trade with native islanders a moot point. Father would theoretically be able to produce a thriving colonial trade outpost without any need to negotiate with 'the natives'. This fantasy would have been appealing to British readers who wished to separate themselves from the practical realities, such as the slave trade, that allowed for much of their commercial success at the turn of the century.
36. Wyss, *The Swiss Family Robinson*, 51.
37. Ibid., 188.
38. Ibid., 285.
39. Ibid., 363.
40. Ibid., 364.
41. Ibid.
42. Loxley, *Problematic Shores*, 107.
43. Catherine Molineux details the complex ideology eighteenth-century Britons negotiated to both criticise the inhumanity of the slave trade while simultaneously arguing for the subjection of native peoples as necessary for imperial commercial expansion. See Molineux, *Faces of Perfect Ebony*.
44. Wyss, *The Swiss Family Robinson*, 429.
45. Ibid.
46. A notable exception to this rule is Robinson Crusoe who is haunted by the need to return to his island colony in the opening of *The Further Adventures of Robinson Crusoe*. Defoe, *Robinson Crusoe and the Further Adventures of Robinson Crusoe*.
47. Seeyle, 'Introduction', xvii.
48. Wyss, *The Swiss Family Robinson*, 433, n. 1. The Baroness Isabelle de Monolieu's version was titled *Le Robinson suisse, ou, Journal d'un père de famille, naufragé avec ses enfans* published in French in 1814. An extended edition appeared in 1824.
49. Green, *The Robinson Crusoe Story*, 77.
50. Wyss, *The Swiss Family Robinson*, ed. John Scieska, trans. William H. G. Kingston, 443.
51. Ibid., 453.
52. Ibid., 464.
53. Ibid.
54. Moore, *New Guinea: Crossing Boundaries and History*, 135.
55. Of the thirty missionaries who boarded the *Duff*, only four were ministers while the rest specialised in trade. As Cousins records, 'There were six

carpenters, two shoemakers, two bricklayers, two tailors, two smiths, two weavers, a surgeon, a hatter, a shopkeeper, a cotton manufacturer, a cabinet maker, a draper, a harness maker, a gentleman's servant who had become a tin-worker, a cooper, and a butcher. Only six of them were married. There were also three children.' Cousins, *The Story of the South Seas*, 6.

56. Williams joined the LMS in July 1816. Along with David Darling, George Platt and Robert Bourne, the LMS sent Williams to revitalise the flagging missions in the Pacific. Williams lived and worked not only in Tahiti, but also in Raiatea, Rarotonga and the Samoan islands among others. His narrative records in detail the lives of the missionaries in all of the various outposts of the LMS. For more on John William's fascinating life, see Prout, *Memoirs of the Life of the Rev. John Williams*.

57. Williams, *Missionary Enterprises*.

58. Edmond, *Representing the South Pacific*, 114.

59. Williams references Cook's journals frequently when describing the islands he encounters. He actually introduces his narrative with 'that truly great man Captain Cook, whose name I never mention but with feelings of veneration and regret. His objects were purely scientific.' Williams, *Missionary Enterprises*, 1–2.

60. These racial categories were made evident in the Western division of the Pacific into Melanesia, the eastern islands from New Guinea to Fiji whose name in Greek means the 'dark islands' or 'dark islanders', and Polynesia, extending in a triangle from New Zealand in the southwest to the Hawaiian islands in the north and back down to Easter Island in the southeast whose name comes from the 'many islands' or 'many islanders' it contains.

61. Williams, *Missionary Enterprises*, 8.

62. Ward, *British Policy in the South Pacific*, 9.

63. Howe, *Where the Waves Fall*, 93.

64. Williams, *Missionary Enterprises*, 577.

65. Ibid., 580.

66. Ibid., 140.

67. Gunson, *Messengers of Grace*, 141.

68. Johnston, *Missionary Writing and Empire, 1800–1860*, 116.

69. Diderot, *Ramaeu's Nephew and Other Works*, 218.

70. Sivasundaram, *Nature and the Godly Empire*, 146.

71. Campbell was a Scottish missionary who became a director of the LMS in 1805. His other publications champion the LMS's work in southern Africa.

72. Campbell, *Maritime Discovery*, ii.

73. Dodge, *Islands and Empires*, 167.

74. Samson, *British Imperial Strategies in the Pacific*, 269.

75. Fulford and Kitson, *Romanticism and Colonialism*, 30.

76. Gunson, *Messengers of Grace*, 214.

77. Campbell, *Maritime Discovery*, 354.

78. It was in fact John Campbell's work in Africa which inspired William Ellis to join the LMS in 1814. Ellis travelled to Tahiti in 1816, where his greatest legacy was installing a printing press at Moorea, allowing documents

to be printed in the Tahitian language. Ellis continued his missionary work in Hawaii in 1822. Due to his wife's ill health, Ellis returned to England in 1825 where the LMS urged him to publish to refute criticism of the missionary efforts. His connection to the LMS remained strong and he served as the LMS secretary in charge of foreign relations from 1830 to 1838. Etherington, 'Ellis, William'.
79. While Ellis's publication date precedes those of Williams and Campbell, his time in Tahiti overlaps with Williams's journeys that inspire *Missionary Enterprises*.
80. Ellis, *Polynesian Researches*, 1, vi.
81. Gunson, *Messengers of Grace*, 183.
82. Ellis, *Polynesian Researches*, 1, ix.
83. Ibid.
84. Rapa is one of the Austral Islands near Tahiti.
85. Ellis, *Polynesian Researches*, 1, 45–6.
86. Ibid., 62.
87. Ibid., 203.
88. Brantlinger, *Dark Vanishings*, 143.
89. Ellis, *Polynesian Researches*, 1, 349.
90. Ibid., 379.
91. Ibid., 450–1.
92. Ibid., 450.
93. Ibid., 390.
94. Houses, like many aspects of Polynesian society, maintained a religious significance for Polynesian peoples. Guardian spirits were often associated with specific households, so the missionaries emphasis on creating new dwelling spaces was likely twofold: to replace traditional huts with more 'European' styles of housing but also to remove the dwelling place from the influence of spirit worship. For more on the importance of dwellings in Polynesian society, see Oliver, *Oceania*, 1, 321–60.
95. Ellis, *Polynesian Researches*, 2, 68.
96. The distribution and nature of farming in the Pacific varied widely from island to island and even between different landscapes on individual islands, making a summation of farming practices among islanders difficult. In general, the islanders tended to individual plants or cuttings, instead of planting seed over prepared ground. The 'intensity' needed to farm various island crops varied widely, which is likely why many missionaries viewed islanders as 'indolent' or unproductive. For more on the nature of food-growing in the Pacific islands, see Oliver, *Oceania*, 1, 185–320.
97. Ellis, *Polynesian Researches*, 1, 444.
98. Sivasundaram, *Nature and the Godly Empire*, 159–60.
99. Ellis, *Polynesian Researches*, 1, 106.
100. Ibid., 453.
101. Ibid., 372.
102. Ibid., 179.
103. A city in Moorea, one of the Society Islands.
104. Ellis, *Polynesian Researches*, 2, 146.
105. Ibid., 196.

106. Of course, the extent to which cannibalism was actually practiced in the Pacific is hotly debated by anthropologists, but for the British reading public, cannibalism was an accepted reality of the Pacific islands. As anthropologist Gananath Obeyesekere succinctly explains, 'Why this British preoccupation with cannibalism? One reason, it seems to me, is clear: cannibalism is what the English reading public relished. It was their definition of the savage.' See Obeyesekere, *Cannibal Talk*, 28. The connection between island 'savages' and cannibalism had been entrenched in British fiction from Robinson Crusoe's encounters with Friday.
107. Ellis, *Polynesian Researches*, 2, 167.
108. Ibid., 214.
109. For more on the debate over Western depictions of cannibalism in the Pacific, and in the British imagination in general, consider Obeyesekere, *Cannibal Talk*; Arens, *The Man-Eating Myth*; Barker et al., *Cannibalism and the Colonial World*; Krieger, *Conversations with the Cannibals*; Lestringant, *Cannibals: The Discovery and Representation of the Cannibal from Columbus to Jules Verne*; Sahlins, 'Cannibalism: An Exchange'; Salmond, *The Trial of the Cannibal Dog*.
110. Ellis, *Polynesian Researches*, 2, 573–4.
111. Ibid., 575–6.
112. Ibid., 576.
113. Edmond, *Representing the South Pacific*, 105.
114. Another LMS missionary, Buzzacott, spent five months in Tahiti before travelling on to Rarotonga in 1828. According to later accounts, he was close friends with John Williams.
115. Sunderland and Buzzacott, *Mission Life in the Islands of the Pacific*, vii.
116. Ibid., viii.
117. Ibid., 26.
118. Ibid., 88.
119. Ibid., 95–6.
120. Sivasundaram, *Nature and the Godly Empire*, 171.
121. Sunderland and Buzzacott, *Mission Life in the Islands of the Pacific*, 211.
122. Ibid., 92.
123. H. E. Maude famously discusses the problematic definition of the beachcomber. As he explains: 'Probably we would all know a beachcomber if we were to see one, yet he is hard to define as a type. The *Oxford English Dictionary* calls him "a settler on the islands of the Pacific, living by pearl-fishing, etc., and often by less reputable means", and this is reasonably accurate, though "resident" would be better than "settler", since many stayed for relatively brief periods. In the more precise terminology of the anthropologist he is a regional variety of the world-wide class of individuals called by Hallowell "transculturites": persons who, throughout history, "are temporarily or permanently detached from one group, enter the web of social relations that constitute another society, and come under the influence of its customs, ideas and values to a greater or lesser degree".' Maude, 'Beachcombers and Castaways', 254.
124. Sunderland and Buzzacott, *Mission Life in the Islands of the Pacific*, 118.
125. Ibid., 238.

Chapter 2

Adventures in the Pacific: The Influence of Trade on the South Seas Novel

Introduction

One of the earliest Pacific adventure stories, full of captures and escapes, cannibals and cutthroats, paradises and purgatories, was written not by an aspiring novelist but by the young missionary George Vason, who 'went native' after initially attempting to convert the islanders of Tonga. When he lands in Noogollefa,[1] Vason is greeted by natives, but he is more interested in describing the two Europeans he meets, Benjamin Ambler and John Conelly, beachcombers who left an American ship to settle on the islands. Vason quickly notes that the two men

> showed themselves to be base and wicked characters . . . it is most likely that they were transported for some misdemeanor, and gladly secreted themselves in this island, where they could indulge, without restraint, in those habits of idleness and profligacy, to which they had been addicted.[2]

While Vason admits that the two men are useful in dealing with the island chiefs, he despises their sin and weakness:

> The dress and carriage of the two Europeans were like [the islanders']: they seemed to imitate them in every thing, and much to exceed them in wickedness. Thinking we were as bad as themselves, they swore with the fluency of abandoned seamen, and probably to give us an idea of the impure freedoms, in which they indulged without control, in Tongataboo, they treated the women with brutish indecorum and cruelty, and told us that one of them had three wives, and the other four. They were soon, however, awed into a more reserved behaviour, by our discountenance and reproof; and before long, became our bitterest enemies.[3]

Vason's use of 'our' underscores his identification with his missionary brethren; he simultaneously identifies himself with the idea of the two wanton Europeans-turned-native. Having already admitted that he enjoyed swearing as a youth in his introduction, Vason is aware that the differences between himself and these two beachcombers are not as distinct as he perhaps would have liked to believe. Rather than pursuing his missionary endeavours, Vason leaves his fellow missionaries to live with the natives, changing the tone of his work. Instead of focusing on 'civilising' island people and bring them to Christ, the style popular in missionary fiction, Vason's narrative highlights instead his many experiences and adventures amongst the peoples of Tonga.

Vason's narrative of his fall from grace stands as a transition point in the literature of the Pacific isles. This trend developed alongside, yet branched away from, the early conversion narratives of missionaries like John Williams and John Campbell, which championed humility and obedience to God as the way to civilise the islanders, adopting instead a secularised style focused on the experiences of foreign travellers in the islands. While the traditional missionary narrative would continue throughout the nineteenth century, in the narratives of William Ellis and Aaron Buzzacott for example, this newer style offered a new way of interacting with and interpreting the island communities, valuing power and control over piety. As the anecdote from Vason's narrative suggests, the new genre of adventure fiction would transform the traders and beachcombers largely vilified in missionary narrative into lead characters and eventually heroes. These new trader/adventurers sought the Pacific deliberately as a source of potential excitement and/or for potential profit.

From the outset, the narrative of the British trader in the Pacific took on a very different tone from that of the missionary. While traders, like missionaries, were interested in describing the fantastic peoples and places they encountered, they focused more on the adventure in and conquest of a hostile and unpredictable landscape. Graham Dawson explains,

> Crucial here is the structurally necessary remoteness of the quest from domesticity, the sphere conventionally associated with femininity and civilization. Since the adventure hero must renounce the relative comfort, security and intimacy of domestic life in order to encounter sufficiently testing conditions, adventure as a form tends to background domestic masculinities, rendering them invisible, unimaginable.[4]

To assert their masculinity, traders described their experience as explorers battling the elements, and more often than not hostile savages, struggling to survive harrowing expeditions. Not surprisingly, the line between fiction and non-fiction became increasingly hard to discern as tales of shipwrecks and shark attacks flourished. Stories like those of former missionary George Vason straddled the line between travel writing and adventure fiction. Such stories, as John M. MacKenzie notes, 'celebrated self-reliance and individualism, competing now not with other classes in their own society but with other races and nationalities in a world-wide context'.[5] The Pacific islands were particularly well suited as the setting of such tales as they were remote enough to provide sufficient adventures, yet small enough to be conquered and controlled.

While missionary narratives, as I explored in Chapter 1, would continue arguing for isolation and moral guidance as the appropriate way to interact with the islands, adventure fiction developed as a separate branch of British Pacific narrative and presented a new way to interact with the islands and their inhabitants. The adventure narrative focused less on the proper way to civilise natives and more on how the island spaces could provide a way to 'civilise' British citizens, especially to rehabilitate the maligned image of the trader (often associated with piracy and other crimes) into a productive citizen of Empire. However, adventure fiction did more than simply revise the image of the adult trader/adventurer in the islands: it also provided a new interpretation of the castaway, transforming the traditional 'Robinson Crusoe' figure from a capable adult into a youthful boy. Even as they seek to reform adults through island adventures, these new novels use the established characters of 'trader' and 'missionary' to provide a template for appropriate masculine behaviour both abroad and at home. Youthful castaways find through their experiences on the island and interactions with usually hostile natives and usually helpful adults, the appropriate way to behave. Thus adventure novels functioned as educational primers, instructing boys in how to act both at home and abroad.

I explore this development of the adventure genre using Fredrick Marryat's *Masterman Ready* and R. M. Ballantyne's *The Coral Island*, *Gascoyne, the Sandal-wood Trader* and *The Island Queen*. In *Masterman Ready*, Marryat presents an early vision of the adventure narrative, still connected to the *Swiss Family Robinson* tradition, where the missionary/philosopher Mr Seagrave and the adventure hero Masterman Ready instruct the boys in proper manly behaviour. In Ballantyne's *The Coral Island*, the boys Ralph, Jack and Peterkin must learn to control their island home without the help of such parental guidance. Instead, they must choose appropriate role models from the island's various inhabitants – missionaries, pirates and natives. *Gascoyne* focuses less on the boys and more on their role models, working to transform the pirate of *The Coral Island* into a productive trader worthy of emulation. Finally, *The Island Queen* questions the dominance of male role models by presenting a female ruler, a stand in for Queen Victoria, as an alternate form of leadership for young boys and even their adult counterparts.

For both the adult trader/adventurer and the boy castaway, the Pacific islands serve as unregulated spaces where boys and men must chose adulthood and/or heroism without the guiding forces of the home government or a paternal stand-in. By investigating the relationships between the Pacific characters of missionary, trader/adventurer and boy/castaway, therefore, I argue that these new adventure narratives created a new narrative of British interactions with the Pacific islands by using the spaces to explore the intersection of issues of national identity, masculinity and trade.

George Vason: The Prodigal Missionary

In many ways, missionaries were the earliest and most pervasive British settlers of the smaller islands of the South Pacific fashioning themselves as new settlers of uncharted territories, bringing civilisation and the gospel to the heathen islanders. The islands of the missionaries were fertile and overflowing with life of all kinds, a paradise worthy of the investment of supporters back home. Spurred by the images of wanton behaviour and cannibalism that flourished in the narratives of Cook and Bougainville, the LMS was quick to gather funds and send a small group of eager missionaries to the heathen islands of the Pacific. Beginning in 1796 with the departure of the mission ship the *Duff*, missionaries and their vision of the gospel-driven Western civilisation spread through the islands of Polynesia. Thirty men, some with their wives and children, boarded *The Duff* to establish missions in the Marquesas, Tahiti, and the Friendly Islands.[6] However, this early missionary effort was dogged by failure due to cultural conflict and internal divisions.

Twenty-four-year-old bricklayer and author, George Vason was among the men who made up the original Pacific mission. Unlike the writings of later missionaries, such as William Ellis or Aaron Buzzacott, Vason's account of his travels is far more personal and more focused on his adventures. As the later accounts show, the stories of the majority of the Pacific missionaries would provide a uniform argument for the correct way to interact with the islands. Vason's account, in contrast, reveals a new trend as it branches away from the missionary narrative, adopting the form of a newly developing genre. Like the others, Vason set out for the Pacific full of noble intentions and missionary zeal, but as he relates, he was soon 'lured' by the Polynesian lifestyle into 'going native' and abandoning the missionary project. As he adopts native traditions and builds a successful plantation, Vason secularises the traditional missionary story. Vason's narrative, therefore, represents an intriguing mix of missionary narrative and adventure story revealing a rare glimpse into a moment in which missionary narrative overlaps with the early adventure narrative, questioning whether Vason's life as a missionary or as an adventurer/trader is more compelling.

Vason's narrative opens with an 'Introductory Essay' outlining the purpose undertaken by the *Duff* and providing a list of the missionaries who volunteered to go on the journey. It takes an interesting detour, however, to describe the life of the ship's commander, a non-believer named Captain Wilson. The narrative relates Wilson's escape from a French prison in India,

> which he did by leaping from the prison walls, a height of forty feet. In his flight the vast Coleroon, a river full of alligators, obstructed his passage; but ignorant of the peril, he plunged into the waters and swam unhurt to the opposite shore.[7]

His adventures incomplete, Captain Wilson is recaptured, 'chained to a soldier, and driven naked, and barefoot, and wounded, a distance of five hundred miles. He was at length loaded with irons of 32 *lbs.*, and thrust into a horrible dungeon called the "Black Hole."'[8] After twenty-two months of torture, 'emaciated, naked, half-starved, and covered in ulcers, with thirty-one companions, who alone remained to tell the dismal tale of their sufferings, Captain Wilson obtained deliverance'.[9] While this story is clearly intended to titillate and excite the reader, Vason is quick to bring the story back to the missionaries. As the introduction explains, one of the missionaries, Mr Thomas, who believed 'he should have more hope of converting the Lascars to Christianity than Captain Wilson',[10] eventually succeeds in converting the wary captain. In the Captain Wilson story, therefore, the narrative draws upon the newly developing genre of the adventure story to enliven its tale of conversion. Still, adventure is not yet fully foregrounded: the narrative records the incident in only a few pages before returning to the style typical of missionary texts, recording the places visited and people encountered.

Like other missionaries' narratives, Vason's is quick to comment upon the indolent and easy-going lifestyles of the native Polynesians. As the introduction notes,

> From the abundance, diversity, nutrition, delicacy and richness of provision to please the palate and promote strength, spontaneously brought forth to gratify the inhabitants of these favoured isles, it would seem as if man here was only made for enjoyment; and utterly exempt from our painful condition of labour and toil.[11]

While the islands may appear Edenic, however, with their proliferation of plants and animals, the narrative is very clear that such abundance leads to moral failings amongst the islands' peoples. The introduction explains:

> This Pacific paradise is one of mere carnal enjoyment, in which the mind is uncultivated, and in which the standard of intellectual acquirement can only be compared to a low stunted shrub, utterly dissimilar, and forming a perfect contrast, with the natural fertility of these climes; for while the luxuriant earth spontaneously brings forth a constant and teeming abundance, the moral condition of the inhabitants presents to the mind of the Christian philanthropist, nothing but the cheerless prospect of a sterile waste, utterly separated and estranged from those exalted principles which dignify and ennoble the man of regenerate heart, and distinguish him from all others, as the most exalted creature of God.[12]

The narrative views the peoples of the Pacific as base savages, unable to perceive the noble morality of the Christian missionaries. Vason's natives are slaves to violence and lust, which overwhelm any moral impulse; 'the choicest pleasures the Polynesian knows', therefore 'are only carnal—the pleasures of a beast'.[13]

It is not only the islanders' lasciviousness that offends, however, but also their penchant for violence. Quoting from the narratives of John Williams and William Ellis, the introduction describes tales of human sacrifice, infanticide and cannibalism. The narrative responds to such atrocities by quoting liberally passages from Isaiah, Exodus and Jeremiah, most of which condemn the Israelites for their idolatry and show God's judgement upon them. The narrative also condemns the islanders in a litany reminiscent of the Old Testament prophets, declaring them

> filled with all unrighteousness, fornication, wickedness, covetousness, maliciousness, full of envy, murder, debate, deceit, malignity, whisperings, backbiters, haters of God, despiteful, proud, boasters, inventors of evil things, disobedient to parents. Without understanding, covenant breakers, without natural affection, implacable, unmerciful; who, knowing the judgment of God, that they which commit such things are worthy of death, not only do the same, but have pleasure in them that do them.[14]

While the vision of islanders as lost souls is common to missionary narratives, such a severe judgement upon them is not. While most missionaries focus on their ability to convert the natives to Christianity, a great many of this narrative's descriptions condemn the natives for their wickedness and their deliberate betrayal of God's commands without seeking to convert them.

Having established the wanton sins of the islanders and the punishments for such disobedience, the introduction explains that it was only through the continued faith and work of dedicated missionaries that Christianity flourished in the islands allowing such heathens to be saved. Subsequently, the text segues into Vason's 'Authentic Narrative'. Vason admits that as a young man he experienced a rocky start with religion, noting that while he was a hard worker, he 'had not the fear of God' in his heart and was 'addicted to swearing and cursing'.[15] After attending worship and having a conversion experience, Vason became inspired to do the work of God by bringing His message to the peoples of Polynesia. Vason's first vision of the islands, however, reveals the possible immaturity of his faith as he begins to doubt the islands' fallen state. He notes,

> Had we not known that Eden was become desolate through the sin of the primeval pair, the abundant fertility that beautified this island, and blessed its inhabitants with ease and plenty, might have led us to call this a second paradise, planted in the watery waste.[16]

Like other missionary narratives, Vason dwells on the beauty and productivity of the landscape, yet despite his knowledge that this paradise is tainted by sin, he finds it an irresistible draw.

Unlike the narrative of John Williams, which focuses primarily on the conversion of islanders and their chiefs, or even that of William Ellis, which includes a great deal of natural history and anthropological study, Vason's narrative is heavily anecdotal and highly personal. Vason seems more interested in describing his reactions to the islands he lands upon than in the islanders' reactions to him. Many of his stories from Tahiti focus less on the natives and more on the missionaries left behind to save them. This shift from an interest in the islanders to a focus on the travellers would become a hallmark of Pacific adventure fiction. More interesting, however, is Vason's description of the second leg of his trip to Tongataboo.[17] Despite its more introspective focus, the first half of Vason's narrative sounds much like any other, but once Vason lands in Tonga, his new home, things slowly begin to change. Soon after coming to live at Tonga, Vason leaves his fellow missionaries to reside with Mulkaamair, the island chief. Vason admits that

> accustomed to these scenes of pleasure, luxury, and amusement, unrestrained by the presence of my companions, unassisted by any public means of grace, having singly to stem the torrent of iniquity, it was not long before I felt the pernicious influence of general example.[18]

Vason blames his weakness, along with his unwillingness to pray, meditate and consult the Bible, for his fall. He explains, 'I began to dislike the means of grace, I never visited the brethren, found delight in the company, manners and amusements of the natives; and soon took too large a part in them.'[19] Having left the company of his fellow missionaries, Vason throws himself more into the power of Mulkaamair.

Soon Vason finds himself 'going native', dressing and acting like one of the local Polynesians, and following more and more of their customs. When Mulkaamair offers Vason a wife, 'a near relation of his', Vason relates,

> My conscience loudly cautioned me, not to be guilty of the sin of cohabiting with a woman without the sanction of marriage, and of taking a wife who was a heathen, and a perfect destitute of every mental, as well as religious endowment; who would most probably lead me still farther from the right way.[20]

While Vason's concerns are deeply personal, they echo earlier visions of the seductive native women.[21] For Vason, his 'marriage' to a native woman marks his inevitable decline and, as he describes, 'I now entered, with the utmost eagerness, into every pleasure and entertainment of the natives; and endeavoured to forget that I was once called a christian, and had left a christian land to evangelize the heathen.'[22] While the missionaries at Tonga were failing, few islanders were converting and others were growing violent, Vason records that he paid little attention at the time, busy pursuing his own pleasure: he builds himself a handsome plantation with the help of the chiefs and island labourers, increases his number of wives, and participates in 'disorderly meetings' and 'nocturnal dances' with other young men of the islands.[23] No longer called to separate himself from such endeavours, Vason opens himself up to the sorts of practices and encounters associated with the 'deviant' traders and beachcombers like Benjamin Ambler and John Conelly.

As Vason becomes more and more accustomed to the habits and practices of the natives, he finds himself more and more enmeshed in their culture, even taking part in a violent battle with Mulkaamair against a rival tribe, a battle that costs the lives of the other three missionaries working at Tonga.[24] Despite the loss of his original brethren, Vason continues to side with the Tongans who eventually defeat their enemies. He reports that the Tongans then 'took the bodies of their slain enemies, dragged them to the sea-shore, and after inflicting every brutal insult of savage cruelty, roasted and ate them'.[25] Vason says little else about this act of cannibalism, neglecting either to confirm his role as a participant in such a ceremony or to decry the custom from his later position as a penitent convert. After the Tongans final victory at Vavou,[26] however, Vason allows the natives to tattoo his full body, a process that takes three days. Even from his penitent viewpoint, Vason appears unashamed of his decision, noting, 'I looked indeed very gay in this new fancy covering.'[27] Historian Rod Edmond notes that tattooing represented the final step necessary to transform a man from a European into a Polynesian. He explains:

> From the Polynesian point of view tattooing involved a reinforcement of the skin, often as protection against threats to the body from gods and other supernatural forces, and was intimately connected with rituals of rebirth and maturation. It always involved a closer integration with the social group. From a European point of view, however, this refashioning of the body surface implied a repudiation of western culture. It had, therefore, an opposite significance, being a rejection of the civilized body and a highly visible move towards assimilation into so-called savage culture.[28]

For Vason, the decision to be tattooed represents more than a simple aesthetic change; it heralds his full rejection of his former life. Vason's tattoos mark him as an islander and embody in many ways his desire to leave 'civilised' society for the life of a native on his prosperous plantation with his wives.

Despite his conversion to the native way of life, Vason remains concerned about the fate of his old friends, the missionaries. Having heard rumours of a European ship in the area, Vason quickly heads to the vessel in hopes of returning to England, as the increased possibility of a tribe of invading natives has made island life uncomfortable. In what Vason interprets as a punishment for his sins, however, the ship departs the next morning with his former brethren, but without him. His fortunes fall further when he finds the natives of the island rebelling against the chiefs with whom he has allied. Desperate to escape the ensuing slaughter, Vason attempts to make peace with the enemy chief by offering to rule one of the islands. Knowing his position is tenuous at best, Vason is overjoyed to find a European ship on the horizon; while Vason has worked hard to identify himself as a Tongan, he has not fully lost his desire to be seen as a European. Unfortunately, upon seeing his dress and manner of speaking, the sailors assume Vason 'was a native who had picked up some European phrases'.[29] Desperate to escape, Vason pleads with God for deliverance and is soon after rescued. Seeing this rescue as a divine act of providence, Vason repents of his native life and returns to his former life and religion, noting, 'I now endeavour, under many infirmities and interruptions, to live to his [God's] praise and glory.'[30] Vason ends his reflections on Tonga with a strong condemnation of 'going native':

> The joy which I felt upon being restored to the comforts of civilized life, a well-ordered government, and the holy duties and services of revealed

religion, compared with that state of precarious subsistence, uncertain safety, corrupt conduct, and savage violence, to which the unfettered inhabitants of lawless islands are subject, is to me a demonstration from experience, that such Utopian felicity never existed, except in the imaginations of discontented and infidel philosophers. We want nothing but an experience of the contrary to make us prize the advantages of British law and British privileges.[31]

Vason asserts that Utopian islands are the construction of idle minds and that, in reality, the islands must be civilised and sanitised by British law and religion, an assertion that fits nicely within the pre-established missionary narrative form. Yet despite these claims, the sheer number and detailed nature of the pages describing his pleasures while living as a native far outweigh his warnings against such behaviour, placing the narrative also into the category of adventure fiction. Vason seems torn between regret over his past decisions and delight over his freedom and wild experiences. Vason's narrative offers a unique look at the transformation of the island narrative, as it blends the missionary narrative with the burgeoning genre of adventure fiction.

While Vason ends his account with a statement championing his conversion, the majority of his text recounts highly secular adventures. Missionaries capitalised on such accounts, issuing cheap biographies like Vason's to raise financial support for their ongoing efforts.[32] However, the popularity of such texts revealed a reading public ready and eager to devour more of such adventures, with or without religious underpinnings. Thus while Vason's text, with its 'conversion' narrative, still adheres to the form of the missionary accounts to establish its legitimacy, other adventurers would begin to publish accounts for less 'pure' motivations, proving that missionaries were not the only ones who could engage the British reading public.

Masterman Ready: Captain Marryat's Reconstructed Robinsonade

Along with non-fictional accounts, the nineteenth century produced a great many fictional stories of the Pacific, for example the writings of naval captain Fredrick Marryat. While Marryat was the first significant Victorian children's author to conceive of the South Pacific as the perfect setting for a boy's adventure novel, he directed his writing to children and thus has been primarily ignored by literary scholarship. Marryat served in the British navy for over twenty years before his experiences inspired him to write novels. Marryat was almost fifty, however, before he published his first real children's novel. Inspired by his own children's request, in 1841 Marryat took up the task of rewriting *The Swiss Family Robinson*.[33] While in the preface to his adaptation, Marryat claims that he can overlook the original text's errors in seamanship, he finds it impossible to ignore 'that much ignorance, or carelessness . . . in describing the vegetable and animal productions of the island on which the family had been wrecked'.[34] Disturbed by the lack of 'accuracy' in Wyss's tale, Marryat rewrote the whole story, transforming it into a new narrative titled *Masterman Ready*. In his work on Victorian children's books, F. J. Harvey Darton has argued that Marryat's revision was 'as realistic as *Robinson Crusoe* itself, but more densely populated and more purposeful'.[35] While still encapsulating many of the original themes of *The Swiss Family Robinson*, Marryat's rewrite reworked the story for Victorian audiences by increasing the authenticity of places and events, exploring the growing sense of connectivity and exchange between Britain and the larger world, and interrogating the new systems of masculinity forming alongside the growth of empire, trends also evident in Vason's narrative. Marryat's revised narrative expanded the story of a missionary family civilising an island into the new adventure genre by including the new character of the trader/adventurer in the form of Masterman Ready and offering him and Father as appropriate masculine role models for the castaway family.

The basic premise of Marryat's narrative is the same as that of his inspiration: a family is shipwrecked on a desert island and forced to build a new civilisation while they await rescue. As literary critic Martin Green notes, Marryat's efforts to update the text were highly successful: in

> the rendering of season and shoreline, food-gathering and hut-building, Marryat is almost on par with Defoe . . . He knows the practical problems the Seagraves would meet on their island, and the solutions he devises for them are both plausible and engrossing.[36]

Marryat, however, does not simply update the flora and fauna. In essentials the shipwrecked family remains familiar: Marryat transforms Father, Mother and their sons Fritz, Jack, Francis and Ernest into Mr and Mrs Seagrave and their sons William, Thomas and Albert. Marryat, though, also makes a few additional changes, adding a daughter, Caroline, a black nursemaid, Juno, and, most significantly for the plot, a new family protector, aged seaman Masterman Ready. Finally, and most significantly, Marryat chooses to split Wyss's Father into two characters, dividing male authority on the island between Mr Seagrave and Ready. While Mr Seagrave still governs his family, it is Ready who fulfils the role of advisor and adventurer, using the knowledge gleaned from his long career at sea to teach the family how to survive on the hostile island.

By dividing the character of Father, the novel is able to explore two visions of masculinity, the evangelical intellectual and the rough and ready explorer (or, essentially, the missionary and the adventurer). The ability to compare the two men is essential for an investigation of manliness. As John Tosh explains, becoming a man

> depended on the recognition of manhood by one's peers in an atmosphere which had as much to do with competition as camaraderie. Attaining manhood could not therefore be blandly described as a natural process, or a matter of filling one's allotted niche. It made more sense to represent it as a period of conflict, challenge, and exertion.[37]

Yet while Marryat offers the two men as competing examples of masculinity, both are intentionally simplified into 'philosophical' or 'action-oriented' stereotypes for the youthful audience to copy. Masterman Ready, for instance, provides youthful readers with an example of a 'rough and ready' masculine script which emphasises action and practicality. Ready is far more cautious than Father about preserving the family's supplies while on the island. Although he is gratified to discover that 'where there are coconut trees in such plenty as there are on that island there is no fear of starvation, even if we had not the ship's provisions', he also later reminds William that 'we could not do very well on coconut milk alone'.[38] Thus Ready galvanises the family into providing for all eventualities, including the rainy season. While the island is stocked with food, from the pigeons, pigs and other livestock left from the wreck to the native foods of turtles, fish, bananas and yams, Marryat is quick to remind his audience that such foods are not fully sustainable or self-replenishing. While Wyss's island provides the Swiss family with a yearlong bounty of infinite variety, Marryat's island conforms more accurately to the realities of island agriculture. The family must tend a garden in order to have a variety of vegetables, and Ready makes both a fish and turtle pond to provide for unlucky days. While the family is constantly finding new resources, these foods are not always currently viable, as in the case of the bananas and peppers that have not fully ripened.[39]

If Ready is the family's practical guide, planning for the upcoming seasonal changes on the island, than Mr Seagrave is the philosophical leader, providing the educational counterpoint to Ready's actions. In many ways, Mr Seagrave's teachings echo those of Wyss's Father, emphasising natural education for the children and the value of labour as a conduit to God.[40] If Father lives in an Edenic paradise full of innumerable plants and animals that simply need his family's tending, Mr Seagrave takes a slightly more conservationist view of his family's island and the balance of nature. Indeed, while unusual in adventure fiction, Marryat, experienced with foreign cultures from his time in the navy, takes a Romantic view of nature. As ecocritics have noted, since the 1790s the Romantics 'appeal[ed] to notions of nature and the natural as norms of health, vitality, or beauty and as precisely what commercial/industrial society represses or destroys, both in the human psyche and in the surrounding environment'.[41] Depictions of the islands of the South Pacific aligned nicely with Britain's need for a philosophical paradisial counterpoint to the Industrial Revolution and working class concerns of the 1830s and 40s. Still, while Marryat shipwrecks his characters in paradise, it is a paradise that only exists when all elements are in harmony. As Mr Seagrave explains to William,

> Examine through the whole of creation and you will find there is an unerring hand which invariably preserves the balance exact; and that there are no more mouths than for which food is provided, although accidental circumstances may for a time occasion a slight alteration.[42]

Although Mr Seagrave does not challenge the rights of men, especially white Englishmen, to control or alter their environment, he does recognise at least the outlines of an ecosystem that only works when multiple elements are in balance. While Victorian critic Patrick Brantlinger has argued that Marryat's novels reflect the sunny optimism of the mid-Victorian age which treated island colonies as perfect examples of 'subduing and planting the entire world', Marryat's novel is surprisingly aware, at least on a basic level, of the impact of cultural exchange.[43] When William inquires why people remark that others are 'as stupid as an ass', Mr Seagrave replies that the animal's intelligence suffers not as a result of any inherent characteristics, but rather as a consequence of its environment. As he explains:

> We have only very sorry specimens of the animal in England; they are stunted and small, and, from want of corn and proper food, besides being very ill-treated, are slow and dull-looking animals. The climate of England is much too cold for the ass; in the south of France and the Mediterranean, where it is much warmer, the ass is a much finer animal; but to see it in perfection, we must go to the Torrid Zone in Guinea, right on the equator, the hottest portion of the globe, where the ass, in its native state and native country, is a handsome creature and as fleet as the wind . . . We must see an animal in its own climate to form a true estimate of its value.[44]

Marryat's analysis of the decline of the ass is notable in the adventure genre, where the white man's (or boy's) right to control, capture and claim the wilderness is treated as innate. While the novel is concerned for the fate of the small island, it always maintains that with proper care, such imbalances need not occur. Escapist fantasies like Marryat's maintained the image of the islands as a 'New England' where labour, love and devotion could produce a utopian society, with plants, animals and humans living in a perfect balance.

If Marryat's narrative, like Wyss's, argues that utopia is possible, his need for accuracy extends beyond the sustainability of the island ecosystem to the political realities of settling an island not as unoccupied as it at first appears. Unlike Wyss's *tabula rasa*, Marryat's island challenges the fledgling colony when of a band of savages arrive. Marryat's descriptions of the islanders, 'all painted, with their war-cloaks and feathers on, and armed with spears and clubs', owes more to the histrionic travel fiction of storytellers like Crusoe's interactions with Friday's brethren than to the scientific realism of Cook's *Journals* or missionary accounts. This philosophy is espoused by the ever-practical Ready, who, upon finding two lost native women, remarks,

> A savage is a savage, and, like a child, wishes to obtain whatever he sees; especially he covets what he may turn to use, such as iron, etc. . . . There is no trusting to them, and I would infinitely prefer defending ourselves against numbers to trusting to their mercy.[45]

In adventure fiction, where the ideological goal is to establish the perfect English settlement, the savage is depicted as nothing more than the hostile Other.[46] While Marryat's natives are hostile and aggressive, they are quickly outsmarted by the superior technology of the white English settlers. Having built a stockade upon arrival, the family is protected from the continuous waves of savage attacks. While muskets do not work to frighten the natives, a fact which, according to Ready, proves they have been in contact with whites before, they do work to thin the seemingly endless number of attackers. The natives seem to have little motivation for their attack, beyond their inherent barbarism and lust for iron. Unlike the more nuanced portrayals of natives in the missionaries' narratives, adventure fiction reduces the islanders to brute savages, violent thieves driven only by primal needs. In doing so, the novel elevates Ready to the position of hero, whose 'physical prowess and readiness for combat' transforms his violence towards the islanders into a sort of manly sport.[47] Marryat also elevates Ready's ability to act as a more masculine, and thus more heroic, trait than Mr Seagrave's philosophical, and often evangelical, musings. The novel thus elevates the trader/adventurer to a higher status than that of the peaceful domestic philosopher/missionary.

While the hostile islanders may seem to be the villains of the piece, the real danger to the family's safety lies not in the attacking horde, but in one small foolish boy. While the family is able to hold off the invaders, they find themselves under siege and limited in their supplies. Soon after, Ready discovers that their precious supply of water has been depleted by none other than little Tommy, who has chosen to slake his thirst rather than consider the needs of his family. In order to save the Seagraves from a terrible death by dehydration, Ready dresses as a native and sneaks out of the stockade to fetch water. While he is successful in his quest, he is ambushed by a savage and killed. Thus, Marryat transforms *The Swiss Family Robinson* from a simple educational treatise on surviving a desert island to a new genre greatly concerned with manliness and the appropriate way to train a boy in his moral duty. The only thing worse than the island savages is the island's savage, little Master Tommy, whose constant foolish and selfish decisions eventually cost Ready, the most helpful and important figure of civilisation on the island, his life. While the family initially shelters the child from the immediate consequences of his actions, Mr Seagrave firmly believes that the knowledge will transform Tommy from an imprudent boy to a wiser man: 'What a lesson it will be to Tommy when he is old enough to comprehend the consequences of his conduct!'[48] As literary historian Alan Horsman has argued, this example of foolishness punished is far from simplistic. He explains:

> The intervening treatment of the culprit [Tommy's] repeated naughtiness is no doubt intended to make the reader award blame; but this, like the crudity of the judgment upon the child in the process of learning, is something added to the action and not essential to it: the action has been concerned with the discipline of reality; from it there stand out clearly the self-centered young child at one end and the mature second mate at the other, while the development of this maturity appears in the narrative of Ready's life. Something more than simple blame arises from a climax in which the mature man is destroyed as a result of the inevitable limitations of someone at the other end of the disciplining process.[49]

I would argue the 'something' Horsman refers to in the consequences of Tommy's actions is an interrogation of manhood and boyhood which would become staples of adventure fiction. As Graham Dawson summarises, 'Adventure narratives about these soldier heroes imagine masculinities which are ideally powerful and free from contradictions. They function, psychically and socially, as wish-fulfilling figures of identification offering the psychic reassurance of triumph over the sources of anxiety.'[50] Unlike *The Swiss Family Robinson,* where Father's judgement and control are absolute, *Masterman Ready* gives power to Tommy, and his choices have very real and lasting consequences. A foolish boy can kill a powerful man, yet even so, the fantasy of perfect education can correct his foolishness. By the end of the narrative, the time on the island proves instructive to all the boys, with William inheriting and wisely managing his father's flocks in Sydney, Tommy 'notwithstanding all his scrapes' joining the army, and little Albert joining the navy and becoming a commander.[51] Whereas the future of the boys at the end of *The Swiss Family Robinson* is fraught with uncertainty, Marryat's boys all become adventurer-heroes, either as triumphant colonisers (in the case of William) or as soldiers of the British Empire.[52] Through wise guidance and hard lessons in a hostile environment, Marryat shows that all young boys, the brave and the foolish, can become true men of empire. While Tommy's actions may appear foolish and misguided, proper role models rehabilitate him into a model adventurer/trader. Like Vason's narrative, Marryat's champions the adventurer as the most appropriate, and most interesting, subject for boy's fiction.

Boys Will Be Boys: R. M. Ballantyne's *The Coral Island*

While Marryat's *Masterman Ready* has been largely ignored, Scottish author Robert Michael Ballantyne's first Pacific novel, *The Coral Island* (1858), has incited a great deal of recent critical interest. Unlike Marryat, whose novel closely echoes *The Swiss Family Robinson*, Ballantyne broke from earlier models of the Pacific by freeing the Victorian boy from the constraints of a role model like Father or Ready. The adventure novel of the 1840s was concerned with defining this new independent 'boy'. As literary critic Rod Edmond explains,

> The new manly boy comprised several rather different, even conflicting, qualities. One set of qualities emphasized physical courage, heart, pluck and guts. Boys being trained to run an empire should be fearless and daring . . . On the other hand, moral responsibility was an essential part of Christian manliness and the manly boy had to learn to temper his physical vigour with the Christian virtues of restraint and piety.[53]

This new interrogation of the 'manly boy' dovetailed nicely with the increased interest in the Pacific. Adventure critic Joseph Bristow notes,

> On islands—geographically sealed-off units—there is the possibility of representing colonialist dreams and fears in miniature. In children's literature, the island regularly serves as an appropriately diminutive world in which dangers can be experienced within safe boundaries. Boy heroes can act as the natural masters of these controllable environments. Islands provide an appositely

"child-like" space which boys can easily circumnavigate without revealing any lack of manful maturity.[54]

Using *The Coral Island* as an example, scholars have developed multiple interpretations of the link between the interest in masculinity and the interest in imperialism. Thus, *The Coral Island* represents an important transition between the family-oriented survivalist tales of the early Victorian age and the new adventure genre, which intended to provide lessons specifically to boys on how to become good citizens of a growing empire. As a Pacific text, *The Coral Island* reveals the increasing secularisation of the South Seas narrative and the real implications of the interactions between religion and trade as revealed through the boys' 'play'.

Unlike Marryat, Ballantyne's original inspiration came not from an interest in foreign places, but instead from a new vision of his home. Having published multiple books based on his experiences adventuring in America, Ballantyne was already a successful children's writer before he conceived of *The Coral Island*. It was in the summer of 1857, however, that he was inspired to create a new adventure outside the scope of his own travel experience. While staying in a seafront house in Burnisland,[55] Ballantyne was able see from his bedroom window the island of Inchkeith. His biographer, Eric Quayle, explains that it was while Ballantyne was

> sitting at his table before the window, idly gazing out to sea, that the sight of the little island shimmering in the distant sunlight brought suddenly to his mind the idea of making the characters of his next tale castaways on just such a place. He decided to make it a tropical island, uninhabited and wild, but crowded with a multitude of dangers.[56]

For Ballantyne, who drew upon outside sources for his descriptions of the Pacific, the differences between the foreign island and the British island outside his window were nominal. His coral island belongs to Ralph, Jack and Peterkin from the moment they land upon it, a metaphorical extension of Britain with coconuts. The boys instantly view any other islanders as savage invaders or, after an appropriate conversion, British subjects.

Unlike Marryat's novel, where, with the exception of William, the children are seen primarily as liabilities hindering Ready and Mr Seagrave in their civilising efforts, the boys of *The Coral Island* are exceedingly capable and no longer require a guiding Father. Instead, as Jack states, 'We are wasting our time in *talking* instead of *doing*.'[57] Jack strongly echoes Thomas Carlyle's philosophy of masculine power as inherently connected to 'doing'. In *Chartism*, Carlyle explains,

He that can work is a born king of something; is in communion with Nature, is master of a thing or things, is a priest and a king of Nature so far . . . Let a man honour his craftsmanship, his *can-do*.[58]

This emphasis on 'doing' offered a new way to move the shipwreck story from a focus on an individual or family to a focus on boyhood. The idea of boyhood in *The Coral Island* has been widely discussed. Martin Green reflects:

In Ballantyne's hands, the Robinson material was reshaped to be boy's reading. It may seem this was no new development, but the readers aimed at by earlier writers like Campe, Wyss, and Marryat were children rather than boys, though certainly male rather than female children. The crucial difference is that 'children' means not-grown-up, or at least innocent, while 'boy,' as the word was so eloquently used by mid-Victorians, connoted more positive qualities. These are the qualities suggested by epithets like lionlike, or noble . . . 'Boy' in this sense is one of the group of words associated with 'manly' and 'manliness.'[59]

Thus, the boys are less concerned than their predecessors with the essentials of survival and more with the pure joy of exploration or, as Susan Maher succinctly states, 'Re-creation is not the order of day in *The Coral Island*, adventure is.'[60] However, while critics like Green have focused on the connection between boyhood and adulthood, I would further argue that boys are equally interested in learning manliness through 'play', the boyish equivalent of the masculine 'to do'. Instead of focusing on building houses or taming creatures, usually under the watchful eye of Father or an equivalent character, *The Coral Island* shows the boys fighting sharks, conducting scientific experiments and exploring for the sheer pleasure of it. In a word, they play. The initial goal of the text is not to build a society, but to build a better boy through natural education: 'the order they impose upon their island world in minimal. The boys themselves, not the island, come to signify their culture's ideology. The order that counts on the Coral Island is order from within.'[61] The boys' adventures or 'play', however, serve not only to educate the fictional characters but also the real British boys at home. Pacific island 'play' informs British island behaviour. In his essay on *The Coral Island*, Martine Dutheil explains,

Ballantyne's narrative in fact addresses its lesson to the British boys whose access to manliness is symbolically achieved through their role as colonial instructors. In *The Coral Island*, this pedagogical impulse translates into detailed descriptions of the fauna and flora of the island, into scientific experiments (such as Ralph's water-tank) and didactic generalizations.[62]

Education is no longer provided by a governing all-knowing Father, but instead is learned by the manly act of 'doing' translated into the boyish act of 'playing'. Boys are encouraged to act, to take charge of their own destinies, and by extension their countries.

While the first half of *The Coral Island* encourages exploration and adventure, Ballantyne reveals the consequences of these actions when 'the boys' dream of isolation is shattered by the realities of empire'.[63] The second half of the novel deliberately introduces the emblematic characters of Pacific island writings: 'the cannibal, the pirate and the missionary'.[64] All three categories invade the boys' island and challenge their developing masculinity. In a sense, British fiction is transformed into a Pacific reality as the boys are forced to test their boyhood 'playing' against the realities of manly 'doing'. The islanders that the boys encounter are of the same mindlessly vicious sort that characterise Marryat's fiction. These natives threaten not only physical danger, however, but psychological trauma, as

> the conjunction of children and island as icons of 'civilised' nature conjures the sense of an interdependent purity which must be safeguarded from the native's corruption. The native is dehumanised in the Empire's endeavour to present itself as taming of the beast or ejection of the serpent from a westernised Christian Eden.[65]

The natives are dangerous not because they may eat the boys, but because they bring out the savage nature hidden within them. Enraged by the natives' acts of cannibalism and infanticide, Jack attacks a band of savages in a fury, killing the chief, and in one of the more problematic scenes in the novel, causing the others to be 'awestruck by the sweeping fury of Jack, who seemed to have lost his senses altogether'.[66] Diane Loxley explains,

> As far as interracial conquest is concerned, it is precisely this fundamental challenge of a superior masculinity and warriorhood which is, in fact, most difficult for the European to assert without, at the same time, effacing the crucial primary distinction between its progress and civilisation as against the non-European's essential savagery.[67]

While such violent actions depict the boys acting as manly warriors, this violence must be tempered with justice to reflect Ballantyne's belief in the moral superiority of the British islanders.[68] Thus the

> cannibals are over-the-top stereotypes of the savage native ... One understands the savage native entirely after reading Ballantyne's description: savage natives are completely 'Other,' closer to animal than to human; they are monsters; they are evil incarnate; they can—and must—be killed with impunity.[69]

Unlike the natives from other parts of the empire, the British designated the Pacific islander as cannibal, the worst sort of savage, next to whom 'the European civilizer is represented as a godlike figure or a "superior being"'.[70] Violence against Pacific islanders was acceptable, even manly, because these savages broke one of the most basic indicators of 'civilization', killing and eating other humans.

While the boys' actions temporarily subdue the islanders' threat, the missionaries on the island must transform fully the hostile savages into peaceful natives. The novel speaks of the LMS with great admiration, arguing that it is only by the grace of God and the work of the missionaries that the people have abandoned their old 'savage' ways and embraced British civilisation. As with the earlier missionary texts, evidence of civilisation is revealed through construction:

> The Christian village is characterized by straightness, order and western taste . . . The implications of the taming of nature are specifically significant as in Ballantyne's story, nature has—like in Defoe's *Robinson Crusoe*—a literal and figurative meaning. Consequently, the orderly village is a symbol of the civilization of both the objective world and the nature of the savages who used to live in the wilderness.[71]

Ralph himself makes clear this distinction between the mission and the primitive villages, stating, 'I was again led to contrast the rude huts and sheds and their almost naked, savage-looking inhabitants with the natives of the Christian village, who, to use the teacher's scriptural expression, were now "clothed in their right mind"'.[72] Roslyn Jolly has argued that such descriptions are unsurprising, given that '*The Coral Island* is animated throughout by the desire to defend and win supporters for the Pacific missions. Much of it is simply missionary propaganda and it borrows heavily from such texts as John Williams's *Missionary Enterprises*.'[73] By championing missionaries, however, Ballantyne also supports an alternative masculinity to that portrayed by his boy heroes. Evangelical manhood developed from an emphasis on reputation to a focus on creating character. John Tosh explains:

> The traditional vocabulary of manliness—words like 'sturdy', 'vigorous' and 'robust'—was redefined to include a moral as well as a physical dimension; this was particularly true of 'courage', now interpreted to mean standing up for what is true and right, rather than showing physical guts. Character was formed by areas of experience, moralized work and moralized home. Work acquired almost hallowed authority. Manly energy was to be focused not on anti-social self-assertion, but on occupation or 'calling'.[74]

While the boys demonstrate the militant, active masculinity of the adventure tradition, the missionaries reveal there was also a place, albeit less heroic, for the domestic man, like Wyss's Father or Marryat's Mr Seagrave, called to lead the home through the example of his righteous character. While it is undoubtedly true that Ballantyne champions the efforts of the South Seas missionaries, he is also very aware of the link between missionary endeavours and colonial ones.

Between the hostile savages and the saintly missionaries, the boys encounter a third, and most contentious, category of island dweller: the trader, who in this case is a ferocious pirate. Bloody Bill and his pirate crew act as the notorious truth tellers of the island, famously stating, 'I don't know and I don't care what the gospel does to them, but I know that when any o' the islands chance to get it, trade goes all smooth and easy.'[75] While the pirates' rough ways are challenged by the boys' inherent nobility and honesty, the novel makes clear the link between trade and religion. According to Neil Rennie, 'These views combine religious ideology and imperialism in a familiar manner for the time. They link the Christian ideal with British nationhood, and allow writers like Ballantyne to identify messages of faith with the propaganda of empire.'[76] Critic Stuart Hannabuss agrees, arguing that only after the missionaries convert the island is it able to function successfully as a British colony.[77] The Pacific lent itself especially well to imperial rhetoric, as unlike larger British colonial prospects, it was entirely possible to convert and control a small island in a manner of years. Yet Bloody Bill calls into question both of the boys' potential role models: the trader/pirate and the missionary. While the missionaries have a righteous agenda and the pirates clearly a malevolent one, both contribute to the introduction of imperial vice in the Pacific. Without missionaries, traders would have a more difficult time dealing with the natives. *The Coral Island* thus destabilises the rosy picture of empire, calling into question the motivations and consequences of both traders and missionaries.

The answer to the thorny problems of imperialism, outlined by their interactions with traders and missionaries, lies with the boys' ability to make proper decisions, 'converting' the pirates and aiding the missionaries. However, the conversion of the natives comes at the end of the text as the civilising power of the missionaries undermines the independent imperial power of the boys to conquer and govern the island space. Rennie argues,

For [Ballantyne] community became utopian when it became Christian. Mixing adventure with religion, he challenged the reader to get himself wrecked on a savage island (where he would be roasted and eaten) as opposed to a Christian island (where he would be fed and clothed and sent on his way rejoicing).[78]

It is only when all three elements are balanced, when the missionaries have converted the islanders making way for proper imperial trade interests (by eliminating the pirates) that the boys' work is complete and that they are able in good conscience to leave their island and return to society. The boys' work is paradoxically to 'play', but their adventures on the island, as Jacqueline Rose has argued in her work on childhood, function as a 'type of "look and learn" where the children acquire knowledge of the natural world and an understanding of their moral superiority over the savages at one and the same time'.[79] Yet 'play' or adventure is not enough; the boys must also assume a more active, can-do, manhood by the end of the novel, asserting themselves against both the hostile pirates and island savagery. While earlier texts, such as Marryat's *Masterman Ready*, provide direct role models for boys in the form of parental figures, *The Coral Island* transitions adventure fiction towards a greater focus on the boys themselves. Unlike their predecessors, Ralph, Jack and Peterkin have direct agency and must make their own choices as to which model of masculinity to follow: adventurer, trader or missionary. While *The Coral Island* stands as a model of Victorian adventure fiction,[80] its vision of boyhood and of possible male role models is complicated by the wider canon of Ballantyne's writing.

Of Trader Kings and Island Queens: Ballantyne's Pacific Tales

While *The Coral Island* has received its fair share of critical attention, scholarship has left the rest of Ballantyne's Pacific fiction in obscurity. By examining two of Ballantyne's later works, *Gascoyne, the Sandalwood Trader* (1864) and *The Island Queen* (1885), this section will provide a more complete look at the evolution of Ballantyne's feelings about British expansion in the South Seas by widening the definition of adventure fiction to include new masculine role models, and rehabilitate established ones.[81] While *The Coral Island* reveals the vulnerabilities of the colonial enterprise, Ballantyne's later works reveal a shift towards an increasingly optimistic view of imperial growth in the Pacific, championing the idea that increased trade will benefit the growing empire. *Gascoyne* and *The Island Queen* both reinterpret the relationship between children, missionaries, traders and islanders first examined by Ballantyne in *The Coral Island* while in *The Cannibal Islands* Ballantyne rewrites Captain Cook's *Journals*, transforming the scientific expedition into a boy's adventure novel. All three texts show Ballantyne's increasing support for the missionary movement in the Pacific and the British right to convert and colonise the fertile islands.

Seven years after his initial success with *The Coral Island*, Ballantyne returned to the islands of the Pacific for his novel *Gascoyne, the Sandal-wood Trader*.[82] His delay is perhaps understandable. Despite his intention, like Marryat, to create a truly accurate narrative, Ballantyne made a mistake in his description 'about coconuts, which he had to repent publically for the rest of his life. It mattered to his audience that he should seem to be dealing in facts.'[83] The error itself is quite minor: Ballantyne has Peterkin cut a hole in a coconut with a penknife. He remarks later in reminiscences that he based the scene on the small coconuts he saw at the grocers rather than the larger, tougher specimens found on the islands.[84] This incident, however, reveals a change in the British reading public: readers had enough access to information about the Pacific both to be aware of Ballantyne's error and to be bothered by it. While adventure stories could push boundaries, it was important that, at least on the surface, they appeared as accurate as possible. Even with such minor mistakes in his early works, Ballantyne resolved not only to research the settings of his books but also to gain first-hand knowledge (either by personal visits or by speaking with people who resembled his characters) before writing.[85] His need for increased research was not the only reason for the delay; Nelson's also commissioned him to write other small works. Ultimately, the additional effort paid off as *Gascoyne*, Ballantyne's second major Pacific novel, was a commercial success for both the author and the press. Ballantyne was paid £80, the most for any of his books to date, and by June of 1864, *Gascoyne* had sold over two thousand copies.[86]

Unlike its predecessor, *Gascoyne* is not a shipwreck tale. Instead, the novel features young Henry Stuart whose mother, the widowed Mrs Stuart, had travelled to the Pacific with a group of missionaries to serve as a schoolteacher. Henry, like *The Coral Island*'s Ralph, is an adventurous young man who spends his time on the island alternately working on the mission settlement and holding the savage natives at bay, especially the wild Keona, Henry's island foil, who exceeds his fellow natives 'in revenge, hatred, and the like' and seeks to murder the brave, kind boy.[87] Despite Ballantyne's instance on Keona's villainy, the only discernible difference between the two youths is that Henry is born British and Christian. *Gascoyne*'s Henry, like the boys of *The Coral Island*, are not in a *bildungsroman* where they develop into better men than their island counterparts. As literary critic Paulette Michel-Michot has argued, 'Ballantyne's characters do not develop; they go through a series of exciting and heroic adventures that leave them unchanged. Logically enough, the boys are finished products, and the novel is a statement of the mid-nineteenth century credo.'[88] Henry enters the novel brave, kind and good and his inherent heroism goes unquestioned throughout the narrative: 'Ballantyne's children are free of evil ... They fear nothing and behave like "gentlemen" towards one another. They embody the sense of superiority, the blind optimism, the self-assurance and complacency of the mid-nineteenth century British empire.'[89] Unlike Ralph, Peterkin and Jack, Ballantyne's Henry is not forced to explore or claim the island; instead he serves as a pre-formed moral compass, an example of proper British boyhood.

The novel's conflict thus arises not from Henry's interactions with the savage natives on the island, but instead with a new arrival to their shores, a black-hulled vessel captained by the enigmatic title character Gascoyne. Unlike Henry, Gascoyne's status is questionable from the moment of his arrival. The very design of his ship is mysterious, its trappings 'we ... associate with the idea of a yacht or a pirate' and its captain 'a man preeminently fitted for the accomplishment of much good or the perpetration of much evil'.[90] Ballantyne's familiarity with the varieties of South Seas trade echoes in the ambiguous nature of the arriving trader. While whaling was the 'longest lived, largest, and most profitable of all Pacific commerce', there was also a great deal of European interest in selling luxury goods such as pearl, *bêach-de-mer*, and of greatest importance to *Gascoyne*, sandalwood.[91] In his history of Hawaii, Douglas L. Oliver writes: 'some sandalwood was spotted and carried along to China for barter. There it was eagerly accepted, so much so that within a few decades there was hardly a stick of sandalwood left in the Islands.'[92] Growing competition for the rare wood and the possibility of earning huge sums in the Chinese market, led sandalwood traders to increasingly harmful and exploitive interactions with the natives who lived on the islands with the precious commodity. Oliver records several incidents of violence and blackmail, and he notes the connection between sandalwood and the arms trade; 'sandalwooders', he reports,

> temperamentally well suited to this commerce, became especially proficient in it and were able to supplement their decreasing profits from the dwindling supply of sandalwood by labor recruiting and by the arms and rum trade. In the Solomons some of them went so far as to join with their favorite clients in head-hunting forays.[93]

Fellow historian John M. Ward supports Oliver's negative portrayal of the sandalwooders, stating,

> The sandalwood traders, certainly the most violent and the most ill-famed of the Europeans then in the South Pacific, used methods in dealing with natives

which the British government, had it intervened, would have been bound to prevent and punish by every means within its power. The traders and seamen were well enough content with conditions as they were.[94]

Ballantyne's decision to make his title character Gascoyne one of the most maligned traders in the Pacific is therefore an unusual choice. Gascoyne's status as a role model is ambiguous, as he is neither instantly praised nor condemned.

While Gascoyne's profession makes him suspicious to the nineteenth-century reader, his actions rehabilitate his shaky reputation. As he tells Captain Edmund Montague, commander of the British navy's HMS *Talisman*, traders often act violently for their own protection and due to the lack of governmental support:

> If I had sought protection from the warships of the king of England, I must have sailed long and far to find it . . . It is no child's play to navigate these seas, where bloodthirsty savages swarm in their canoes like locusts. Moreover I sail, as I have told you before, in the China Seas where pirates are more common than honest traders.[95]

As Gascoyne reveals to Henry's mother (later revealed to be his wife), however, he is not simply a trader, but also Durward the pirate.

In many ways, Gascoyne is similar in character to *The Coral Island*'s Bloody Bill. Both are sandalwood traders and both masquerade as legal traders to avoid confrontations with the British government. Yet in *Gascoyne*, Ballantyne's intention is to redeem the selfish and bloodthirsty pirate character from his earlier fiction. Bill participates in piracy purely for profit, and he sees the island missionaries (like Henry and his family) only as avenues to increased trade. As Bill states, 'We find that wherever the savages take up with Christianity they always give over their bloody ways, and are safe to be trusted. I never cared for Christianity myself.'[96] Bill explains that he was forced into piracy and held prisoner until he 'became reckless and at last joined them. Since that time, [his] hand has been steeped in human blood again and again.'[97] Ralph tries to save Bill's soul after natives wound him, but Bill responds, 'it's not for the likes o' me'.[98] Ballantyne leaves Bill's eternal fate a bit ambiguous. While he inquires with his last words whether the Bible says a man like him can be saved, he makes no formal conversion before he dies. In contrast, while Gascoyne, like Bill, is deceived into a life of piracy, he chooses to repent of his actions. Instead of killing for profit, Gascoyne states, he 'determined to become merely a *robber* and use the proceeds of my trade to indemnify those to whom injustice had been done . . . I called myself in jest, a tax-gatherer of the sea.'[99] After heroically defending the mission settlement from an attack by natives, Gascoyne willingly accepts arrest by Captain Montague. Such is the nobility of Gascoyne's actions that even the morally impeachable Henry recognises he should be set free. After Henry stages a daring prison break, and despite Gascoyne's initial protests that he deserves jail, Gascoyne and his family and friends escape to start a trade outpost and missionary school on the small Green Isle in the South Seas. Ballantyne's rationale in redeeming the pirate's character is clear: even the worst and most maligned traders of the South Pacific can be reclaimed by the moral guidance of missionaries and the inherent nobility of their British heritage. In *Gascoyne*, therefore, trade is purified by and inherently linked with the mission's project. Fulfilling the predictions of John Williams and William Ellis, Ballantyne's fictional Pacific missions have opened up the Pacific to a new era of British trade wherein even the most hardened of pirates can be converted into a loyal and productive citizen of the empire.

The British public was captivated with *Gascoyne* and books like it. According to Martin Green,

> by the mid-nineteenth century, the South Sea islands were well established in the Western imagination as *the* setting for Robinson adventures, and indeed for fantasies of various kinds, ranging from heroic thoughts of missionary martyrdom, via Crusoe, to licentious dreams of unlimited sex.[100]

In order to transform these savage islands of the Pacific, *Gascoyne* called out for white leadership from the new men of empire. By 1885, however, Ballantyne had significantly revised what that leadership might look like in his new novel, *The Island Queen*, responding to the ever-increasing power of the British Empire and new developments in the Pacific. While his previous novels had argued that the hope for transforming the island natives rested with white men, the actual conquest of the Pacific had been far less noble. Although the French had been actively securing their claims to islands across the Pacific, including in British-dominated Polynesia, Britain's response to French expansion was minimal, establishing consuls to keep the status quo.[101] Trade was also developing at a rapid pace. According to historian John Ward,

> Whereas in the 'forties island trade had consisted mainly of the supply of provisions to whalers and the acquisition of sandalwood, the growth of trade based on Australia, New Zealand and North and South America during and after the 'fifties made the Pacific a commercial highway in which island bases were sought as coaling stations and ports of refreshment.[102]

Yet despite the new forms of trade, and the increase in traders, for the most part, 'the new industrial and trade developments in the South Pacific produced no immediate change in British policy'.[103] Britain maintained its policy (or perhaps non-policy) of detachment, preferring to let the islands govern themselves. Instead of 'taking things already available and making fast turn-arounds—large profits derived from quick exchanges . . . More white traders moved in and islanders became less eager to sell out to the first bidder.'[104] The new plantation economies were brutal, mostly run by 'individuals with more hope than capital' and leading to a new island exploiter, the 'blackbirder' who 'induced' natives from other islands to work the plantations in Polynesia, in effect creating a new slave trade.[105] Instead of revealing himself as the noble saviour of the islands, the white British coloniser was far more likely to be a degenerate mutineer, a con-artist or a scheming businessman hoping for a quick profit – in other words, a Bloody Bill.

In *The Island Queen*, Ballantyne responds to such colonisers by arguing that the problem of foolish men in the Pacific stems from bad leadership. While noble boys still exist, when there is trouble amongst the men, the answer lies in feminine, not masculine, leadership, undoubtedly reflecting the influence of Queen Victoria over the growth of the British Empire.[106] *The Island Queen* harkens back to *The Coral Island*, shipwrecking three youths on a deserted Pacific island. In this case, however, the survivors are not solely male; along with Dominick and young Otto, Ballantyne's third victim is their sister, Pauline. Pauline is not the first female to be shipwrecked on an island; indeed the genre is dominated by matrons, such as Wyss's loving Mother in *The Swiss Family Robinson*, or small children, such as Marryat's Caroline in *Masterman Ready*. Nonetheless, Pauline is the first young woman in Ballantyne's canon to feature as a main character and leader. In the initial chapters of the novel, Pauline functions as do many of the other female shipwreck victims, as mother and moral guide. Later, however, after the children are joined by a group of shipwrecked emigrants, including several violent and cantankerous men, the islanders declare Pauline queen; it is the female monarch who finally secures the island.

Pauline is an intriguing mix of wilting maiden and just and fair ruler of a complicated and dangerous situation. In many ways, she is the guiding force of civilisation on the island. While the boys are distressed by momentary concerns (getting dry, finding shelter), Pauline always focuses on the long term. She is the keeper of the faith on the island, reminding the boys to pray and thank God for their deliverance (a role originally held by Father in *The Swiss Family Robinson*).[107] Her religious devotion inspires her to keep a calendar, one of the few tenuous links that connect the new island community with their old life in England.[108] Pauline, or 'Pina' as her brothers call her, is quickly made the unofficial ruler of the small island and she orders the boys to

'Go forth and subdue the land', though when pressed, 'she was rather puzzled, as rulers sometimes are when required to tackle details.'[109] For assistance, she designates Dominick her prime minister and Otto her army and sends them off on an exploratory mission. While the boys are made servants of the empire, off to 'practical' errands like supplying food and claiming land for the new monarchy, Pauline reminisces, and 'as she gazed over the sand, and across the sea, her thoughts assumed the wings of the morning and flew away over the mighty ocean to old England'.[110] Thus Pauline is a thoughtful monarch whose primary duty is to remember England and impose a similar system of government and religion on the oftentimes unruly boys.[111]

Later, Pauline's 'play' monarchy with her brothers becomes quite real when their island is invaded by a group of shipwrecked emigrants. As with the boys in *The Coral Island*, 'playing' quickly turns to 'doing' as Pauline is forced to decide how to manage these new subjects. Ballantyne's depiction of Pauline's rulership articulates larger concerns about the ruling female monarch, Queen Victoria. On the one hand, it is Pauline's shy, retiring femininity that allows her to control the rough men. Upon meeting the shipwrecked crew,

> with a natural tact and grace of manner which had the appearance of, but was not meant for, dignity, [Pauline] advanced and offered her little hand to Malines [a crewmember], who seemed to fear that he might crush it unintentionally, so slight was the shake he gave it.[112]

Pauline's beauty also instantly silences the ship's doctor, John Marsh, who, upon beholding her, is 'reduced to that condition which is variously described as being "stunned," "thunderstruck," "petrified," and "struck all of a heap" with surprise'.[113] In many ways Marsh's admiration is that of the Victorian chivalric tradition; he may admire and love the maiden from afar, but would never dream of a physical relationship with her.[114] It is not just Pauline's physical appearance, however, that stuns; her presence both in body and mind in such a hostile place renders the men speechless. In fact, her difference is what initially inspires the men to make her Queen, stating that

> nothing short of a power standing high above them and out o' their reach will have any influence with them at all. There are so many strong, determined, and self-willed men amongst them that there's no chance of their ever agreeing to submit to each other; so, you see, you are a good angel, before whom they will be only too glad to bow—a kind of superior being, whom they will reverence, and to whom they will submit.[115]

Yet while Otto believes that Pauline's power derives from her femininity, and therefore moral superiority, Pauline sees her role as a sovereign duty. When Pauline makes an unpopular decision to choose one of the crewman over her brother as her premier, Otto inquires, 'Were you not made queen for the purpose of carrying out their [the men's] wishes?' Pauline replies,

> Certainly not . . . I was made queen for the purpose of ruling. They told me they had confidence in my judgment, not in my readiness to carry out their wishes. If my judgment, coupled with that of my advisers, does not suit them, it is open to them to unmake me as they made me, and appoint a king or president, but my judgment I cannot alter.[116]

The conflict between Pauline as the sweet mothering 'good angel' and the unassailable British monarch echoed the complicated views of the British reading public towards Queen Victoria. The popular vision of Victorian gender roles, espoused by thinkers like John Ruskin in his lecture series *Sesame and Lilies*, is that:

> The man's power is active, progressive, defensive. He is eminently the doer, the creator, the discoverer, the defender. His intellect is for speculation and invention; his energy for adventure, for war, and for conquest, wherever war is just, wherever conquest necessary. But the woman's power is for rule, not for battle,—and her intellect is not for invention or creation, but for sweet ordering, arrangement, and decision. She sees the qualities of things, their claims, and their places. Her great function is Praise: she enters into no contest, but infallibly judges the crown of contest. By her office, and place, she is protected from all danger and temptation. The man, in his rough work in open world, must encounter all peril and trial: to him, therefore, must be the failure, the offense, the inevitable error: often he must be wounded, or subdued; often misled; and always hardened. But he guards the woman from all this; within his house, as ruled by her, unless she herself has sought it, need enter no danger, no temptation, no cause of error or offense. This is the true nature of home—it is the place of Peace; the shelter, not only from all injury, but from all terror, doubt, and division.[117]

Of course, Victoria herself complicated this binary; as monarch, she had power and authority over the men surrounding her (including in her complicated relationship with Prince Albert) and she served as the leader of the powerful British army and navy. Victoria also presented herself paradoxically, as literary scholar Adrienne Auslander Munich argues,

> replicating the language of femininity, virtually erasing the possibility of using her physical body to represent authority. In 1852, after she had been a monarch for fifteen years she stated, 'I am every day more convinced that *we women, if* we are to be good women, *feminine* and *amiable* and *domestic,* ares [sic] not *fitted to reign.*'[118]

The Victorians thus struggled to reconcile the seemingly inseparable roles of 'ruler' and 'woman'. For Ballantyne, the answer was to portray

Pauline as the sweet, noble antithesis of the men's inherent rowdiness. While the men compete with each other, Pauline is set apart as a pure and youthful, and thus untouchable, ruler. In a very Ruskinian fashion, Pauline is left to 'order' the island, making judgements about how the islanders live, work and play. The men control any violence on the island, then once the situation is under control, bring the offenders to Pauline for final judgement. Ballantyne argues that to run an island colony smoothly requires a mix of masculine adventuring and female ordering. Pauline, for instance, remains firmly queen, even as a volcano threatens the safety of the islanders. She tells the overly worried Dr Marsh, 'I am not a mere puppet, sir ... My place is here till all my subjects are safe! And your duty is to assist in the embarkation, not to offer advice to your queen!'[119] In fact, Pauline's rulership is so appreciated that the men offer her the chance to continue on as Queen in their next island home. Away from the freedom (and necessity) of the island, Pauline chooses her loyalty to her family instead. She ends her adventure by returning to the domestic sphere, a dutiful daughter rather than a potential wife. Ballantyne's novel thus leaves his position on female monarchy highly ambiguous. Is Pauline able to rule so successfully because she is a woman or in spite of her gender? Is her choice to return to her family at the end of the text a sign of her strength or her weakness as a woman? While Ballantyne had strong opinions on the heroism of boys, *The Island Queen* investigates his intriguing but confused vision of similar qualities in a female heroine. One reading of *The Island Queen* offers the hope that though traders and plantation owners may struggle, England could succeed and prosper in the South Seas islands with the help and guidance of a strong female monarch.

As trade in the Pacific increased, first with the whaling industry in the 1840s and later with luxury goods like sandalwood and plantations through the mid-to-late Victorian era, depictions of the British South Seas began to incorporate these new experiences. Focusing on adventure and conquest, the new stories created by real travellers like George Vason and John Coulter created a thirst for hyper-masculinised stories of glory and grandeur. This new non-fiction induced British novelists like Fredrick Marryat and R. M. Ballantyne to create their own versions of the Pacific experience. While these fictional narratives depicted the islands as commercial havens where boys played at manhood and eventually became men by protecting and reproducing miniature versions of the English empire, they were also testing grounds for theories of masculinity, heroism, foreign policy and rulership. As we shall see in the next chapter, however, missionaries and traders were not the only visitors to the islands. By mid-century the exotic tales of new peoples and animals on far away islands had attracted the attention of Victorian scientists. Early biologists and naturalists like Charles Darwin and T. H. Huxley changed the course of the natural sciences based largely on their experiences on small Pacific islands. The travel writings of these early scientists offered yet another vision of the Pacific to the curious home audience – a vision that transformed these promised paradises into something far more curious and far more dangerous. Novelists too began picking up on the more ominous themes of evolutionary science in texts like H. G. Well's *The Island of Doctor Moreau* and began arguing that perhaps paradise hid a darker secret.

Notes

1. Now Nuku'alofa, the capital of Tonga, located on Tongatapu.
2. Vason and Orange, *Life of the Late George Vason*, 101.
3. Ibid.
4. Dawson, 'The Imperial Adventure Hero', 46–7.
5. MacKenzie, *Propaganda and Empire*, 207.
6. Captain Cook named Tonga 'The Friendly Islands' because of the pleasant reception he received.
7. Vason and Orange, *Life of the Late George Vason*, 14.
8. Ibid., 15.
9. Ibid., 15–16.
10. Ibid., 16.
11. Ibid., 26.
12. Ibid., 28.
13. Ibid., 29.
14. Ibid., 35.
15. Ibid., 61.
16. Ibid., 88.
17. Captain Cook gave the main island of Tonga, now Tongatapu, this name on his voyages.
18. Vason and Orange, *Life of the Late George Vason*, 129.
19. Ibid.
20. Ibid., 132.
21. For example, Bougainville describes Tahitian women as beautiful, submissive and highly sensual. He records that 'the endeavours to please, are their most serious occupation . . . the wives owe their husbands a blind submission; they would wash with their blood any infidelity committed without their husband's consent . . . an unmarried woman suffers no constraint on that account; every thing invites her to follow the inclination of her heart, or the instinct of her sensuality'. Lansdown, *Strangers in the South Seas*, 80.
22. Vason and Orange, *Life of the Late George Vason*, 133.
23. Ibid., 141.

24. The missionaries were Samuel Harper, a twenty-six-year-old cotton manufacturer, Daniel Bowel, a twenty-two-year-old shopkeeper, and James Gaulton, age unknown, the cook's assistant on the *Duff*.
25. Vason and Orange, *Life of the Late George Vason*, 175.
26. Vavou is another of the Tongan islands.
27. Vason and Orange, *Life of the Late George Vason*, 179.
28. Edmond, *Representing the South Pacific*, 71.
29. Vason and Orange, *Life of the Late George Vason*, 197.
30. Ibid., 196.
31. Ibid., 196–7.
32. Bradley, *The Call to Seriousness*, 77–8.
33. It is unclear which edition of *The Swiss Family Robinson* Marryat's children were referencing, though presumably it was an English translation.
34. Marryat, *Masterman Ready*, 5.
35. Darton, *Children's Books in England*, 116.
36. Green, *The Robinson Crusoe Story*, 84.
37. Tosh, *A Man's Place*, 110–11.
38. Marryat, *Masterman Ready*, 37, 58.
39. Ibid., 165.
40. Like Father, Mr Seagrave is constantly tying the natural world to God's absolute control and authority. See for example his conversation with William where he remarks, 'The principle of order is everywhere—everything is governed by fixed laws, which cannot be disobeyed. We have order in the seasons, in the tides, in the movement of the heavenly bodies, in the instinct of animals, in the duration of life assigned to each of them . . . Does this not give you some idea of the vastness, the power, and the immensity of God?' Ibid., 129.
41. Clark, *The Cambridge Introduction to Literature and the Environment*, 13.
42. Marryat, *Masterman Ready*, 15.
43. Brantlinger, *Rule of Darkness*, 29.
44. Marryat, *Masterman Ready*, 214.
45. Ibid., 180–1.
46. The idea of the Pacific savage or cannibal conformed easily to established British prejudices. As postcolonial critic Ania Loomba explains, 'The late medieval European figure of the "wild man" who lived in forests, on the outer edges of civilization, and was hairy, nude, violent, lacking in moral sense and excessively sensual, expressed all manner of cultural anxieties. He and his female counterpart were "others" who existed outside civil society, and yet they constantly threatened to enter and disrupt this society.' See Loomba, *Colonialism/Postcolonialism*, 57.
47. Tosh, *A Man's Place*, 111. Graham Dawson also explores this idea of the adventure hero explaining, 'The condition of his triumph, however, is the denigration and defeat of an other: one who is all that he is not, and who, by virtue of this difference, may legitimately be triumphed over and destroyed.' See Dawson, 'The Imperial Adventure Hero', 48.
48. Marryat, *Masterman Ready*, 252.
49. Horsman, *The Victorian Novel*, 18.
50. See Dawson, 'The Imperial Adventure Hero', 48.

51. Marryat, *Masterman Ready*, 255.
52. Caroline, in contrast, fulfils her domestic duty by 'marr[ying] a young clergyman and ma[king] him an excellent wife'. Ibid.
53. Edmond, *Representing the South Pacific*, 143.
54. Bristow, *Empire Boys*, 94. Bristow's study continues to discuss the connection between the Victorian adventure novel and boyhood at length.
55. A Scottish city located across the Firth of Forth from Edinburgh.
56. Quayle, *Ballantyne the Brave*, 114.
57. Ballantyne, *The Coral Island*, 24.
58. Carlyle, *Thomas Carlyle*, 167.
59. Green, *The Robinson Crusoe Story*, 113.
60. Maher, 'Recasting Crusoe', 172.
61. Ibid.
62. Dutheil, 'The Representation of the Cannibal in Ballantyne's "The Coral Island"', 110.
63. Ibid., 109.
64. Ibid.
65. McCulloch, '"The Broken Telescope"', 139.
66. Ballantyne, *The Coral Island*, 203. For more on Jack's degeneracy, see Webb, 'Corrupting Boyhood in Didactic Children's Literature.
67. Loxley, *Problematic Shores*, 118.
68. The boy's violence towards the savages was a hallmark of juvenile literature, especially the adventure novel 'replete with militarism and patriotism, in which violence and high spirits became legitimated as part of the moral force of a superior race'. See MacKenzie, *Propaganda and Empire*, 499.
69. Kutzer, *Empire's Children*, 7.
70. Obeyesekere, *Cannibal Talk*, 18.
71. Siegl, *The Robinsonade Tradition*, 60.
72. Ballantyne, *The Coral Island*, 346.
73. Jolly, 'South Sea Gothic', 84. *The Coral Island* is not the only Ballantyne text to single out John Williams for praise. In his 1871 text *Jarwin and Cuffy*, Ballantyne's heroes actually meet the famous missionary. See Hannabuss, 'Ballantyne's Message of Empire'.
74. Tosh, *A Man's Place*, 112.
75. Ballantyne, *The Coral Island*, 243.
76. Rennie, 'The Palm-Tree Shall Grow', 34. Fiona McCulloch has also argued that 'another ambiguity on which *The Coral Island* plays is the dichotomy of legitimate and illegitimate trade: colonialism and piracy. The latter is the dark side of colonialism . . . problematising chivalric intention. Instead of maintaining a polar distinction between them, they seem inadvertently, if not deliberately, confused, reinforcing the aforementioned link between Christianity and colonialism as a potentially illegitimate alliance.' See McCulloch, '"The Broken Telescope"', 141.
77. As Hannabuss explains, the boys' coral island is 'an island paradise which at the same time can serve as a British colony, having successfully been indoctrinated by British missionaries'. See Hannabuss, 'Islands as Metaphors', 77.
78. Rennie, 'Far-fetched Facts', 33.
79. Rose, *The Case of Peter Pan or the Impossibility of Children's Fiction*, 79.

80. Joseph Kestner, for example, refers to *The Coral Island* as 'a signature text of mid-century Victorian adventure narrative . . . because it established motifs such as islands, voyaging and encounters with racial Others'. See Kestner, *Masculinities in British Adventure Fiction*, 18.
81. Unlike Marryat, Ballantyne was a prolific writer of South Seas fiction. His other Pacific works include *Fighting the Whales* (1863), *Sunk at Sea: Adventures of Wandering Will in the Pacific* (1869), *The Cannibal Islands* (1869), *Jarwin and Cuffy* (1878), *Philosopher Jack: A Tale of the Southern Seas* (1879), *The Lonely Island or The Refuge of the Mutineers* (1880), *The Madman and the Pirate* (1883), *Blown to Bits or The Lonely Man of Rakata* (1889) and *The Coxswain's Bride* (1891). While all provide an interesting look at British constructions of the South Pacific, the two novels I have chosen to discuss provide a relative sample of the general themes and characters reflected in Ballantyne's body of work.
82. Ballantyne published one South Seas story, *Fighting the Whales*, in this period, but while the story takes place in the Pacific Ocean, it is primarily an educational treatise on whaling. Other than having a young male protagonist, it has no connection to *The Coral Island*.
83. Green, *The Robinson Crusoe Story*, 116.
84. Ballantyne, *The Coral Island*, 35. For Ballantyne's admission of his mistake, see Quayle, *Ballantyne the Brave*, 145.
85. Quayle, *Ballantyne the Brave*, 145.
86. Ibid., 161, 94.
87. Ballantyne, *Gascoyne*, 24.
88. Michel-Michot, 'The Myth of Innocence', 40–1.
89. Ibid., 39.
90. Ballantyne, *Gascoyne*, 11, 18.
91. Howe, *Where the Waves Fall*, 93.
92. Oliver, *The Pacific Islands*, 51.
93. Ibid., 67.
94. Ward, *British Policy in the South Pacific*, 45.
95. Ballantyne, *Gascoyne*, 159.
96. Ballantyne, *The Coral Island*, 250.
97. Ibid., 297.
98. Ibid.
99. Ballantyne, *Gascoyne*, 256.
100. Green, *The Robinson Crusoe Story*, 111.
101. Ward, *British Policy in the South Pacific*, 155.
102. Ibid., 158.
103. Ibid., 162.
104. Oliver, *The Pacific Islands*, 121.
105. Ibid.
106. In 1877, Britain proclaimed Queen Victoria Empress of India. In 1884–85 Britain solidified its interest in Africa at the Berlin Conference.
107. Ballantyne, *The Island Queen:*, 48. Interestingly prayer was one of the tenets of Evangelical masculinity, as 'there were few occasions on which a Victorian father could assert his dominance over his wife, his children and his servants so effectively as when he led them in family prayers'. See Bradley, *The Call to Seriousness*, 180–1.

108. Ballantyne, *The Island Queen*, 101.
109. Ibid., 64.
110. Ibid., 65.
111. The idea of the domestic female ruler as connected to imperialism was not a foreign idea to the Victorians. As Kutzer explains, 'British imperial relations were often presented in familial terms, with England as the "mother country" and her colonial subjects as dependent children needing to be led to higher moral ground. The civilized values Britain wanted to bring to the colonies were often bound up with images and issues of family life.' Kutzer, *Empire's Children*, 5.
112. Ballantyne, *The Island Queen*, 124.
113. Ibid., 136.
114. For more on the chivalric tradition in Victorian literature see Girouard, *The Return to Camelot*.
115. Ballantyne, *The Island Queen*, 191.
116. Ibid., 219.
117. Ruskin, 'Lilies: Of Queens' Gardens', 149–50.
118. Munich, 'Queen Victoria, Empire, and Excess', 265.
119. Ballantyne, *The Island Queen*, 280.

Chapter 3

Islands of Discovery: Scientific Curiosity in the Works of Darwin, Huxley and Wells

Introduction

One of the most influential ideas of the nineteenth century began not through a study of apes, but of plankton. Before Charles Darwin formulated his landmark theories on the evolution of species, he was nothing more than a curious young companion collecting marine life aboard the HMS *Beagle*. One of his greatest supporters, naturalist and philosopher T. H. Huxley, had equally humble beginnings working as a surgeon's mate on the HMS *Rattlesnake*, largely to pay off his debts. Both men set off into the vast waters of the Pacific with only modest goals, having little idea that the ideas they would develop on their journeys among the islands would challenge the very basis of Victorian science and religion. It was these journeys that helped to inspire the vast genre of 'science fiction' which took the theories developed on these early voyages and transformed them into hopeful or horrifying views of the future. For novelist H. G. Wells, the scientific Pacific of Darwin and Huxley was not a place of discovery, but of nightmare.

Earlier struggles in the Pacific occurred mainly between missionaries who sought to convert the islanders and traders who sought to profit from them. By mid-century, the British reading public had access to accounts from both groups and demand grew for more tales of islands and islanders. Yet a subset of the English population found depictions of new flora and fauna more than a passing amusement for a dull evening. Victorian naturalists began to conceive of the Pacific as an encouraging locus of possibility for new scientific discovery. The Royal Navy proved invaluable as it sent a number of surveying expeditions between 1820 and 1860 to explore various Pacific islands and all carried naturalists.[1]

Charles Darwin and Thomas Henry Huxley both joined expeditions to the newly discovered islands and their findings would permanently change the face of Victorian society. While the scientific texts produced by both men have been studied extensively by a variety of critical fields, their travel narratives have received far less attention, especially as Pacific narratives.[2] This chapter will argue that both Darwin's *The Voyage of the Beagle* (1839) and Huxley's *The Voyage of H.M.S. Rattlesnake* (1852) merge popular tropes of missionary and adventure fiction with a newly developing genre of scientific narrative. Like earlier Pacific explorers, Darwin and Huxley comment extensively on the morals and customs of the islanders they encounter in their travels and provide detailed descriptions of the natural landscape of individual islands. They differ from their predecessors, however, in applying new scientific principles to their observations and drawing intriguing conclusions about both natural and social forms of evolution. While missionaries and traders needed to depict themselves as heroic settlers and adventurers to gain financial support for their endeavours, scientists were able to portray more honestly the realities of life in the islands. Independently, both men conclude that while exploring the islands can have great commercial and scientific benefits, there are often dangerous consequences.

With the publication of travel narratives and later scientific essays, the Victorian community quickly became embroiled in debates over evolutionary theory and social progression. By the end of the nineteenth century, the idyllic Pacific paradise had become a breeding ground for new theories of cultural degeneration and potential regressive evolution. Edwardian authors in the growing genre of science fiction, such as H. G. Wells, were quick to explore these innovative themes. Critics of Wells have extensively analysed his books for their pronouncements on and predictions of science and pseudo-science as well as their commentary on British culture. His 1896 novel *The Island of Doctor Moreau* still stands as one of the best-known investigations of Darwinism and British colonialism at the turn of the century. Despite the volume of critical attention the novel has received, however, *The Island of Doctor Moreau* has yet to be examined specifically as a work of Pacific fiction, even though Well's investigation of regressive evolution clearly resonates with the British fears of degeneration in the Pacific also found underpinning the works of contemporaries Stevenson and Conrad.[3] Wells deliberately sets his novel near the Galapagos Islands, a Pacific group not usually considered in discussions of island narratives. The geographical location connects the British narrative with Darwin's theories of evolution and with Wells's investigations of and responses to those theories. The novel also manifests a new trend in British Pacific narratives that focuses not on trade and commercialism, but instead on the dangers of new scientific theory which posited that British men might be physically 'degenerating' into lesser forms. This chapter will thus argue that Wells's work establishes the Pacific as a place of scientific barbarism intimately connecting the shifting boundary between the 'civilised' and the 'savage' with the ongoing debate over whether the British were evolving forward or backward.

The Origin of *Origins*:
Charles Darwin's *The Voyage of the Beagle*

In December of 1831, Charles Darwin boarded a survey expedition on the HMS *Beagle* and would spend almost five years onboard cataloguing the natural phenomenon they discovered on their journeys. Over the course of his observations, Darwin came to realise that instead of simply cataloguing species he must analyse them, and as Allan Christensen has argued, 'must therefore write a history of dynamic processes in which the boundaries between biological categories are in constant flux'.[4] While the narratives of missionaries and traders conformed to very strict purposes, Darwin's scientific writings were constantly adapting and evolving conclusions based on newly discovered data. While often considered only for their scientific merit, the scientific writings of Darwin deserve consideration as literary texts as well. As George Levine argues, echoing Gillian Beer,

> Darwin's language is not distinct from the ideas it expresses but intrinsic to them; it cannot be skimmed off. Alive with metaphor, twists, and hesitations, the prose is saturated with aesthetic, intellectual, and ethical energy, and with the sorts of ambivalences and multi-valences characteristic of literature.[5]

By considering *The Voyage of the Beagle* as connected to a longer tradition of British Pacific narrative, we can see how Victorian science writing shifted perspectives on the Pacific islands. Darwin's narrative constantly reinvents his vision of the Pacific islands and islanders, bringing a new instability to the British perspective of cultural superiority.

As a scientist, Darwin was less interested in the myth of the idyllic Pacific paradise and more in the realities of the islands' development. As he writes,

> The often repeated description of the stately palm and other noble tropical plants, then birds, and lastly man, taking possession of the coral islets as soon as formed, in the Pacific, is probably not correct; I fear it destroys the poetry of this story, that feather and dirt-feeding and parasitic insects and spiders should be the first inhabitants of newly formed oceanic land.[6]

For the literary tradition of the British Pacific, such statements were as radical as Darwin's evolutionary theories. By replacing the 'noble' narrative of gradual settlement with the darker reality that Pacific was originally settled by the 'lower' life forms of insects and spiders, Darwin writes a new version of the Pacific where the settlement of paradise is less beautiful than the British would have liked to imagine.

Earlier narratives imagined the islands as untouched paradises filled with new experiences. Darwin instead practically described the landscape based on familiar images of home, continually describing 'new' island discoveries with metaphors drawn from Britain. Sometimes he used these metaphors to show the vast bounty of the Pacific islands, as when he explains,

> In Brazil I have often admired the varied beauty of the bananas, palms, and orange-trees contrasted together; and here we also have the bread-fruit, conspicuous from its large, glossy, and deeply digitated leaf. It is admirable to behold groves of a tree, sending forth its branches with the vigour of an English oak, loaded with large and most nutritious fruit.[7]

Darwin connects the breadfruit with the liveliness of the oak, but also adds that the bounty of breadfruit in Tahiti adds an increased value, noting, 'However seldom the usefulness of an object can account for the pleasure of beholding it, in the case of these beautiful woods, the knowledge of their high productiveness no doubt enters largely into the feeling of admiration.'[8] Darwin argues that while the islands resemble his own island home, they produce new and exciting crops. The breadfruit improves upon the English oak as its stately beauty also provides a useful product.

Darwin does not only use these connections with England to describe the beauty and usefulness of islands. While he looks favourably upon the productive groves of Tahiti, he has a less charmed view of the more rugged islands of the Galapagos. His description notes:

> The entire surface of this part of the island seems to have been permeated, like a sieve, by the subterranean vapours: here and there the lava, whilst soft, has been blown into great bubbles; and in other parts, the tops of caverns similarly formed have fallen in, leaving circular pits with steep sides. From the regular form of the many craters, they gave to the country an artificial appearance, which vividly reminded me of those parts of Staffordshire, where the great iron-foundries are most numerous.[9]

Instead of a poetic description, Darwin elucidates the less picturesque elements of the scene, connecting the large lava craters with the foundries instantly recognisable to British readers. Darwin showed that the islands could be artificial or even ugly and that not every island was a bountiful paradise full of goods for British consumption.

The need to show both the extreme beauty and potential flaws of

Pacific islands extend also to Darwin's depictions of animals. His account records his fascination with the tameness of the native birds but also retains a sense of menace in how easy it is for invaders to overwhelm them. As Darwin explains,

> All of [the birds] are often approached sufficiently near to be killed with a switch, and sometimes, as I myself tried, with a cap or hat. A gun is here almost superfluous; for with the muzzle I pushed a hawk off the branch of a tree . . . I often tried, and very nearly succeeded, in catching these birds by their legs.[10]

While Darwin is fascinated by his ability to interact with the local animals he also recognises 'Formerly the birds appear to have been even tamer than at present', acknowledging, to a small extent at least, that outside interaction is changing the natural reactions of the local species as they learn they have reason to fear the new invaders.[11] He expands on this problem later in his description of New Zealand explaining,

> It is said that the common Norway rat, in the short space of two years, annihilated in this northern end of the island, the New Zealand species. In many places I noticed several sorts of weeds, which, like the rats, I was forced to own as countrymen. A leek has overrun whole districts, and will prove very troublesome, but it was imported as a favour by a French vessel. The common dock is also widely disseminated, and will, I fear, for ever remain a proof of the rascality of an Englishman, who sold the seeds for those of the tobacco plant.[12]

Darwin recognises that while Europeans, including the British, brought outside species to 'aid' the islands, these invasive species were largely damaging to the local environment. Rather than a civilising influence, the British had often proved to be detrimental to local crops and peoples.

Yet while Darwin is largely sceptical of the influence British sailors have had on local species, he occasionally argues that such interference may be beneficial to the islands or islanders. In Tahiti, he writes,

> In front of us there was an extensive brake of wild sugar-cane; and the stream was shaded by the dark green knotted stem of the Ava,—so famous in former days for its powerful intoxicating effects. I chewed a piece, and found that it had an acrid and unpleasant taste, which would have induced any one at once to have pronounced it poisonous. Thanks to the missionaries, this plant now thrives only in these deep ravines, innocuous to every one.[13]

In Darwin's opinion, the missionaries have done good work by removing this offensive tasting plant to less populated areas and replacing it with more healthful foods such as yams and bananas.

While Darwin's descriptions of the island landscapes provide a glimpse into his consistent practice of viewing the islands, and the Europeans who influenced them, as both helpful and hostile, he truly begins to expand upon these ideas when describing native islanders. Darwin admits that his perception of the Pacific has already been influenced by reading prior narratives of the islands. He explains before visiting Tahiti:

> From the varying accounts which I had read before reaching these islands, I was very anxious to form, from my own observation, a judgment of their moral state,—although such judgment would necessarily be very imperfect. First impressions at all times very much depend on one's previously acquired ideas. My notions were drawn from Ellis's *Polynesian Researches*—an admirable and most interesting work, but naturally looking at everything under a favourable point of view; from Beechey's Voyage; and from that of Kotzebue, which is strongly adverse to the whole missionary system. He who compares these three accounts will, I think, form a tolerably accurate conception of the present state of Tahiti.'[14]

Darwin's assumptions that reading such accounts would influence his judgements prove true. For example, he remarks,

> The Tahitians have the dexterity of amphibious animals in the water. An anecdote mentioned by Ellis shows how much they feel at home in this element. When a horse was landing for Pomarre in 1817, the slings broke, and it fell into the water; immediately the natives jumped overboard, and by their cries and vain efforts at assistance almost drowned it. As soon, however, as it reached the shore, the whole population took to flight, and tried to hide themselves from the man-carrying pig, as they christened the horse.[15]

While Darwin bases his initial impression of the Tahitian's abilities on his own observations, he is supported not just by the facts at hand, but by the stories of prior explorers. While Darwin is attempting to write a scientific narrative, he cannot help but be influenced by the narratives of explorers, missionaries and traders that made up his first impressions of the islands.

Even though Darwin draws on the experiences of others, he is very willing to correct his impressions based on his own unique experiences. While influenced by Beechey and Kotzebue to think poorly of missionary endeavours, Darwin later remarks,

> One of my impressions, which I took from the two last authorities, was decidedly incorrect; viz., that the Tahitians had become a gloomy race, and lived in fear of the missionaries. Of the latter feeling I saw no trace, unless, indeed, fear and respect be confounded under one name. Instead of discontent being a common feeling, it would be difficult in Europe to pick out of a crowd half so many merry and happy faces.[16]

While Darwin clearly is connected to a history of Pacific narrative, he is also writing his own story which defies even his own predictions of Pacific behaviour.

As he continues in his journeys, Darwin forms an overall positive view of the Polynesian islanders. On one of his first nights in Tahiti, Darwin records,

> In returning in the evening to the boat, we stopped to witness a very pretty scene. Numbers of children were playing on the beach, and had lighted bonfires which illumined the placid sea and surrounding trees; others, in circles, were singing Tahitian verses. We seated ourselves on the sand, and joined their party. The songs were impromptu, and I believe related to our arrival: one little girl sang a line, which the rest took up in parts, forming a very pretty chorus. The whole scene made us unequivocally aware that we were seated on the shores of an island in the far-famed South Sea.[17]

Darwin's account seems almost surprised at the pleasantness of the scene, as if he is experiencing a chapter from one of his predecessor's accounts. His language in describing the Tahitians is reminiscent of early mission texts as he notes, 'The Tahitians, with their naked, tattooed bodies, their heads ornamented with flowers, and seen in the dark shade of these groves, would have formed a fine picture of man inhabiting some primeval land.'[18] It is during these experiences in Tahiti that Darwin begins to argue that perhaps the development of man could be traced through the islands. As he argues,

> I did indeed admire this scene, when I compared it with an uncultivated one in the temperate zones. I felt the force of the remark, that man, at least savage man, with his reasoning powers only partly developed, is the child of the tropics.[19]

He begins to more strongly develop this idea after observing the peoples of New Zealand, where he explains,

> Looking at the New Zealander, one naturally compares him with the Tahitian; both belonging to the same family of mankind. The comparison, however, tells heavily against the New Zealander. He may perhaps be superior in energy, but in every other respect his character is of a much lower order. One glance at their respective expressions, brings conviction to the mind that one is a savage, the other a civilized man.[20]

It was observations such as these which would change Victorian thought at home, as later scientists and philosophers would argue over developing ideas of racial hierarchy and cultural evolution.

Darwin largely describes the peoples of Polynesia as pleasant and noble, yet he does not present the same image of all islanders, as we see with his description of New Zealanders. While he does not find any evidence to support claims that the missionaries have tainted the people of Tahiti, he is far more concerned about the European influence in the Galapagos. When visiting Charles Island he explains,

> This archipelago has long been frequented, first by the bucaniers, and latterly by whalers, but it is only within the last six years, that a small colony has been established here. The inhabitants are between two and three hundred in number; they are nearly all people of colour, who have been banished for political crimes from the Republic of the Equator.[21]

Darwin first notes that the island has largely been used for trade by pirates and whalers and then concludes with its new status as a penal colony. Instead of an island transformed by missionary zeal or useful as a potential trading partner, Darwin shows Charles Island as occupied first by greed and then by crime. While traders and missionaries argued that British influence was transforming the islands into more 'civilised' spaces, Darwin's narrative also shows the negative consequences that outside interest could have for the islands.

This quickly becomes a pattern in his descriptions of the Galapagos, as Darwin allows himself both to record the great beauties of the islands but also their often hidden perils. When visiting Charles Island, Darwin accompanies a group of Spaniards to a salina, or salt-producing lake. He records,

> The water is only three or four inches deep, and rests on a layer of beautifully crystallised, white salt. The lake is quite circular, and is fringed with a border of bright green succulent plants; the almost precipitous walls of the crater are clothed with wood, so that the scene was altogether both picturesque and curious. A few years since the sailors belonging to a sealing-vessel murdered their captain in this quiet spot; and we saw his skull lying among the bushes.[22]

Darwin again juxtaposes two contradictory visions of the Pacific as both an island paradise and a place of potential danger and death.

Darwin is quick to recognise the limitations of his impressions of the islands. He views the islands, like the crew of the *Beagle*, as brave visitors in a vast and often hostile ocean. When seeing the Lagoon Islands, Darwin writes in awe,

> These low hollow coral islands bear no proportion to the vast ocean out of which they abruptly rise; and it seems wonderful, that such weak invaders are not overwhelmed, by the all-powerful and never-tiring waves of that great sea, miscalled the Pacific.[23]

Later as the *Beagle* sailed to New Zealand, Darwin reflected:

It is necessary to sail over this great ocean to comprehend its immensity. Moving quickly onwards for weeks together, we meet with nothing but the same blue, profoundly deep, ocean. Even within the archipelagos, the islands are mere specks, and far distant one from the other. Accustomed to look at maps drawn on a small scale, where dots, shading, and names are crowded together, we do not rightly judge how infinitely small the proportion of dry land is to the water of this vast expanse. The meridian of the Antipodes has likewise been passed; and now every league, it made us happy to think, was one league nearer to England. These Antipodes call to one's mind old recollections of childish doubt and wonder. Only the other day I looked forward to this airy barrier as a definite point in our voyage homewards; but now I find it, and all such resting-places for the imagination, are like shadows, which a man moving onwards cannot catch.[24]

Darwin is impressed both by the islands' ability to endure in the rough environment of the Pacific but also just how distant they really are from his home. While on the one hand, trees and caverns remind him of England, on the other hand he recognised how much of these associations are simply his own fancy, his own imaginings, rather than hard scientific evidence.

While Darwin is able to reflect poetically on the limitations of his Pacific journey, he is still able to draw new scientific inferences based on the data he is able to gather. In observing a variety of Pacific peoples from Polynesia to New Zealand, Darwin begins to arrive at conclusions that will lead to his widely discussed theory of natural selection. As he remarks towards the end of his voyage,

Wherever the European has trod, death seems to pursue the aboriginal. We may look to the wide extent of the Americas, Polynesia, the Cape of Good Hope, and Australia, and we find the same result. Nor is it the white man alone that thus acts the destroyer; the Polynesian of Malay extraction has in parts of the East Indian archipelago thus driven before him the dark-coloured native. The varieties of man seem to act on each other in the same way as different species of animals—the stronger always extirpating the weaker.[25]

Darwin does not simply blame the problems in the Pacific on European influence, but also recognises that the islanders themselves were constantly in conflict. This does not mean that Darwin removed the British from consideration of the problems between invading and existing islanders. His writing is often conflicted, as when he explains,

All the aborigines have been removed to an island in Bass's Straits, so that Van Diemen's Land enjoys the great advantage of being free from a native population. This most cruel step seems to have been quite unavoidable, as the only means of stopping a fearful succession of robberies, burnings, and murders, committed by the blacks; and which sooner or later would have ended in their utter destruction. I fear there is no doubt that this train of evil and its consequences originated in the infamous conduct of some of our countrymen.[26]

To an extent I agree with John Tallmadge that Darwin continually espouses 'the belief that England is the finest country on earth and that English civilization is superior to any other', yet he still concedes that the English have made some poor choices, especially in the Pacific.[27] Darwin believes, for example, that removal of the natives was the only way to guarantee British safety in Tasmania, but also recognises that many of the violent actions of the natives were precipitated by British occupation.

Darwin feels sympathy for the islanders who suffer from British invasion while at the same desires to be part of a new wave of invaders using the Pacific to benefit the British homeland, this time through scientific discovery. As a scientist, Darwin finds the islands of the Pacific to be a fascinating home of new and exciting species that inspire innovative reflections and theories as to the development of organic life. He is constantly aware, however, that the Pacific is far from an idyllic paradise and that dangers as well as discoveries exist on the islands. Darwin presents an often contradictory view of the Pacific as a place of great beauty that harbours dark problems, often brought by explorers like himself, and remained torn between wanting to preserve his discoveries and believing that stronger species would always eventually cause damage to weaker ones.

'Darwin's Bulldog' Goes to Sea: T. H. Huxley's *The Voyage of H.M.S. Rattlesnake*

Before Huxley earned his nickname for his 'dogged' advocacy of Darwin's theories, he too sailed to the far islands of the Pacific, serving as an assistant surgeon on the HMS *Rattlesnake*. While Darwin's connection to evolutionary biology can be seen in his travel writing through his detailed descriptions of the development of islands and islanders, Huxley's narrative while also connected to the new science of biology subtly differs in its emphasis. As a surgeon, Huxley largely focused on the natural sciences, especially anatomy, and his account details his opinions on the moral and social development of island peoples. His detailed descriptions inspired Grafton Elliot Smith to argue in 1935 that this journey made Huxley into an anthropologist.[28] Darwin had filtered his opinions of native islanders through his developing theory of natural selection, where stronger species naturally dominated weaker ones. Huxley, in contrast, constantly fluctuates between describing the Pacific islanders and the British islanders as the more 'evolved' species. Huxley's narrative reveals the growing scepticism amongst British scientists in viewing cultural superiority as limited merely to geographic location. Instead, Huxley argues that it is largely behaviour not birth that indicated the 'civilised' nature of a given people.

As he set out on a voyage of discovery into the open waters of the Pacific, Huxley, like Darwin, recognised that his perceptions were influenced by the narratives of earlier explorers. When he reached Lizard Island in 1848, he remarked,

> The natural beauty of the scene was heightened by the recollection that one stood on ground rendered classical by the footsteps of the great Cook, who from this height sought some exit from the dangers which had so nearly put an end to him and his glory.[29]

Huxley draws on the memory of Captain Cook both to emphasise the beauty and excitement of visiting the islands but also to remind himself and his readers of the peril that such beauty could hide. Even with the fear of hostile natives, Huxley seems enchanted by the islands and later remarks, 'If I had been Robinson Crusoe I certainly should never have been troubled with his yearnings after society, or else the mass of men are very different from those whom I have seen.'[30] In this early section of his narrative, Huxley echoes the missionaries and traders before him by viewing the islands a paradise where man can live a simple life.

Yet while Huxley imagines the islands as peaceful havens, he also records the legacy that missionaries especially have had on the islands. When visiting Port Essington in Australia, he visits the solitary home of the Catholic missionary Don Angelo. Huxley records:

> He got the natives to build his house for him, and he lived wholly in their manner—rather priding himself upon so doing, though there can be little doubt that he thereby hastened his end. He continued to teach the black-fellows to say a few prayers, of whose meaning they had not the remotest notion: indeed I was told that they were occasionally to be heard repeating them in the square of the settlement with many gestures as rather a good joke than otherwise. And he took care of their children, for which the gins were doubtless much obliged to him. He hoped to make more impression upon the children than on the adults and he was doubtless right enough, but I fear he has done very little, and that little is a mere mechanical repetition of formulae.[31]

Huxley, who in 1869 would coin the term agnostic to describe his beliefs, did not think highly of the missions projects in the Pacific.

Instead, as in the Australian anecdote, he saw the missionaries as well-meaning but ineffectual and that it would be scientists who would take true advantage of what the Pacific had to offer.[32] Huxley would argue that the islanders of New Guinea lived in an almost perfect society and that European interference in their customs would be a tiresome mistake. As he explains,

> The people seem happy, the means of subsistence are abundant, the air warm and balmy, they are untroubled with 'the malady of thought,' and so far as I see civilization as we call it would be rather a curse than a blessing to them. I could little admire the mistaken goodness of the 'Stigginses' of Exeter Hall, who would send missionaries to these men to tell them that they will all infallibly be damned.[33]

Unlike Darwin, who believed 'civilisation' would always come to 'weaker' societies whether it was wanted or not, Huxley advocates against mission efforts expanding in the Pacific and argues for the preservation of the current island societies.

Huxley seems on paper at least to champion a more modern sensibility towards preserving native cultures, yet he based these assumptions on an often faulty and contradictory set of claims about islanders. Huxley did often describe the islands as peaceful paradises, but he was not always so naive when it came to their inhabitants. Sometimes he simply viewed the islanders' actions with a sense of paternalistic humour. Huxley records with amusement trading axes with a native named 'Kai-oo-why-who-ah' writing:

> Brady drew ten lines on the sand, and laid an axe down by them, giving 'Kai-oo-why-who-ah' who had hold of his arm to understand that when there was a 'bahar' (yam) on every mark he should have the axe. He understood directly and bolted off as fast as he could run, soon returning with his hands full of yams which he deposited one by one on the appropriate lines, then fearful lest some of the others should cut him out of the axe, he caught hold of Brady by the arm and would not let him go until he got yams enough from the others to make up the number and the axe was given to him. The yell of delight the blackie gave! He jumped up in the air, flourished it, passed it to his companions, tumbled down and kicked up his heels in the air, and finally catching hold of me we had a grand waltz with various poses plastiques for about a quarter of a mile.[34]

Like a great many earlier explorers, Huxley takes delight in what he sees as the 'childish' enthusiasm for iron the natives display. Iron was and is scarce in the Pacific islands so explorers and traders often recorded natives willing to trade high sums or fight in order to gain such advantageous weapons.

The anecdote of the axe merely presents islanders as foolish children, but Huxley and the crew of the *Rattlesnake* did occasionally have more sinister and dangerous interactions with islanders as well, especially in the islands near New Guinea. While 'Kai-oo-why-who-ah' is willing to trade for his axe, other islanders were not so patient. On Rossel Island (now Yela), Huxley records,

> They were very greedy for iron and stole one of the crutches wh. happened to be lying loose on the thwart of a boat astern. Like any dexterous London thieves they passed it from hand to hand and concealed it at the far end of their canoe, and when charged with the theft looked as innocent and impassive as M. de Tallyrand himself could have looked under similar circumstances.[35]

Huxley remains unsurprised at the natives thievery, largely as similar accounts occur in many explorer narratives like Cook's and as it was an oft cited vice in missionary texts.

Huxley is more concerned by the interactions between their ship and the armed and sometimes hostile natives they encounter. The party lands on a 'small green island' to trade with locals when the business begins to sour. The local chief

> did not seem much inclined to trust us, and the whole party went jogging on until they were joined by a good many more who came over the hills armed with their spears; by this time there were some 30 or 40 natives, almost all with their spears, and one had a carved and pointed wooden sword. This gentleman from his extreme blackness and ugliness and the peculiarity of his weapon was immediately named the 'Jack of Clubs.'[36]

While Huxley largely inscribes his own fears onto natives, attempting to diffuse the tension with a clever nickname, other situations were more serious. After a successful trading venture with the people of Chaumont, the crew of the *Rattlesnake* returns to their ship, sending the wrong message to the islanders. Huxley records the tense moments that follow as

> they must have imagined that we were taking French leave with their cocoanuts and yams. One of them who was in advance appeared very angry and scowling and poising his spear made up to Robinson. Robinson took it very coolly, just bringing his gun to his hand in readiness and looking that the fellow, who on coming closer thought better of it. As it was, it was as well there was no firing, though had I been in Robinson's place I should most undoubtedly have shot the man. I don't see the fun of waiting till you have the spear through you before you fire.[37]

While Huxley remains in good humour, it is clear he is aware that there are very real dangers in his choice to sail to the islands.

While intimidated, Huxley and his party bring out their trade goods and are surprised to find a lack of enthusiasm. Huxley describes in detail one item of interest,

> There was one tooth in the jaw and the circlet was completed by a small bone apparently not of some animal lashed to the coronoid process. The old fellow would not part from it for love or money. Hatchets, looking-glasses, handkerchiefs, all were spurned and he seemed to think our attempts to get it rather absurd, turning to his fellows and jabbering, whereupon they all set up a great clamour, and laughed. Another jaw was seen soon in one of the canoes, so that it is possible the custom there to ornament themselves with memorials of friends or trophies of vanquished foes.[38]

Not only are these islanders well-armed, they are not easily bought by British trinkets, especially in trade for items taken from defeated enemies. Huxley seems impressed by the islanders and notes, 'The blackies behaved very honestly with us, not attempting to take anything without giving a proper equivalent.'[39] Instead of viewing the islanders as foolish children or hostile warriors, Huxley begins to respect them as members of a fellow, if different, type of civilisation. While Huxley does record islanders who arm themselves upon seeing the *Rattlesnake* land on their shores, more often he notes the peaceful and warm spirit of the peoples he encounters. After visiting Brumer Island, Huxley notes,

> We were all so pleased with the primitive simplicity and kind-heartedness of these people that we gave them three cheers on our departure, a proceeding which astonished them not a little. During our visit we saw no arms of any kind in the hands of any of the males.[40]

Unlike earlier explorers, such as Cook, who were often surprised by native violence, Huxley presents the islanders as primarily peaceful and only inclined to attack upon provocation.

In his narrative, Huxley often records details to undermine the simplification of islanders into 'uncivilised' barbarians in need of British culture. While visiting the Louisiade Islands near New Guinea, Huxley records,

> Not very far from the huts and cocoa-nut patches one might occasionally see a clear patch of land exhibiting many parallel rows of something or other, concerning which a great controversy has arisen, some maintaining them to be cleared and cultivated fields, planted in rows like any dibbled farm-ground, others, that it is a mere natural result, a sort of lusus . . . I incline to the cultivation-party, and put it down as a fact: *'The Louisiadians cultivate the Ground.'*[41]

Missionaries often cited the lack of Western agriculture in the Pacific to support claims that islanders were indolent and needed Christian discipline to become a productive people.[42] Huxley, in contrast, presents Pacific islanders who do in fact cultivate fields just like their British islander counterparts. In doing so, he undermines a basic tenant that underpins the assumptions that native peoples are lazy or uncivilised.

Huxley's narrative is also more complimentary towards island women than earlier accounts which focused primarily on their reputation for sexual proclivity and lack of Western dress. Unlike the famous descriptions of warm-blooded island beauties by explorers such as Bougainville, Huxley is more impressed by the women's actions than their features. Near S.W. Island he relates,

> In some of the canoes they brought off some specimens of their ladies; they were ugly enough but not quite so bad as the Australians. They were a girdle from which long grassy fibres depend as far as the knees so as to from a kind of petticoat . . . They never stood up in the canoes as the men do but always kept sitting and sometimes shading themselves with a piece of matting.[43]

For Huxley, the most interesting feature of these native women is their dress which he connects to the petticoats of British women. Instead of looking for differences between island women and British women, Huxley repeatedly remarks on their similarities, not only in habits of dress but in social custom. During a dance on an island near New Guinea, Huxley remarks,

> The girls were very merry and unconstrained though perfectly modest in their behaviour. They seemed half inclined to have a dance too but had not the courage. It amused me very much to see how perfectly women are women all the world over. There was the same incessant flow of small talk among themselves, the same caressing and putting their arms round one another, as would have been seen in *any* other group from London to Sydney.[44]

Hardly wild and unrestrained, the island women of Huxley's travels display the same behaviours and decorum as any 'civilised' group of women in society.

Perhaps the strongest evidence Huxley presents as to the civility of the islanders, both men and women, is when he records the tale of a shipwrecked white women they discover in their travels. As she relates to Huxley's party, she had left her father in Australia to run away with her lover and join his companions on a voyage to salvage the remains of a wrecked ship off an island in the Torres Straits.[45] Her companions are killed in a storm and she is shipwrecked on an island near New Guinea. The islanders adopt her and

> they treated her very kindly, fed her and protected her from insult. One of the old chiefs, who had lately lost a daughter, persisted, according to

their common belief that white people are the ghosts of black, that she was this very daughter 'jump alive again' and she seems to have been regularly adopted among them, so that she talks of her brothers, nephews etc.[46]

Far from the position of veneration that whites legendarily took on in Pacific fiction, Mrs Thomson finds herself treated 'quite as a pet' and

she never shared in the labours of the women but stayed in the camp to look after the children while they went out on 'hospitable cares intent.' Of the kindness and good disposition of the men she speaks in the highest terms, and of the women too she speaks well but says that some of them were not so kind.[47]

The story has all the hallmarks of classic British adventure fiction with a dangerous shipwreck and a survival amongst natives on a foreign shore. Yet instead of a white conqueror who tames the uncivil natives and creates a new colony, Huxley's story of Mrs Thomson shows a white who is not inherently of higher value than islanders, and in fact functions only as a charming novelty. Far from cannibals or cutthroats, the islanders prove peaceful and largely welcoming and treat the ship-wrecked woman kindly until she is able to return to her people (though they are hesitant to part with her).

If Huxley is notable for presenting a great deal of evidence to under-mine the supposition that all islanders were barbarous and uncivilised, he also makes great strides in challenging the British position as superior civiliser. His account often presents his own actions, as well as the actions of the crew and captain, as running the gamut from foolish to downright dangerous. When first landing on a 'small green island' near New Guinea, Huxley records the crew's ignorance in the correct way to communicate with the potentially hostile islanders. He writes,

As soon as [the islanders] saw us on this territory they advanced slowly towards us—one bright copper-coloured gentleman who appeared like Paul to be "the chief speaker" bearing a green branch in his hand which he fre-quently waved. We too gathered branches and waving for the dear life and making all sorts of unearthly noises, supposed to express our pacific disposi-tion, went towards them.[48]

Instead of presenting himself as a heroic adventurer, Huxley expresses the comedy inherent in the British communications with native peoples. He relates a similar story in Chaumont Island where

several blacks came down, but each party was rather suspicious of the other, the skipper with his usual want of savoir-faire looking as stupid as a stock-fish, and the niggers not knowing precisely what we wanted to be about. After awhile it occurred to me in my presumption that this was not the way to do any good . . . . I began to dance and the niggers began to dance, and then we sat down and began to draw some of them, and then some more of the officers came ashore and we were very good friends.[49]

Huxley draws on a common racial stereotype, the black islanders' love of dance, but instead presents an often comic and childish derogatory image as a point of connection between two dissimilar groups of people. Huxley comes off looking like a fool but it is his very foolishness that creates peace and 'makes friends'. By using stock racial stereotypes, Huxley presents the white invaders as equally foolish as the local natives.

Occasionally, however, Huxley presents the natives as far wiser than him or his companions. Never overly impressed with the captain of the *Rattlesnake*, Huxley loses patience with the man's continual assumptions that all natives are hostile fools. On Middle Island, Huxley records,

> The natives did not remain long after the arrival of the cutter, but seeming in doubt of *our* intentions, moved off to the weather island. To hear the Captain talking in the evening you would have imagined that a bloody battle had taken place at the least, or at any rate must have taken place had it not been for his extreme care and providence setting the cutter. What a Sir Joshua Windbag the little man is![50]

Huxley strongly empathises with the islanders' lack of trust in white visitors, especially after listening to the captain's version of events. Huxley also recognises that men like the captain edit Pacific narratives to transform real events to present themselves as heroic conquerors of hostile peoples. In one disastrous encounter, the captain fires on a group of friendly natives invited on board by a crew member. Huxley ponders,

> Suppose we landed at a village, the natives received us with every appearance of friendship, took one or two of our number up to their houses, and then as we were shoving off treated us to a shower of spears? What should we say? When should we have held forth sufficiently about their treachery? And yet some day or other a big book will appear with a statement to the effect that 'every effort was made to conciliate the natives and treat them kindly.'[51]

Huxley's implications are twofold: one, that much of the 'treachery' of islanders may have been invented by foolish explorers and two, that statements that present such evidence in Pacific accounts may have been exaggerated or even invented for effect. Not only does Huxley undermine the validity of earlier explorer accounts, he also recognises the negative effects such voyages may have had on the islanders as when he remarks, 'One of the natives had picked up some English words (as I suppose from the *Bramble*), "Me very bad," "Me negar."'[52] For Huxley, the British assumptions of a hostile and uncivilised island populace could prove to be a self-fulfilling prophecy.

While Huxley is easily able to see how his companions make unsupported assumptions about the islanders they encounter, he is not always aware that he occasionally shares similar impulses. Like Darwin, Huxley is prone to connecting island experiences with memories from home, though he tends to choose social rather than biological examples. In Brumer Island, he begins referring to one islander as the 'dandy' describing him as

> looking at once friendly and martial, the former feeling being expressed in his countenance and gesture, the latter by means of a large wooden sword, with which on his shoulder he strutted about. He had a young girl on each arm, one of them my friend of the previous day, and these he gave us to understand were his wives.[53]

While only having a limited acquaintance with the man, Huxley feels comfortable assigning him the role of the dandy. As he walks back to the camp with the dandy and his ladies, Huxley records,

> The Dandy ... [kept] last between us and the ladies, and as we went he explained to me some story in a private and confidential manner. What it might mean, of course, I can't pretend to say but it appeared to be something to this effect. 'Really my dear friend, I am very sorry to be obliged to treat you in this inhospitable manner, but you see, our acquaintance is so *very* slight, and the ladies are so unprotected here, that the other gentleman would be angry if they found you here.'[54]

While Huxley expresses annoyance at the captain and earlier explorers for writing Pacific histories based on faulty impressions, he suffers from the same folly by translating the story told to him by the dandy based simply on his feelings. While wishing to portray a realistic narrative of the Pacific islands, Huxley too is often trapped by his own cultural assumptions.

Charles Darwin's *Voyage of the Beagle* was one of the first British scientific narratives of the Pacific islands and would greatly influence his later theories and by extension the British reading public. By examining the islands without the artificial constraints of the missionary or trader narrative, Darwin was able to see the harsher realities of Pacific development and such revelations led to his famous publications later in the century such as *Origin of the Species* and *The Descent of Man*. More interested in the moral and social ramifications of biological theories, T. H. Huxley's *The Voyage of H.M.S. Rattlesnake* also attempted to present a more accurate version of Pacific peoples than the accounts of his predecessors. While Huxley suffered from his own inescapable biases, his account undermined traditional definitions of 'civilised' and 'savage' islanders and argued that the Pacific islands may fare better without the interference of British invaders. With scientists bringing the debate about what truly constituted 'advanced' cultures, especially by the turn of the century, it was not long before fictional authors turned to Pacific islands to test some of these new radical ideas. The growing genre of science fiction attracted authors like H. G. Wells to test just how far evolutionary theory could go.

The Rise of the Mad Scientist:
H. G. Wells's *The Island of Doctor Moreau*

Published in 1896, H. G. Wells's *The Island of Doctor Moreau* undoubtedly helped to cement Wells's reputation as 'the inventor of the "scientific romance", a combination of the adventure novel and philosophical tale in which the hero becomes involved in a life-and-death struggle resulting from some unforeseen scientific development'.[55] The 'scientific development' highlighted in this novel is Darwinian theory, and specifically its connection to the fear that man could 'regressively evolve' to a more primitive or bestial form. Influenced by his trip to the Galapagos Islands, Darwin published *Origin of the Species* in 1859 and *The Descent of Man* in 1871. Both texts shocked Victorian audiences and sparked an intense debate as to the place of man in the evolutionary hierarchy. Wells himself would study under T. H. Huxley, who famously connected Darwin's theories of evolution with the Edwardian fear of degeneration. Huxley believed that 'human evolution depended very directly on moral struggle against the animal from which we have sprung. The alternative to this struggle, passive progressivism, could lead to regressive evolution in which humanity became ever more like lower animals.'[56] Literary critics have extensively interrogated Wells's interpretation of Darwinism which underpins the novel.[57] While it is not my intention to re-tread such well-explored critical ground, I do think critics have missed a vital perspective in failing to consider the novel as a Pacific text, even though many critics have noted that the coordinates given in the novel correspond to a section of the Pacific Ocean very near the Galapagos Islands. Examining the novel in the context of changing attitudes towards Pacific islanders and the burgeoning discipline of Edwardian anthropology, Wells's investigation of the possible slippage between white men, islanders and animals takes on an intriguing new dimension.

The narrative opens with three men shipwrecked and floating alone in a small dinghy.[58] The opening recollects a long tradition of British

Pacific fiction, from the three boys in Ballantyne's *The Coral Island* to the three beachcombers of Stevenson's *The Ebb-Tide*. Unlike these earlier texts, however, Wells's begins with a decidedly darker tone, as the three men discuss their starvation and the undeniable need for 'the thing we all had in mind', cannibalism.[59] While cannibalism was associated with primitive peoples in general, the Victorians especially connected the practice with Pacific islanders.[60] The choice to have Prendick consider cannibalism at such an early stage in the novel is interesting for two reasons. First, it shows that the men are becoming 'savages' even before they reach the island, or as Robert Philmus summarises, 'Their actions eliminate any clear distinction between man and beast. Prendick thus arrives on Moreau's island having already lost any firm sense of the norms of civilized behaviour.'[61] Unlike the contemporary fictions of Stevenson and Conrad, these men are savages before they reach the island, not because of their experiences on it.[62] The second point of interest is that Wells chooses to break down the boundaries between white men, islanders and animals even before the latter two categories enter the novel. As Michael Parrish Lee argues, cannibalism becomes central to the novel's conception of civilisation and savagery. Lee states,

> From the outset, the text makes cannibalism synonymous with revelation and depicts open channels of understanding as being highly invasive—violating the boundaries between self and other, much as the cannibalistic desire that they circulate threatens to violate these boundaries. And so the violent union demanded by same-species hunger is formally replicated in the violently harmonious understanding between individuals who want to eat each other.[63]

The break between 'self and other' manifests itself later in the novel when Prendick discovers Moreau's beast-men eating other animals. Lee continues,

> The breaking of a cannibalistic eating taboo now becomes the central problem of the narrative, with Moreau and company seeking proof of cannibalism among the 'savages.' The trial scene violently pries cannibalism out of the realm of secrecy and subtext, tearing open the intrigue-laden world of the island until it resembles the strangely open world of the dinghy.[64]

From the outset, this is not a 'traditional' Pacific narrative where white men invade an island and 'civilise' the native islanders. The potential for savagery is open to all who come to the island, an island which functions as the testing ground for the inner nature of mankind. While the novel makes it very clear that Prendick intends to eat one of his companions, he is saved from the act of 'savagery' by an accident: the other two men kill each other and fall overboard. Thus Prendick arrives on the island tainted but not condemned, questioning his actions and his position as a 'civilised' man of society and already fearing that he is beginning to degenerate into a bestial state.

Like Prendick, the half-savage half-civilised invader, the island itself is not typical of other British Pacific narratives. Unlike the islands of Polynesia, Melanesia, Micronesia and the Malay Archipelago, the Galapagos Islands had no native islanders and a harsh, unforgiving landscape 'in the Pacific dry belt, [where] most of the terrain . . . is semi-desert low-land'.[65] Moreau's island is both beautiful and deadly, a paradise that turns hellish in an instant. Moreau's assistant Montgomery warns Prendick on his first day that he will 'find this island an infernally rum place'.[66] Moreau later remarks, 'I never asked you to come upon this island . . . This island is full of . . . inimical phenomena.'[67] Yet even without the strange inhabitants, the island is hostile to invading species. On his first night, Prendick notes that 'In spite of the brilliant sunlight and the green fans of trees waving in the soothing sea-breeze, the world was a confusion, blurred with drifting black and red phantasms.'[68] Paradise continually transforms to reveal purgatory. Prendick finds the lush green forest turns into 'a precipitous ravine, rocky and thorny, full of a hazy mist that drifted about me in wisps . . . I was astonished at this thin fog in the full blaze of daylight.'[69] Another trail leads into a dense thicket with 'fronds flicking into our faces, ropy creepers catching us under the chin or gripping our ankles, thorny plants hooking into and tearing cloth and flesh together'.[70] This is not the island of Ballantyne or Wyss, Cook or Crusoe, calmly waiting to be 'civilised' by a superior force; this is the island of Stevenson's *Vailima Letters*, violently, almost militaristically attacking any 'invaders' that attempt to explore too deeply. While earlier texts hopefully argued that the British could control and civilise these 'savage' islands, the blatant hostility of Moreau's island suggests that such a project is doomed to failure.

Though hostile and unforgiving, the island cannot resist invasion by Moreau and his companions. In fact, Moreau sees the island much as earlier colonists did, as virgin land ready to be inhabited and used by a superior race. He tells Prendick, 'It is nearly eleven years since we came here, I and Montgomery and six Kanakas. I remember the green stillness of the island and the empty ocean about us as though it was yesterday. The place seemed waiting for me.'[71] Wells, however, turns the traditional narrative of Pacific colonisation into a horrifying farce. Instead of populating the island with 'civilised' Englishman, Moreau fills it instead with the mutilated beast-men of his vivisection experiments.[72] Moreau's experiments are so appalling that they scare away the 'savages' with their savagery. As Moreau records,

> The Kanakas, too, had realized something of it. They were scared out of their
> wits by the sight of me. I got Montgomery over to me—in a way, but I and
> he had the hardest job to prevent the Kanakas deserting. Finally they did, and
> so we lost the yacht.[73]

Before the imported islanders left in the yacht, Moreau allowed them
to interact with one of his experiments, a gorilla-man whom Moreau
considers 'a fair specimen of the negroid type when I had done him'.[74]
Wells presents Moreau as creating a breed of islander that ranks far
lower in the traditional Victorian racial hierarchy than his 'Kanakas',
or Polynesian islanders, essentially participating in regressive evolution.[75] The South Sea islanders take on the role originally held by British
colonisers: 'they received [the gorilla-man] and took his education in
hand'.[76] The gorilla-man demonstrates his progress by building a hovel,
a traditional sign of British civilisation reaching all the way back to
Crusoe. One of the islanders takes on an even greater role as 'a bit of a
missionary, and he taught the thing to read, or at least to pick out letters,
and gave him some rudimentary ideas of morality'.[77] Intriguingly, it is
the Polynesian islanders who have the strongest grasp of what the British
see as the essence of civility: education, cultural elevation and moral
structure. Despite their efforts, Moreau notes the futility of teaching
the gorilla man as 'the stubborn beast flesh grows, day by day, back
again'.[78] While the islanders have a firm understanding of 'civilised'
behaviour, Moreau's creation cannot learn as they have. Wells's story is
clearly not one of progression; Moreau notes,

> All the Kanaka boys are dead now. One fell overboard the launch, and one
> died of a wounded heel that he poisoned in some way with plant-juice. Three
> went away in the yacht, and I suppose, and hope, were drowned. The other
> one . . . was killed.[79]

Moreau explains that his later creations are even more spectacular failures than the gorilla-man and that one, a horrible serpentine monstrosity, kills the last South Seas islander. On this island, a dark parody of
Darwin's Galapagos, life is not continually evolving forward but instead
is destroyed.

If Wells portrays the imported islanders as failed attempts at enacting
the traditional role of colonisers, then Prendick's position on the island
remains ambiguous; he is neither fully coloniser nor fully islander. He is
certainly not a dashing explorer like *The Coral Island*'s Ralph. Instead
he arrives on the island weak and helpless, as 'hunger and shortage of
blood-corpuscles take all the manhood from a man'.[80] This deprivation
of some essential 'manliness' characterises Prendick's later actions on
the island as well. When Moreau finally dies, a victim of his own savage

handiwork, Prendick has a chance to rule the beast-men and colonise the island as the evolved superior, holding the 'vacant scepter of Moreau', but his cowardice prevents his ascension to island master and Prendick subsequently records that he 'sank to the position of mere leader among my fellows'.[81] To his horror, Prendick begins to recognise how few boundaries separate him from the beast-men. Forced to live among them, Prendick notes, 'I became habituated to the Beast People, so that a thousand things that had seemed unnatural and repulsive speedily became natural and ordinary to me.'[82] Prendick exemplifies Wells's fears of the degeneration of man; the intrepid coloniser of early Pacific fiction has regressively evolved into a cowardly fool who 'became as one among the Beast People in the Island of Doctor Moreau'.[83] Prendick is the fictional representation of degeneration, proving Wells's theory in his 1891 essay 'Zoological Retrogression' that

> There is . . . no guarantee in scientific knowledge of man's permanence or permanent ascendancy. He has a remarkably variable organisation, and his own activities and increase cause the conditions of his existence to fluctuate far more widely than those of any animal have ever done.[84]

In Wells's novel, it is not the inevitability of science but the foolishness of man's choices that determine his eventual downfall.

Wells's *The Island of Doctor Moreau* offers a vision of the frightening degeneration not only of mankind, but of the traditional Pacific narrative of British colonisation. While earlier fictions featured heroes of the 'civilising mission' or wild adventurers seeking liberty and excitement on untamed islands, Wells's fiction is far darker, showing the British as creating greater 'savagery' on the islands than is possible in the islanders' native state. Yet science fiction was not the only genre exploring the potential dangers of Pacific settlement and Wells's contemporaries Joseph Conrad and Robert Louis Stevenson also investigated the perils of the Pacific in their narratives. While Stevenson imagined a hybrid Pacific where whites and islanders could potentially learn to live together in peace, Conrad instead viewed the enterprise as doomed by greed and warned that only destruction lay ahead for the British invaders.

Notes

1. For more on these expeditions, see Thomas, *Islanders: The Pacific in the Age of Empire*, 153.
2. The texts have been slightly more popular in scientific writing looking to find antecedents for Darwin's theories, but have yet to be considered as a literary representation of the Pacific. For a summation of the role of

The Beagle in the debate over the development of Darwin's theories see Sulloway, 'Darwin's Conversion'. Literary studies have been far less kind to the diaries, even Gillian's Beer's landmark work on Darwin's influence on Victorian culture only briefly touches on *The Beagle*. See Beer and Levine, *Darwin's Plots*.

3. I will be discussing the Pacific works of Stevenson and Conrad in my next chapter.
4. Christensen, 'Textual Voyages of Self-Formation and Liberation', 253.
5. Levine, 'Reflections on Darwin and Darwinizing', 226.
6. Darwin, *The Voyage of the Beagle*, 21.
7. Ibid., 426–7.
8. Ibid., 427.
9. Ibid., 396.
10. Ibid., 422.
11. Ibid.
12. Ibid., 451–2.
13. Ibid., 433. Ava is another name for Kava, or the *Piper methysticum* plant, which was often prepared in Polynesian societies as a communal or ceremonial beverage.
14. Ibid., 436–7.
15. Ibid., 431.
16. Ibid., 437.
17. Ibid., 428.
18. Ibid., 436.
19. Ibid., 434.
20. Ibid., 444.
21. Ibid., 397.
22. Ibid., 399.
23. Ibid., 425.
24. Ibid., 440.
25. Ibid., 459.
26. Ibid., 471.
27. Tallmadge, 'From Chronicle to Quest', 342.
28. See Smith, 'The Place of Thomas Henry Huxley in Anthropology'.
29. Huxley, *Voyage of H.M.S. Rattlesnake*, 109.
30. Ibid., 135–6. While Crusoe was shipwrecked on an Atlantic island, his narrative became the classic example of an island text in the British imagination and was often referenced in Pacific narratives.
31. Ibid., 116–17.
32. Huxley explains his term 'agnostic' in an essay, 'When I reached intellectual maturity and began to ask myself whether I was an atheist, a theist, or a pantheist; a materialist or an idealist; Christian or a freethinker; I found that the more I learned and reflected, the less ready was the answer; until, at last, I came to the conclusion that I had neither art nor part with any of these denominations, except the last . . . So I took thought, and invented what I conceived to be the appropriate title of "agnostic." It came into my head as suggestively antithetic to the "gnostic" of Church history, who professed to know so much about the very things of which I was ignorant.' See Huxley, *Science and Christian Tradition*, 237–9.

33. Huxley, *Voyage of H.M.S. Rattlesnake*, 175.
34. Ibid., 155.
35. Ibid., 142.
36. Ibid., 145.
37. Ibid., 159.
38. Ibid., 149.
39. Ibid.
40. Ibid., 172.
41. Ibid., 139–40.
42. I discuss the missionaries' discussions of Pacific agriculture in Chapter 1.
43. Huxley, *Voyage of H.M.S. Rattlesnake*, 150–1.
44. Ibid., 178.
45. These types of illegal salvage operations were not uncommon in the Pacific. Robert Louis Stevenson writes about a similar plot in his novel *The Wrecker*.
46. Huxley, *Voyage of H.M.S. Rattlesnake*, 190.
47. Ibid.
48. Ibid., 143.
49. Ibid., 153.
50. Ibid., 163.
51. Ibid., 184.
52. Ibid., 162.
53. Ibid., 172.
54. Ibid., 173.
55. Wells, 'Biographical Note', ix.
56. Asker, 'H.G. Wells and Regressive Evolution', 17–18.
57. Examples include Glendening, '"Green Confusion"'; Haynes, 'The Unholy Alliance of Science'; Jackson, 'Vivisected Language'; Kemp, *H.G. Wells and the Culminating Ape*; McLean, 'Animals, Language and Degeneration'; Redfern, 'Abjection and Evolution'; Reed, *The Natural History of H. G. Wells*; Vint, 'Animals and Animality'.
58. Prendick makes a point of clarifying there were only three men in the dinghy, the fourth having died jumping off the ship. See Wells, *The Island of Doctor Moreau*, 7.
59. Ibid., 8.
60. I discuss the British fascination with Pacific cannibalism and the validity of their claims in Chapter 1. The connection between cannibalism and South Seas islanders was still alive and well in the British consciousness at the turn of the century, for example see Brown, 'The Solomon Islands as They Are'; Crawfurd, 'On Cannibalism in Relation to Ethnology'; M, 'Cannibalism in Queensland'; Watt, 'Cannibalism as Practised on Tanna, New Hebrides'.
61. Philmus, 'The Satiric Ambivalence of "The Island of Doctor Moreau"', 6.
62. I discuss the Pacific works of Stevenson and Conrad in my next chapter.
63. Lee, 'Reading Meat in H.G. Wells', 257.
64. Ibid., 259.
65. Stewart, *Galapagos: The Islands that Changed the World*, 30.
66. Wells, *The Island of Doctor Moreau*, 29.
67. Ibid., 67–8.
68. Ibid., 38.

69. Ibid., 63.
70. Ibid., 92.
71. Ibid., 75. 'Kanaka' was a British term for a South Seas islander.
72. Wells's novel joins a large movement in British society to stop vivisection at the turn of the century. The 1876 Act to Amend the Law Relating to Cruelty to Animals had officially restricted the practice, but not ended it. In 1898 protestors would form the National Vivisection Society with the goal of abolishing vivisection entirely. For more on the history of vivisection and its connection to British literature, see Lansbury, *The Old Brown Dog*.
73. Wells, *The Island of Doctor Moreau*, 76.
74. Ibid. Early Pacific anthropologists/cultural historians used the phrase 'negroid' to describe the islanders of Melanesia who they considered less evolved than their Polynesian counterparts. See Brown, 'Melanesia'.
75. Victorian pseudo-science and racial theory routinely referred to the lighter-skinned islanders of Polynesia as more 'racially evolved' than the darker skinner islanders of Melanesia and Australia. Darwin himself linked gorillas with 'primitive' dark-skinned peoples, especially those of Australia. Wells also connects Australians, albeit more ironically, with a regressively evolved mud-fish. The underlying fear in Edwardian theories of degeneration was that man could possible evolve into a more 'primitive' people, one they believed closely linked with apes. See Darwin, *The Descent of Man*; Wells, 'Zoological Retrogression'. I am following in the tradition of critics of Wells who use the term 'regressive evolution' interchangeably with 'degeneration'. See Asker, 'H. G. Wells and Regressive Evolution'; Morton, *Vital Science*.
76. Wells, *The Island of Doctor Moreau*, 76.
77. Ibid.
78. Ibid., 77.
79. Ibid.
80. Ibid., 24.
81. Ibid., 117.
82. Ibid., 84.
83. Ibid., 118.
84. Wells, 'Zoological Retrogression', 12.

Chapter 4

The Price of Paradise: Robert Louis Stevenson, Joseph Conrad and British Expansion in the Pacific

Introduction

By all accounts, 3 December 1894 was a solemn day in Upolu, Samoa. Along the high hillsides of Mount Vaea, only the sounds of men clearing a path to the summit broke the silence. Originally planned as a tribute to the strange white visitor who had made his home at an estate in Vailima, some forty island chiefs were now completing the lonely road.[1] That visitor, the elusive Robert Louis Stevenson, had entrenched himself in Samoan affairs and become a fixture of the landscape, earning the poetic nickname Tusitala or 'Teller of Tales' because of his attempts to record, explore and relate stories of the South Seas. Ultimately, however, his time at Vailima was short; a mere four years after he settled in Samoa for health reasons, Stevenson succumbed to his lifelong illness and breathed his last.[2] After finishing their sombre road to the summit, a party of Samoans carried the coffin of Stevenson up the mountainside, bidding farewell to their respected friend.[3] Stevenson's funeral, like his life, was romantic and surprising, a fitting tribute to one of Britain's finest commentators on life in the South Seas.

Though he spent only a short time in the islands, Robert Louis Stevenson's work was the first to provide an in-depth and geographically specific criticism of British settlement in the South Seas. Stevenson's life in the Pacific has recently received new critical inquiry due to a surge of interest in the Pacific as a region and a revival of Stevenson criticism. Respected literary scholars Roslyn Jolly, Ann Colley, Timothy S. Hayes, Oliver S. Buckton and Robert Irwin Hillier, among others, have argued the for importance of Stevenson's South Pacific canon, providing new insights into and readings of these final works.[4]

While this large body of scholarly work has provided multiple ways of interpreting Stevenson's work, few critics have noted that Stevenson brought an environmental sensitivity to his work in Samoa that seems in many ways ahead of its time. While I do not wish to argue that Stevenson was an environmentalist in our modern sense of the term, I do believe his works herald a growing interest in understanding the physical environment of the islands, and that he used the relationship between mankind and the landscape to comment upon his political and ideological goals. Using what ecocritics Catrin Gersdorf and Sylvia Mayer have termed a 'sociopolitical' ecocriticism, I will be examining Stevenson's Pacific works based on 'criteria such as their attention to natural phenomena, their degree of environmental awareness, their recognition of diversity, their attitude to nonhuman forms of life, [and] their awareness of the interconnectedness between local and global ecological issues'.[5] It is my belief that Stevenson's non-fiction writings as well as his novellas and short stories reflect his transformation from an observer of Pacific life to a participant in it. Viewed in this light, Stevenson's writings align with modern ideas of preservation and conservation and show that, by the end of the century, Victorians were beginning to critique the imperial project through its environmental impact.

Another titan of Edwardian fiction, Joseph Conrad, would pick up this tension between the need to settle islands and the social and environmental ramifications of doing so and paint an even darker picture of the interactions between islanders and Europeans. Conrad moves the Pacific narrative from the beaches of Samoa and the coral islands of Polynesia to the Malay Archipelago, introducing new challenges to the 'rightful' settlers of the Pacific. While the commercial failure of these stories may be blamed on the author's unwillingness to cater to fickle, ever-changing public tastes, the lack of critical attention paid to Conrad's later Pacific fiction results largely from Thomas C. Moser's now famous achievement-and-decline theory of Conrad's works, which argued that Conrad's writings markedly declined after 1910.[6] While Conrad's contemporaneous Pacific novel *Victory* eventually garnered critical attention from scholars like Frederick R. Karl and Tony Tanner, who argued for its status, like Conrad's earlier works, as a rich and complicated novel, the short stories have not received similar critical attention. Studies have relentlessly analysed the 'quality' of Conrad's writings over decades, arguing for the merits and weaknesses of individual episodes, paragraphs and even sentences. Not surprisingly, Conrad's more 'romantic' or 'popular' texts often do not meet such rigorous criteria. It is not my intention, however, to engage in yet another round of this sort of critique. Instead, I am more interested in recent work like that of Andrew Pursell; in his article '"People Don't Die Here Sooner Than in Europe": Conrad, Australia and Contexts of Race and Place in

"The Planter of Malata"', Pursell argues that while 'Planter' is 'judged a critical failure by the standards set by his earlier fiction, in terms of the historical issues to which it is attuned "The Planter of Malata" stands on its own as a work of considerable richness.'[7] I agree with Pursell that 'Planter,' along with 'Because of the Dollars' and *Freya of the Seven Isles* which I will be discussing in this chapter, offer vital commentary on the Pacific situation in the Malay Archipelago,[8] specifically in relation to British identity and issues of commerce, gender, and settlement.

While Pursell focuses primarily on British colonialism in Australia, I would like instead to focus critical attention on these neglected texts to explore the intersections of trade, gender and identity in Conrad's increasingly negative portrayal of European expansion in the smaller Pacific islands. While Stevenson worked to create a Pacific where settlers, islanders and islands could co-exist in a peaceful and productive relationship, Conrad's fiction, in contrast, warned that such an idyllic future was impossible. In his texts, the competition between men for trade supremacy turns them into island 'savages' that destroy not only their own lives but the women and islands for which they are competing. For Conrad, therefore, Pacific settlement was a doomed enterprise and men, women and islands were all tainted by association with British Pacific trade.

By examining the environmental sensitivity of Robert Louis Stevenson's Pacific texts and the interactions between men, women and trade in Joseph Conrad's, this chapter shows how contemporary criticism of the imperial project moved from focusing on islanders to the actual islands themselves and a growing need to preserve or protect them. The British vacillated between an optimistic image of trade and contact presented by early adventure fiction and a growing unease amongst some British authors about the true consequences of British involvement in the islands.

'Our Strangling Enemy': Stevenson's *Vailima Letters*

As was also the case with his predecessors, Stevenson's love affair with the Pacific began with the romantic image of a beautiful paradise just waiting to be explored. Charles Warren Stoddard, Stevenson's American friend, 'was known among San Franciscans as a peerless raconteur of Pacific tales' and shared his vision with Stevenson.[9] Stevenson's doctor advised him to go abroad for both his emotional and his physical health after his father died in May 1887. When publisher S. S. McClure offered to fund a series of travel sketches, McClure and Stevenson decided mutually on the Pacific as a fitting choice. After a few delays, Stevenson and his party set sail on the *Casco* in June of 1888 on a path that would take them through the Marquesas to Hawaii and eventually to Samoa.

While Stevenson's experiences on this first journey undoubtedly inspired his interest in the peoples and places of the South Seas, ill health forced him to take up permanent residence in Apia, on the Samoan island of Upolu in 1890. From their first landing, the planter lifestyle attracted the Stevensons. In his account of Stevenson's life, David Daiches explains:

> Louis liked the idea of settling in a climate that was obviously good for his health—it was too humid at sea level but up on the slopes it was very agreeable—and at the same time near a port that had good steamer connections . . . Fanny, who had always fancied herself a pioneer, liked the idea of growing things in the tropics. So they were not put out by general doubts about the practicability of the various cash crops (cocoa, pineapple, vanilla) suggested, by the dubious labour situation, and by the even more dubious political situation, with which inevitably Louis soon got himself involved.[10]

While Stevenson was impressed with the Pacific landscape from his first days on ship, it was only when he began to build a home in Samoa that he started to get a feel for the practical demands of living in the Pacific. Stevenson's *Vailima Letters*, a collection of correspondence begun in 1890 between the author and his friend Sidney Colvin, thus reveals Stevenson's deepening understanding of the connection between himself and the landscape he was turning into home.

From his first days in Vailima, Stevenson seemed torn between his appreciation for the beauty of the landscape surrounding him and the hostile reality of attempting to carve out a living there. On 2 November 1890, he commented,

> This is a hard and interesting and beautiful life that we lead now. Our place is in a deep cleft of Vaea Mountain, some six hundred feet above the sea, embowered in forest, which is our strangling enemy, and which we combat with axes and dollars.[11]

Stevenson uses a martial metaphor to describe his project, defeating the native landscape with a colonial arsenal of weapons and cash. Stevenson depicts himself as the prototypical British planter, following the footsteps of Ballantyne's boys. The Pacific planter, however, as historian Douglas Oliver observes was

> a new kind of person: unlike the whaler and the itinerant trader he was not drawn to the Islands as places of refreshment or sources of native goods, and he was less interested in the Islanders' souls than in their labour. He was a colonist, there to stay, at least until he could return in style to Sydney or Liverpool, Bordeaux or Hamburg.[12]

While idea of the planter's life charmed Stevenson, the physical realities of clearing the land disrupted his peaceful fantasy.

According to *Vailima Letters*, Stevenson's first profound interior reflections occurred as he attempted to clear a garden (an act highly reminiscent of missionaries who, as I show in Chapter 1, also saw building gardens as essential to the taming of the wild islands).[13] He views the act of clearing a garden as a soothing therapeutic alternative to writer's block. Later on 2 November he records that he walked outside

> to see where Henry and some of the men were clearing the garden; for it was plain there was to be no work to-day indoors, and I must set in consequence to farmering. I stuck a good while on the way up. For the path there is largely my own handiwork, and there were a lot of sprouts and saplings and stones to be removed. Then I reached our clearing just where the streams join in one; it had a fine autumn smell of burning, the smoke blew in the woods, and the boys were pretty merry and busy.[14]

The garden is both a place where Stevenson can assert his dominion over the land, and a place where he can keep his workers 'merry and busy'. At the same time, working in the garden also challenges Stevenson's peaceful belief that he is in control of his island home. On 4 November he explains,

> Right in the wild lime hedge which cuts athwart us just homeward of the garden, I found a great bed of kuikui[15] – sensitive plant – our deadliest enemy. A fool brought it to this island in a pot, and used to lecture and sentimentalise over the tender thing. The tender thing has now taken charge of this island, and men fight it, with torn hands, for bread and life. A singular, insidious thing, shrinking and biting like a weasel; clutching by its roots as a limpet clutches to a rock.[16]

While Stevenson declares the landscape an enemy, it is the plant's foreignness and invasiveness that makes it so. His letter contains a strong indictment of the 'fool' who brought a non-native plant to the Samoan islands, an indictment that transforms the 'enemy' from the plants he must eradicate to the foreigners who so unthinkingly imported such troubles to the islands. Stevenson sees himself as an exception to such impulsive visitors, aligning himself instead with the islanders who have no choice but to react to hazardous invaders.

Stevenson's thoughts on the 'kuikui' reflect a larger movement in British thinking. As a result of increased forays into the Pacific islands, the British had to reconsider their assumption that the islands remained an untamed paradise. Ecocritic John Parham explains,

> Environmental awareness did not arise – as is so often assumed – in the odorous atmosphere of the London sewers, but under far distant palm trees,

on exotic islands, out of an awareness of threatened dreams of paradise. It was there that people first experienced – or believed they were experiencing the connection between rapid deforestation, the drying up of springs, the desiccation of the soil, and a change in climate.[17]

The experience of clearing land for his estate brought Stevenson into direct contract with the consequences of foreign exchange. Biologically speaking, the island demonstrated the effects of colonisation and exploration. As Parham continues,

> *islands* became the exemplary cases: these small, isolated worlds created virtual laboratory conditions for the study of ecological interrelationships . . . On small islands it was possible for the forest to be completely destroyed within a short period of time; no wind-born seed from neighboring regions was able to regenerate it.[18]

Not surprisingly, scientists like Charles Darwin found the islands indispensable for proving theories like natural selection as I show in Chapter 3.

The Pacific islands were not simply of interest to biologists and naturalists, however; they were also, as Richard Grove summarises in *Green Imperialism*, important 'mental symbols' that 'continued to constitute a critical stimulant to the development of concepts of environmental protection as well as of ethnological and biological identity'.[19] While on the one hand, Stevenson is concerned with the practicality of clearing land for a garden, such ruminations inevitably lead him to question his purpose as a planter in Samoa. As Grove argues,

> The landscapes of island and garden were metaphors of mind. Anxieties about environmental change, climatic change and extinctions and even the fear of famine, all of which helped to motivate early environmentalism, mirrored anxiety about social form (especially where the fragile identity of the European colonist was called into question) and motivated social reform, At the core of environmental concern lay anxiety about society and its discontents.[20]

For Stevenson, concerns about modifying his island home quickly transform into larger concerns about his position as a coloniser/leader. As Stevenson moves to a more isolated part of the island, he also finds himself questioning his own motivations in clearing the land. On 3 November 1890, he records:

> A strange business it was, and infinitely solitary; away above, the sun was in the high tree-tops; the lianas[21] noosed and sought to hang me; the saplings struggled, and came up with that sob of death that one gets to know so well; great, soft, sappy trees fell at a lick of the cutlass, little tough switches laughed at and dared my best endeavour. Soon, toiling down in that pit of verdure, I

heard blows on the far side, and then laughter. I confess a chill settled on my heart. Being so dead alone, in a place where by rights none should be beyond me, I was aware, upon interrogation, if those blows had drawn nearer, I should (of course quite unaffectedly) have executed a strategic movement to the rear; and only the other day I was lamenting my insensibility to superstition! Am I beginning to be sucked in? Shall I become a midnight twitterer like my neighbours? At times I thought the blows were echoes; at times I thought the laughter was from birds. For our birds are strangely human in their calls.[22]

While Stevenson still seems to be at war with Samoan vegetation, this metaphor masks a real sense of anxiety about the colonial project. Without reinforcements, he is suddenly vulnerable to attack, both on his physical person and his mental state. Not only does the environment violently resist his attempts to conquer it, but it also fights back, attempting to hang him and laughing at his attempts to cultivate the land. This physical anguish quickly translates into mental confusion, as Stevenson hears sounds he cannot fully explain. He begins to question both his desire to be alone in his island habitat and his sense of superiority over his neighbours, a move which subverts the traditional colonial narrative of earlier island works like *The Swiss Family Robinson*. As Grove's argument suggests, Stevenson's anxiety about his appropriate relationship to the native environment leads him to question his larger place in the social order: is he going to become a superstitious native? Are the sounds he hears made by humans or animals, and is there such a difference between their languages?

As Stevenson continues on with his project, similar concerns haunt him. A few days later he records

My long, silent contests in the forest have had a strange effect on me. The unconcealed vitality of these vegetables, their exuberant number and strength, the attempts – I can use no other word – of lianas to enwrap and capture the intruder, the awful silence, the knowledge that all of my efforts are only like the performance of an actor, the thing of a moment, and the wood will silently and swiftly heal them up with fresh effervescence; the cunning sense of the tuitui,[23] suffering itself to be touched with wind-swayed grasses and not minding – but let the grass be moved by a man, and it shuts up; the whole silent battle, murder, and slow death of the contending forest; weigh upon the imagination.[24]

While Stevenson may have initially envisioned himself as a triumphant conqueror, carving an island paradise from the mountainous slopes of Upolu, the resistance of the local landscape quickly changes his mind. Rather than a valiant explorer, Stevenson becomes a solitary 'intruder', an 'actor', whose attacks on the forest can only be viewed as 'battle, murder, [and] slow death'. He thus displays a growing awareness of the follies inherent in attempting to modify paradise.

Eventually, the physical nightmare of clearing the ground transforms into actual nightmares. On 19 March 1891, Stevenson reflected on how deeply disturbing his work has been to his mental and physical health:

> I said I was tired; it is a mild phrase; my back aches like toothache; when I shut my eyes to sleep, I know I shall see before them . . . endless vivid deeps of grass and weed, each plant particular and distinct, so that I shall lie inert in body, and transact for hours the mental part of my day business, choosing the noxious from the useful. And in my dreams I shall be hauling on recalcitrants, and suffering stings from nettles, stabs from citron thorns, fiery bites from ants, sickening resistances of mud and slime, evasions of slimy roots, dead weight of heat, sudden puffs of air, sudden starts from bird-calls in the contiguous forest—some mimicking my name, some laughter, some the signal of a whistle, and living over again at large the business of my day.[25]

Stevenson's war on the natural world had clearly taken its toll. He is haunted by his experiences, unable to rest without conjuring up images of the day's battles. The struggle between the pressing need to cultivate Vailima and the guilt and hardship of actually doing so weigh heavily on Stevenson's conscience. Later in the same letter, he wonders,

> if anyone had ever the same attitude to Nature as I hold, and have held for so long? This business fascinates me like a tune or a passion; yet all the while I thrill with a strong distaste. The horror of the thing, objective and subjective, is always present to my mind; the horror of creeping things, a superstitious horror of the void and the powers about me, the horror of my own devastation and continual murders. The life of the plants comes through my finger-tips, their struggles go to my heart like supplications. I feel myself blood-boltered; then I look back on my cleared grass, and count myself an ally in a fair quarrel, and make stout my heart.[26]

The idea of warfare had become much more literal for Stevenson. On the one hand, he feels very strongly that his violence against the island is both cruel and wrong. He intensely anthropomorphises the plants he destroys, seeing them as murdered bodies oozing blood. The landscape has become a horror from which he cannot seem to escape.[27] On the other hand, the duty he feels to build a home for his wife and his 'family' of natives in Vailima bolsters his resolve to continue, despite his self-image as the island foliage's most brutal serial killer. Stevenson originally constructs himself as the conquering male hero taming the wild island landscape, drawing on the role models of earlier narratives from *The Swiss Family Robinson* to adventure novels like those of R. M. Ballantyne. As he engages with the material nature of the surrounding landscape, however, Stevenson views himself as more pirate than pioneer leading him to question his role, and the role of Britain, as 'civilisers' of the Pacific.

The Devil in the Woods: Stevenson's *The Beach of Falesá*

Torn between the necessity of taming the wild landscape and the horror implicit in destroying the native plants, Stevenson found himself inspired to write the first of his two most influential Pacific novellas, *The Beach of Falesá* and *The Ebb-Tide*.[28] Stevenson's original title for *Falesá*, *The High Woods of Ulufanua*, proceeds directly from his admiration for the island scenery. As Stevenson records in September of 1891,

> Ulufanua is an imaginary island; the name is a beautiful Samoan word for the *top* of a forest; ulu – leaves or hair, fanua = land. The ground or country of the leaves. 'Ulufanua the isle of the sea,' read that verse dactylically and you get the beat; the u's are like our double *oo*; did ever you hear a prettier word?[29]

While Ulufanua exists only Stevenson's imagination, he clearly constructed it with the Samoan language and culture in mind, grounding his fiction in Pacific fact. Stevenson makes clear that he is attempting to break both with the romance tradition at large and with his own past works, creating a realistic portrayal of life in the South Seas, or, as Stevenson critic Oliver Buckton neatly summarises, 'an antidote to the romance of South Seas fiction'.[30] As Stevenson himself explained,

> [*The Beach of Falesá*] is the first realistic South Sea story; I mean with real South Sea character and details of life. Everybody else who has tried, that I have seen, got carried away by the romance, and ended in a kind of sugar-candy sham epic. And the whole effect was lost – there was no etching, no human grin, consequently no conviction. Now I have got the smell and look of the thing a good deal. You will know more about the South Seas after you have read my little tale than if you had read a library.[31]

A similar need for 'realistic' depictions of the South Seas underlies early British travel narratives, such as the anthropological journals of missionary William Ellis, but realism was often sacrificed in adventure narratives due to ignorance or the vagaries of plot. Stevenson's time in Samoa, however, lent him a unique perspective on the physical realities of life on a Pacific island.

To achieve his goal, Stevenson worked to create a story where not only the characters and the plot but the very landscape itself mirrored the complex environment in which he found himself. While Stevenson's original title hints at a beautiful Polynesian forest, his eventual choice to rename the text *The Beach of Falesá* echoes his disenchantment with the idea of a Pacific paradise. While the forest is the secret heart of the island, the place where Stevenson feels most like a destructive invader, the beach is the point of invasion and discovery, a place where the foreign and the native collide. Greg Dening describes this interaction in his book on the Marquesas:

> Beaches are beginnings and endings. They are the frontiers and boundaries of islands. For some life forms the division between land and sea is not abrupt, but for human beings beaches divide the world between here and there, us and them, good and bad, familiar and strange. On land, behind the beach, life is lived with some fullness and with some establishment. On the sea, beyond the beach, life is partial and dependent. Ships are distorted segments of living—all male, disciplined, parasitic on the land, not productive. Those who come on them—sailors, missionaries, traders, soldiers—proffer very singular gestures about themselves. They display their cultures but not whole.[32]

In changing focus from the forest to the beach, Stevenson suggests the text will concern itself with the boundaries of the British Pacific experience. The novella's narrator, Wiltshire, finds from his first introduction to Falesá that the island is marked by these boundaries. He notes that he

> saw that island first when it was neither night nor morning. The moon was to the west, setting, but still broad and bright. To the east, and right amidships of the dawn, which was all pink, the daystar sparkled like a diamond.[33]

Stevenson critic Ann C. Colley is struck by the hybridity of this scene, noting that from his arrival, Wilshire

> confronts a society that is constantly being redefined by its crossbreeding . . . Both narrator and reader are thus introduced to the sometimes harmonious, but often cacophonous conjoining of European (Western) and Pacific (Eastern) ways. This hybridic light will illuminate Wiltshire as he moves through his account of mingling and hobnobbing with natives, missionaries, tradesmen, and beachcombers.[34]

Of course, living on the boundaries is not new to Wiltshire, who 'had been for years on a low island near the line', or a coral island near the equator.[35] In leaving the ship and crossing the beach of this new volcanic (or 'high') island, Wiltshire recognises that he is approaching a 'fresh experience', an experience reflected in his vision of the new landscape: 'the look of these woods and mountains, and the rare smell of them, renewed my blood'.[36] Not only does this experience reflect in some part Stevenson's own experiences with the landscape of Samoa (a volcanic island) but it also departs from earlier adventure texts like Ballantyne's that had primarily focused on coral islands. Like Wiltshire, the Victorian audience was being transported to a new and fresh part of the Pacific, a place that would fittingly present a new interpretation of the British experience in the islands.

From Wiltshire's first moments in this setting, however, it is clear this new island is not a perfect paradise. While Wiltshire is struck by the 'strong [smell] of wild lime and vanilla', it also 'set [him] sneezing'.[37] Although this incident by itself seems innocent enough, the captain soon informs Wiltshire that the last island trader died from 'some kind of sickness'.[38] Again the beach is a place of intersection, a place where whites refresh themselves, but also place themselves at risk for disease. The idea of environmental responsibility for illness was deeply entrenched in Victorian medical theory. Historian Philippa Levine explains:

> The idea that climate and the physical environment affected the bodily and mental constitutions of individuals was deeply ingrained in British medical theory and practice. Thus, being 'out-of-place' was understood as a biological and medical (and later a psychological) problem, literally productive of disease or ill-health. Unsuitability of certain peoples to particular climatic conditions proved to be a long-lasting political and legislative rationale for controlling non-white peoples' movement in the Empire and Commonwealth.[39]

This dichotomy between the island as paradise and the island as place of disease is also reflected in Wiltshire's relationships with the natives. On the one hand, the image Wiltshire constructs of the natives living on the beach is one of humans in harmony with nature. He remarks, 'It was good to foot the grass, to look aloft at the green mountains, to see the men with their green wreathes and the women in their bright dresses, red and blue.'[40] However, the vision of untainted paradise quickly sours when Case suggests a marriage between Wiltshire and the native girl Uma. Case is a shady figure whom Wiltshire both admires for his hospitality and, presumably, his similar background. Yet Wiltshire is wary of this other white trader and quickly states, 'He had the courage of a lion and the cunning of a rat; and if he's not in hell today, there's no such place.'[41] When Case suggests a marriage to Uma, Wiltshire recognises on some level the irreverence of the affair. He remarks,

> I must have been taken with Uma from the first, or I should certainly have fled from that house, and got into the clean air and the clean sea, or some convenient river—though, it's true, I was committed to Case; and besides, I could never have held my head up in that island if I had run from a girl upon my wedding night.[42]

Wiltshire knows that there is something unclean or impure about his marriage, but his desire for the native girl and his loyalty to his fellow white trader overcomes his reservations. He 'illegally' marries Uma 'for one night'.[43] For Wiltshire, the island and the islanders provide a refreshing change, even as they are tainted by the presence of white traders. While Wiltshire can recognise the impurity of Case's interference, he seems blind to his own. Stevenson thus portrays the Pacific islands as a place where harmony with nature is possible, but where lust or greed can quickly corrupt paradise.

The day after his marriage to Uma, Wiltshire has high hopes for success on the island, at least if he can break away from Case. In retrospect, however, his dream seems rather strange. As Wiltshire recalls,

> I felt as if I was in the right place to make a fortune, and go home again and start a public house. There was I, sitting in that veranda, in as handsome a piece of scenery as you could find, a splendid sun, and a fine fresh healthy trade that stirred up a man's blood like sea-bathing; and the whole thing was clean gone from me, and I was dreaming England, which is, after all, a nasty, cold, muddy hole, with not enough light to see to read by; and dreaming the looks of my public, by a cant of a broad high-road like an avenue, and with the sign on a green tree.[44]

The idea of making his fortune by trading copra in the South Seas intrigues Wiltshire.[45] At this point, Wiltshire is concerned primarily with success in England, the island being merely a means to an end, with status in England counting far more than status in the Pacific.[46] Yet Stevenson criticises the foolishness of dreaming of a polluted city while surrounded by a clean and refreshing paradise.

Ecocritical scholars have been quick to comment on the connection between the problems of industrialisation in England and the desire for a cleaner environment. As John Parham explains of the Victorian Age

> Urban expansion created problems around housing, working conditions, unemployment, and what we would now more specifically understand as ecological problems – sanitation, air quality, disease, deforestation. Consequently, it became an age of observation, investigation, and social responsibility, in turn, prompting campaigning, political intervention, and legislation. This impulse to intervene, to say and do something, permeated Victorian literary culture.[47]

While domestic novelists focused on changing public opinion towards the preservation of rural landscapes, a more seductive dream for the middle class was to get away from all the chaos at home by escaping, even if only in novels, to a foreign, uncorrupted paradise. The Pacific was a perfect location for fantasy, as 'The Europeans' encounter with tropical forests and tropical forest peoples, the naked "savages," imparted a magical attractive power to the ideal of paradisiacal nature and of the unspoiled, natural human being.'[48] Yet actually living in a mythical paradise quickly revealed the ways in which the practical realties of settlement and colonisation compromised such lofty ideals. Later settlers of the South Seas, Stevenson included, worried that trading exchanges and settlements were ruining the islanders, even while recognising the islands' importance to the British economy. While early in the century missionaries dreamed of islands 'civilised' by the British but uncorrupted by materialism, by the end of the century the dream more closely resembled a nightmare of greed and avarice.

While Stevenson developed a detailed understanding of South Seas trade, he was not fully supportive of Britain's policies, even on his imaginary islands. Wiltshire and Case are fictional representations of the very real competition being waged over these small South Seas islands. Robert Hillier reveals,

> Studies of specific colonial trade practices verify Stevenson's observations from *In the South Seas* and reveal how accurately he captures the lives of traders in *The Beach of Falesá*. The United States, France, England, and Germany all competed for South Seas trade, with religious leaders of the United States and England uniting their missionary enterprise against the French Catholics, and Germany generally eschewing the evangelical. Through combined force and negotiations France gained control over Tahiti, the Tuamotus, and the Marquesas, leaving the other countries to dispute control of the remaining Pacific islands, especially the Gilbert Islands and Samoa, where German traders first arrived in the 1850's and by 1875 controlled most of the Samoan trade.[49]

For Stevenson, islands

> would become his site of bliss and serve as the setting for his most powerful late works of fiction. Yet Stevenson was not content to rest with the 'pleasure' of the South Seas. Discovering that many of the region's problems, such as disease, depopulation, and war, had resulted from European colonialism, Stevenson would probe beneath the surface of island beauty in his fiction to examine a more sinister reality.[50]

Thus unlike in Ballantyne's Pacific, where righteous manliness could reform corrupt trading practices, Stevenson's Pacific reveals the tension between wanting to live and thrive in a paradise and realising that such actions undermine the very nature of that paradise. As Buckton explains, this tension resonates throughout Stevenson's writing:

> There is an apparent contradiction in Stevenson's travel writing between, on the one hand, a discourse of oppression by bourgeois respectability and the impulse to escape to a 'primitive' culture and, on the other, an ideology of national expansion with which his travels are complicit and which assumes a position of racial and cultural superiority.[51]

In *The Beach of Falesá,* this conflict manifests itself in Wiltshire's desire both to marry Uma and live in paradise on the beach, but also to thrive as a colonial trader and possibly return a wealthy and successful man to England. Building on Buckton's argument, I argue that this conflict plays out in the geographical locations Stevenson's characters choose to inhabit: the beach, the forest or the ocean. Each location represents a different facet of the British interaction with the islands.

Still on the beach, Wiltshire soon finds that his hasty marriage to Uma has compromised his lofty dreams of success, as Uma is 'tabooed'. This status prevents the other natives from trading with her husband. Faced with the prospect of losing his bride, Wiltshire proclaims, 'I would rather have you than all the copra in the South Seas.'[52] Still, despite his marital happiness, Wiltshire is outraged upon discovering that Uma was shamed when her first fiancé Ioane deserted her, and that her only remaining friend is Case. While Wiltshire seems to abandon his schemes of trading, he is not able to conquer his jealousy of the island's other inhabitants. When a missionary arrives soon after his discovery, Wiltshire asserts,

> I'm no missionary, nor missionary lover; I'm not Kanaka, nor favourer of Kanakas—I'm just a trader; I'm just a common, low, God-damned white man and British subject, the sort you would like to wipe your boots on. I hope that's plain![53]

While Wiltshire determinedly clings to his status as a white British trader, he quickly reveals that he cares less for lifting the taboo on his goods and more for lifting the taboo on his wife. He reveals that he's 'what you call a sinner—what I call a sweep—and I want you to help me make it up to a person I've deceived'.[54] While Wiltshire does not wish to admit it, the island is changing both his identity and his priorities from those of a simple trader.

With no natives willing to trade with him, Wiltshire is forced to process copra himself. Thus he finds himself working alongside Fa'avao, Uma's mother, and Uma herself,

> mak[ing] copra with our own hands. It was copra to make your mouth water when it was done—I never understood how much the natives cheated me till I had made that four hundred pounds of my own hand—and it weighed so light I felt inclined to take it and water it myself.[55]

Wiltshire originally claims a sense of moral and racial superiority as a trader, free from the demeaning realities of physical labour, but finds after experiencing island culture that he would much prefer to act like a native, watering down copra he himself owns and plans to sell. Instead of vilifying the natives as 'cheats', Wiltshire begins to admire them as fellow, and perhaps cleverer, businessmen.

While working as an islander for the first time, Wiltshire contemplates hunting in the forest. Although he has hunted along the periphery of the forest before, he has not ventured inland:

> the whole 'eye' of the island, as natives call the windward end, lay desert. From Falesá round about to Papamalulu, there was neither house, nor man, nor planted breadfruit tree; and the reef being mostly absent, and the shores bluff, the sea beat direct among crags, and there was scarce a landing spot.[56]

Having learned a little of the native language, Wiltshire inquires about the forest where no humans go, only to be told the forest is inhabited by devils. After investigating, he discovers they are not just any devils, but Tiapolo or chief devils, controlled only by the powers of Case. While the island seems to belong to the natives, the only safe and profitable dwelling place is along the beach, while the heart of the island is a place of monsters.

Despite Uma's warnings, Wiltshire believes he has no choice but to confront Case in the heart of the island, but upon entering the deep woods, he realises he does not belong. While he is able to describe the flora and fauna he encounters, he also remarks

> The queerness of the place it's more difficult to tell of, unless to one who has been alone in the high bush himself. The brightest kind of day it is always dim down there . . . It is all very well for him to tell himself that he's alone, bar trees and birds; he can't make out to believe it; whichever way he turns the whole place seems to be alive and looking on. Don't think it was Uma's yarns that put me out; I don't value native talk a fourpenny-piece; it's a thing that's natural in the bush, and that's the end of it.[57]

Unlike earlier depictions of South Sea islands, where colonisers felt free to carve settlements out of the wilderness without repercussion, Wiltshire recognises the danger in invading this island. Case, in contrast, has no such fears. Instead, he has occupied the forest and built a fake shrine in order to frighten the natives into doing his will. In his work on Stevenson's fiction, Timothy Hayes suggests that 'Case appears both to be in harmony with nature and quite capable of making nature (especially the forest) seem more foreboding through the clever use of simple objects.'[58] While I agree that Case seems the most able to use the forest, this usage does not necessarily imply 'harmony'. Instead, Stevenson seems to suggest that humans, whether native or foreign, can only find harmony and peace when they stick to the beach and the nearby environs. Stevenson reveals Case's colonisation of the interior of the island as morally objectionable, even though it increases British control over the islanders. Wiltshire's understanding that he must remove Case from the forest shows his growing hybrid status as islander/invader who, perhaps against his will, is 'going native'. Case himself recognises this transformation and taunts Wiltshire, stating,

> You don't hinder me any. You haven't got one pound of copra but what you made with your own hands, like a negro slave. You're vegetating—that's what I call it—and I don't care where you vegetate, nor yet how long.[59]

Wiltshire's native qualities, his work amongst the people and his new island relations, mark him as distinct from Case. Unlike his enemy, who is actively working to dominate the people, he is vegetating, a term that Case presumably chooses to imply inactivity, but which also implies that Wiltshire is literally 'growing' into the island. Thus Wiltshire recognises that the best thing for the island is also the best thing for his personal interests: the removal of Case.

The climax of the story is the confrontation in the deep woods between Wiltshire and Case. After Wiltshire blows up Case's shrine, a violent fight ensues wherein Case wounds Wiltshire in the leg with his rifle. Still, Wiltshire eventually manages to sneak up on Case and stab him to death. In the dark of the woods, nothing exists but violence and death. While such an episode could easily dissolve into melodrama, Stevenson focuses on the horror of the hatred between the two men. He ends the scene with Wiltshire fainting from the pain after giving Case 'the knife again a half-a-dozen times up to the handle. I believe he was dead already, but it did him no harm and did me good.'[60] Unlike the violence of Ballantyne's boys, which ultimately champions the power of white empire over 'savagery', the violence in Stevenson's novella is localised between two factions of white invaders.[61] Literary critic Patrick Brantlinger explains,

> In *Falesá*, adventure has given way to trade (although it sneaks in through the back door because trade gives way to crime). A felt contradiction between trade and the heroic, aristocratic significance of adventure results in a narrative that links together imperial domination, the profit motive, moral degeneracy, parasitism, and ultimately murder or attempted murder.[62]

The need to expand the empire into the Pacific has turned paradise into purgatory, while the influx of trade leads only to violence. While earlier depictions of traders, like those in Ballantyne's later novels, worked to downplay the connection between trade and moral degeneracy, Stevenson directly confronts the darkness inherent to imperial commerce.

Yet Stevenson does not end his narrative with the bleakness of the murders, instead offering a potential solution to the problem of white settlement. After the bold confrontation in the woods, no place remains for whites who cannot embrace native culture, at least to some extent. The other non-Polynesians on the island drift away, and soon Wiltshire is 'left alone in [his] glory at Falesá', presumably with full control over the island.[63] Graham Tulloch has argued that

> uninhabited space is again an empty space into which human evil can flow, as with *Treasure Island*. But Wiltshire literally opens up this uninhabited space by blowing up the underground shrine and exposing it for the local people to visit it by daylight. The inhabitants can presumably return to this part of the island, and the whole island can become inhabited.[64]

I think, however, this reading oversimplifies the colonial experience that Stevenson is questioning. While Case's death does open the island up as a profitable trading post once again, there is no evidence that Wiltshire seeks to retake the 'desert' in the centre of the island and no indication that the natives have any desire to seek it out either. Instead, Wiltshire remains happily in control of his station on the beach, the environmental equivalent of hybridity, halfway between the ocean that brings foreign invaders and the heart of the island. This in-between status defines the Wiltshire who narrates the text as well. As Hillier argues, 'To survive in the South Seas, an imperialist must assimilate. And through his narration Wiltshire's point of view slides between his attitudes upon arriving at Falesá and the not wholly different attitudes he holds as he tells his story.'[65] Such assimilation is reflected in Wiltshire's changing racial attitudes; as Colley explains, 'Living on islands teaches [Wiltshire] that there is no such thing as a pure white in such contact zones where Westerners and native peoples mix to create hybrids and where, consequently, the balance of power can be easily unsettled.'[66] Wiltshire is, of course, a hybrid being himself and thus unable to return to the London of his dreams, not because he is not successful, but because he loves his new family and believes island life is the best thing for it. As he states,

> My public-house? Not a bit of it, nor ever likely. I'm stuck here, I fancy. I don't like to leave the kids, you see: and . . . they're better here than what they would be in a white man's country.[67]

Still, Wiltshire ends the novella bothered by the implications of his hybrid status. He ponders,

> What bothers me is the girls. They're only half-castes, of course; I know that as well as you do, and there's nobody thinks less of half-castes than I do; but they're mine, and about all I've got. I can't reconcile my mind to their taking up with Kanakas, and I'd like to know where I'm going to find the whites?[68]

On the one hand, Wiltshire's experiences among the natives have allowed him to mentally elevate his daughters, but on the other hand, he cannot escape his prejudice against the marriage of islanders and whites (despite being content in his own marriage). Roslyn Jolly argues,

> Uma's fertility and the appearance of the Wiltshires' half-caste children suggest the future of a hybridized, post-contact Pacific which defies the assumption, voiced by [Pierre] Loti and so many other nineteenth-century Europeans, that an inevitable historical or evolutionary logic would bring about the extinction of the Pacific islanders.[69]

I agree, but such a hybrid Pacific can only exist in a hybrid location, the *beach* of Falesá. Stevenson, undoubtedly influenced by his own hybrid status as an invader/islander, writes the *Beach of Falesá* as a hopeful vision of a Pacific where British citizens and islanders can find a harmonious way to live and work together, breaking down some of the binaries that divide them.

Towards the end of his life, Stevenson fought valiantly for Samoan independence. In his *Address to the Chiefs on Opening the Road of Gratitude* he remarked,

> You Samoans may fight, you may conquer twenty times, and thirty times, and all will be in vain. There is but one way to defend Samoa. Hear it before it is too late. It is to make roads, and gardens, and care for your trees, and sell their produce wisely, and, in one word, to occupy and use your country. If you do not others will.[70]

As Stevenson saw it, whoever cared for and developed the land in the wisest way would be the one to control it. In order to convince British islanders thousands of miles away of the importance of protecting the tropical island on which he lived, therefore, Stevenson took great pains to balance his poetic use of plot and character with the real details of his lived experience on the island of Upolu. These details are not always geographically specific, and I agree with Hillier that the island 'setting, while distinctly Pacific, tells surprisingly little about Polynesia, but rather functions allegorically as Stevenson juxtaposes it with otherwise intense realism'.[71] Even so, Stevenson was very careful that the *The Beach of Falesá* would resemble his experiences in Samoa. In January of 1893, Stevenson wrote to Colvin, 'I am greatly pleased with the illustrations [in *The Beach of Falesá*]. It is very strange to a South-Seayer to see Hawaiian women dressed like Samoans, but I guess that's all one to you in Middlesex.'[72] While on the one hand, Stevenson wished his stories to convey universal truths about all Polynesian islands, he also wanted them to resonate strongly with the landscape he observed daily and loved until the day he died. By portraying the islands as actual physical places, instead of just fantastical settings, Stevenson could address the realities of the political and economic situation that faced the Pacific.

By reading Stevenson's *Vailima Letters* and *The Beach of Falesá* in proximity to previous British visions of the Pacific and through the lens of ecocriticism, we are clearly able to see a shift away from the assumption of the right of British occupation in the islands to a questioning of such actions as just, good or even possible without significant change. While many nineteenth-century readers (as well as some modern critics) dismissed Stevenson's Pacific fiction as 'too marginal, too eccentric, to be the setting for important literature', a close reading instead reveals that it is essential to understanding both the growing resistance to South Seas occupation and questioning the nature of British Imperialism at large.[73] Stevenson's contemporary Joseph Conrad also suffered ignominy at the hands of critics both contemporary and modern for his Pacific tales, especially his short stories like *Freya of the Seven Isles* and 'Because of the Dollars' yet they too offer surprising insight into the realities of British settlement in the Pacific islands.

Ladies of the Isles: Joseph Conrad's Late Malay Fiction

'Look here. The straight truth of it is that I am now writing a silly story', wrote Joseph Conrad to Edward Garnett on 12 January 1911.[74] Speaking of the story that would eventually become *Freya of the Seven Isles* (1912), Conrad wrote with a confused mixture of pride and shame about his new 'silly story'. After finishing the piece on 15 February, he referred to it as 'Quite good magazine stuff, quite Conradesque (in the easier style), – "no blush to the cheek of the young person" sort of thing. Perfectly safe. Eastern sea setting, but not too much setting.'[75] Later, on 28 February, he called it an 'Eastern seas tale—quite a novel in character and quite suitable for serializing'.[76] Conrad conceived of *Freya* as both an exciting romance ready for serialisation and a story engaged with and defined by its Pacific setting. Yet *Freya*'s publishing history, like its critical reception, was less than ideal. Although the author sought to maintain his exacting personal standards while deliberately writing for magazines, he was only able to get *Freya* published in the *Metropolitan Magazine of New York*, a popular casual publication. Conrad was less than enthusiastic about adapting his artistic endeavours to the whims of publishers and the public, and thus despite a terse request from the publishers, he refused to rewrite *Freya* with a happy ending.[77] *Freya* did not achieve the popularity or profits for which Conrad was hoping, and it quickly and quietly faded into critical obscurity. The fate of Conrad's later Pacific short fiction suffered much the same ignominy as *Freya*; neither 'Because of the Dollars' (1914) nor 'The Planter of Malata' (1914) became commercial or critical successes.

While earlier adventure texts like the journals of Captain Cook or the novels of R. M. Ballantyne had championed British men as successful traders and colonisers of island spaces, by the late nineteenth century authors like Robert Louis Stevenson had begun to question this assumed moral and cultural supremacy. Joseph Conrad, however, breaks with this British/Pacific literary tradition in two key ways. First, Conrad travelled both in person and in his literature through the western Pacific islands of the Malay Archipelago, unlike his predecessors who primarily wrote about the eastern islands of Polynesia. Secondly, Conrad includes not only male protagonists in his Pacific tales, but white eligible British women, a notable addition very rarely found in British Pacific writing.

Not surprisingly then, Conrad's later Pacific fiction approaches colonial concerns in the Pacific islands from a very different perspective than that of his contemporaries. Stevenson had argued that weak British men and their lust for goods had corrupted the Pacific islands, but that there was hope for the region if the British could learn to balance their needs with those of the island communities. Conrad's fiction, in contrast, focuses less on British interactions with native islanders and more on the interactions between British men, British women and other colonial forces.[78] In his texts, men compete for trade supremacy in order to take possession of both the island territories and the British women who live in those territories (and thus function, by extension, as imperial property). These conflicts force men to degenerate into island 'savages' – overly passionate, superstitious and violent. These men are destroyed both literally and figuratively, and their conflicts taint both the women and the territory, thus rendering them unworthy of possession. For Conrad, therefore, trade and competition serve to destroy not only island communities, but British identity, transforming the 'superior' British islanders into savages and their possessions into worthless dross. While earlier Pacific narratives largely considered the negative consequences of island trade for missionaries and native peoples, Conrad instead explores the connection between trade and the personal relationships of European men and women to criticise imperial commerce. With this choice, Conrad places the blame for the damaging effects of life in the Pacific islands solely on the immoral characters and poor choices of the Europeans who fight to claim island territory for self-interested reasons.

Sense and Sensibility:
Gender and Commerce in *Freya of the Seven Isles*

Conrad critics have long considered *Freya of the Seven Isles* little more than melodrama for the masses, and poorly written melodrama at that. Lawrence Graver declared the novella, 'One of the most clumsily protracted of all Conrad's stories, [which] customarily reduces critics to compassionate silence.'[79] This silence has meant that outside a few comments on its publishing history, very few Conradians have explored *Freya* as a work of critical importance. Yet for all its literary flaws and narrative missteps, *Freya* is significant to the continuing lineage of British Pacific fiction, one of the first stories both in Conrad's canon and in the British Pacific tradition at large to feature a plot that revolves around a single, eligible, reasonable, white British woman. Despite the attention it pays to her, however, Freya functions, as Monika M. Elbert argues, primarily as a means

> to explore to the masculine psyche of [the narrator], as well as the fragmented masculinity of the three male protagonists (extensions of himself) who are ostensibly enamored of Freya—but who are interested in her insofar as she serves to allow their own self-definition.[80]

Although I agree with Elbert, I would add that the Seven Isles, and the Malay Archipelago in general, represent an extension of the inter-male conflict over control of Freya. The conflict between Nelson,[81] Jasper and Heemskirk for the control of the islands of the Archipelago directly influences Freya's behaviour, leading to the disastrous and destructive consequences at the end of the story. As the competition for Freya begins to degenerate into the same savage patterns that characterise competition for the island, Freya's outsider status as a creature of reason becomes increasingly compromised and eventually even she is no longer able to prevent savagery from overcoming reason.

The novella opens not with a description of Freya, but with the story of her father, Nelson, a great Danish explorer of the Archipelago. Nelson's background is in keeping with those of many previous incarnations of adventure heroes:

> He had come out East long before the advent of telegraph cables, had served English firms, had married an English girl, had been one of us for years, trading and sailing in all directions through the Eastern Archipelago, across and around, transversely, diagonally, perpendicularly, in semi-circles, and zigzags, and figures of eights, for years and years.[82]

Yet unlike the British traders in Polynesia who had full control over the islands, Nelson must deal with non-English authorities in the

Archipelago. Nelson avoids the Philippines 'from a strange dread of the Spaniards'[83] but cannot avoid those other masters of the Archipelago, the Dutch. The narrator records:

> He was in general afraid of what he called 'authorities'; not the English authorities, which he trusted and respected, but the other two of that part of the world. He was not so horrified at the Dutch as he was at the Spaniards, but he was even more mistrustful of them. Very mistrustful indeed. The Dutch, in his view, were capable of 'playing an ugly trick on a man' who had the misfortune to displease them. There were their laws and regulations, but they had no notion of fair play in applying them.[84]

Nelson's fears intensify after he

> bought, or else leased, part of a small island from the Sultan of a little group called the Seven Isles, not far north from Banka. It was, I suppose, a legitimate transaction, but I have no doubt that had he been an Englishman the Dutch would have discovered a reason to fire him out without ceremony.[85]

As a Dane, Nelson finds himself an outsider caught in the middle of a conflict between Dutch and British authorities over the control of the Pacific, a conflict that will have profound ramifications for both his life and his daughter's. While earlier Pacific texts had sought to legitimise Pacific trade as a heroic venture, Conrad presents the competition over island resources as a nasty, brutal and personally demoralising conquest which turns once brave adventurers into fearful shadows of themselves. From its earliest pages, *Freya* destabilises the masculine tradition of heroic manhood by presenting Freya's father as politically weak and fearful, a position that makes him, and Freya under his protection, vulnerable to outside manipulation.

Freya's opening reflects the very real implications of international politics in Malaysia for the sailors and traders of the Archipelago. Sumatra, where Conrad sets the 'Seven Isles' of the title,[86] serves as a perfect example of the Anglo-Dutch conflict. The Dutch first visited Sumatra in 1596, but it was only after the Dutch East India Company signed a 1662 trade treaty with the British that protracted trade with the island began.[87] At the end of the eighteenth century, the British began to compete with the Dutch for control of the East Indies, including Sumatra. Although his actions were unsupported by the British government, beginning in 1812 the Governor of Java, Sir Stamford Raffles, attempted to extend British influence through a variety of tribal alliances. These efforts proved in vain, and in 1824 the Dutch signed a treaty with the British stipulating that Britain could introduce neither British factories nor British treaties to Sumatra. The Dutch solidified their power with an 1871 treaty in which the British granted them full control over the island.

While the Dutch maintained a powerful presence in Southern Malaysia, the British concentrated their efforts after 1880 on increasing their power in the Malay Peninsula north of Sumatra, and the northern part of the island of Borneo, east of Sumatra. By 1919, the British finally gained controlled of the entire Malay Peninsula, while an 1891 treaty divided the island of Borneo between the British and the Dutch.[88] These complicated and continued negations thus forced independent traders like Conrad's Nelson to manoeuvre between multiple systems of colonial rule, even before they entered into negotiations with the local peoples. Thus while Nelson's dread of Dutch authority is a personal and often debilitating fear, it also reflects the very real uncertainty and shifting nature of island possession and control throughout the late nineteenth century.

If Nelson responds to island politics with fear, Freya's English lover Jasper has no such concerns. Described as a daredevil, Jasper flaunts rules and regulations, participating with his tobacco plantation in a wilder and more dangerous form of trade than Freya's father.[89] With his relationship with the Dutch authorities precarious at best, Nelson fears with good reason Jasper's risky behaviours. The narrator explains,

> It is a fact that the Dutch looked askance at the doings of Jasper Allen, owner and master of the brig *Bonito*. They considered him much too enterprising in his trading. I don't know that he ever did anything illegal; but it seems to me that his immense activity was repulsive to their stolid character and slow-going methods.[90]

Even Jasper's brig, meant to carry him and Freya off to their romantic future, has a disreputable air. The narrator describes the *Bonito* as

> all black and enigmatical, and very dirty; a tarnished gem of the sea, or, rather, a neglected work of art . . . My opinion is that she was old enough to have been one of the last pirates, a slaver perhaps, or else an opium clipper of the early days, if not an opium smuggler.[91]

Jasper's brig recalls the ships of earlier heroes of the romantic adventure tradition, like the black pirate vessel belonging to Ballantyne's rehabilitated lead character in *Gascoyne, the Sandal-wood Trader*. While his derring-do aligns him with the romantic adventure tradition and endears him to Freya, Jasper's independent ways alienate him from her father. The conflict between Jasper's '*caballero*' attitude towards Dutch authority and Nelson's fears of political repercussions leads Freya to place on temporary hold her plans to leave with her dashing lover.[92]

While in older adventure fiction Jasper's actions would have proven him a heroic figure worthy of Freya's love, in the political realities of a contested Pacific, such actions are cause for concern, not congratulations. Fear defines and undermines Freya's father Nelson, but her lover Jasper is equally dangerous both to the stability of Pacific trade and to Freya's future.

Freya's future becomes even more precarious when third male presence, a Dutch naval officer, hears of the pretty girl of the Seven Isles and comes to call. Unlike Jasper, the dashing British adventure hero, Heemskirk is a dutiful officer of the law,

> commanding the *Neptun*, a little gunboat employed on dreary patrol duty up and down the Archipelago, to look after the traders. Not a very exalted position truly. I tell you, just a common middle-aged lieutenant of some twenty-five years' service and sure to be retired before long.[93]

Despite being surprised by this rude and uninvited guest, Nelson allows Heemskirk to stay on at the isle because of his position as a Dutch officer. The narrator records:

> He ought to have been kicked, if only for his manner to Miss Freya. Had he been a naked savage, armed with spears and poisoned arrows, old Nelson (or Nielsen) would have gone for him with his bare fists. But these gold shoulder-straps—Dutch shoulder-straps at that—were enough to terrify the old fellow; so he let the beggar treat him with heavy contempt, devour his daughter with his eyes, and drink the best part of his little stock of wine.[94]

Significantly, Conrad portrays Heemskirk as more dangerous than the island savages, as his relatively minor position of colonial authority renders Nelson helpless in his presence.[95] Because Heemskirk is so completely able to control her father's opinion, Freya sensibly determines that the best choice for all three men is to capitulate to her father's fear and see Heemskirk. Were she to defy her father, Jasper would likely become aware of Heemskirk's advances and fly into a jealous rage, ending any hope of a future together and destroying her father's career in the islands. When the narrator points out that Jasper's rage would allow him to 'squash Heemskirk like a blackbeetle', Freya responds, 'That wouldn't do . . . Imagine the state poor papa would get into. Besides, I mean to be mistress of the dear brig and sail about these seas, not go off wandering ten thousand miles away from here.'[96] Thus the men find themselves at the centre of a romantic triangle for control of the lovely Freya, and a political triangle for control of the island; whoever rules Freya also rules the island. It is only Freya's ability to remain sensible in the face of the men's conflict that keeps the peace.

On an island full of men, Freya is the only character to exhibit the stereotypically masculine characteristic of good sense.[97] As Elbert argues,

> Freya appears male, at least initially, in being able to control her emotions; the men appear female, though, in giving in to turbulent feelings. Freya is merely used to generate feelings, as men discover their potential for emotional depth. Indeed the uniting force has been Freya: she is the medium, whereby the three men are drawn together . . . she becomes the mirror for men's emotions.[98]

While I agree that Nelson, Jasper and Heemskirk's complex emotional responses to Freya unite and feminise the men, this unity cannot be divorced from Freya's connection to the island and from the conflict between civilised reason and barbaric savagery. Whoever controls Freya also, by extension, controls the Seven Isles either by colonial control (Heemskirk), trading influence (Nelson) or eventual inheritance (Jasper). The conflict between the men is not only a conflict over a woman, but a conflict over territory, a conflict which Conrad presents as devastating to rather than empowering of the traditional masculine bonds of adventure fiction.

As the men fight for possession of Freya, they begin to degenerate, revealing even more clearly their inner weaknesses. Heemskirk quickly recognises that Nelson is ruled by his fears and begins a campaign of vicious badgering. The narrator records,

> [Heemskirk] had frightened old Nelson very much by expressing a sinister wonder at the Government permitting a white man to settle down in that part at all . . . He had also charged him with being in reality no better than an Englishman. He had even tried to pick a quarrel with him for not learning to speak Dutch.[99]

This bullying reveals not only Heemskirk's increasing savagery, but also Nelson's who frets, '[Heemskirk] was as savage with me as if I had been a Chinaman.'[100] On the one hand, Conrad depicts Heemskirk as the worst sort of coloniser, brutal and power-mad; on the other hand, Nelson is a foolish islander, ignorant and fearful.[101] Jasper is also ruled by his base and 'savage' emotions, his reckless passion for Freya. When Freya insists that they wait to run away together, partly out of fear for her father and partly out of concern for her reputation, Jasper ignores social convention and capitulates to desire, embracing Freya on a public verandah.[102] Heemskirk catches a glimpse of the two lovers, igniting his rage against his rival. While her father insists that Freya 'was too sensible to fall in love with anyone', Freya uses her powers of 'sense' to manage the three men.[103] She continually works to regulate Jasper's desire, deflect Heemskirk's rage and lustful advances, and soothe her father's fears, deferring without disappointing any of the three. By using 'sense' to take a position of power, Freya, not the men, serves as the traditional 'masculine' presence on the island, soothing the men's 'savage' behaviour – forcing the rationally colonised into the role of coloniser. Conrad presents this negotiation as unstable, however, and puts intense strain upon the girl; 'she became anxious. The absurdities of three men were forcing this anxiety upon her: Jasper's impetuosity, her father's fears, Heemskirk's infatuation. She was very tender to the first two, and she made up her mind to display all her female diplomacy.'[104] What Freya describes as 'absurdities' – recklessness, irrational fear, rage and lust – are all traditional hallmarks of island 'savagery'.[105] As the men fight for Freya, they resemble 'rational' Europeans less and less and Malay 'savages' more and more.

The degeneration of the more noble impulses of the men of the Seven Isles leads to disastrous consequences, with savagery eventually undermining civilised sense. Freya's continued denial of Heemskirk's advances and acceptance of Jasper's goads the lieutenant into levelling threats against Jasper. He tells Freya directly that Jasper is nothing but 'an English trading skipper, a common fellow. Low, cheeky lot, infesting these islands. I would make short work of such trash!'[106] Heemskirk's hatred of Jasper stems both from his 'low-class' origins and from his position as an English trader – an 'invader' of the Dutch islands. Unable to gain Freya's attention with threats, Heemskirk attacks the girl verbally, stating, 'The heathen gods are only devils in disguise, and that's what you are, too—a deep little devil.'[107] Up to this point, Freya has been set apart from the men's foolish behaviour, but Heemskirk preys upon the uncertainty of her ability to maintain 'sense' in the face of the conflict. For the first time, Freya responds passionately rather than rationally, striking Heemskirk across the face as he leans in for a kiss. Despite her earlier protestations that 'no one could carry me off . . . I am not the sort of girl that gets carried off',[108] Freya remarks in this moment that she is glad Jasper is not present, or else 'she would have thrown her consistency, her firmness, her self-possession, to the winds, and flown into his arms'.[109] Unable and unwilling to explain her actions to her father, Freya attempts to internalise her emotions, hiding in her room and making 'faint, spasmodic sounds of a mysterious nature, between laughter and sobs'.[110] With Freya's move from sense into sensibility, 'feminised' by her emotions, there is nothing left to protect Jasper or her father from Heemskirk's retribution. Without Freya's sensible negotiations, the men are no longer protected from their 'savage' impulses – fear, desire and rage – placing both Freya and the island at the mercy of the inevitable conflict to come as the last man standing will claim both 'prizes'. The imperial desire for men to conquer both land and lady leads only to degeneration and despair.

While Heemskirk's actions transform Freya's usual sensible state into one of sentimentality, her prior rationality has served to arm Jasper against such emotional responses. Unaware of Freya's position, Jasper remains on the *Bonito* dreaming of her loveliness. In Jasper's mind, Freya is intimately connected with the landscape of the islands. He reflects,

> Everything in the world reminded him of her. The beauty of the loved woman exists in the beauties of Nature. The swelling outlines of the hills, the curves of the coast, the free sinuosities of a river are less suave than the harmonious lines of her body, and when she moves, gliding lightly, the grace of her progress suggest the power of occult forces which rule the fascinating aspects of the visible world.[111]

In her work on Conrad's female characters, Jennifer Turner argues that Conrad finds Jasper most vulnerable when he dreams of Freya: 'Women and money seem to represent the two main contaminating shore influences, severing the bond between sailor and sea and destabilizing a traditional masculinist mythology of toil and reward.'[112] I disagree – while Jasper's love of Freya equates with a love of the islands, it does not necessarily restrict his life as an adventurer/trader of the seas. Jasper's weakness instead stems from his highly emotional desire for Freya; it is only her 'masculine' ability to remain rational that protects Jasper from harm and turns him from a passionate savage to a noble knight. It is Jasper's move from potential possessor to poet, from imperial conqueror to the even older masculine script of the charming courtier, that redeems him. Envisioning his lady as a person not a prize controls Jasper's recklessness and when Heemskirk arrives unannounced, 'Jasper remembered her earnest recommendation to be guarded and cautious in all his acts and words while he was from her.'[113] Yet while Freya's words inspire Jasper to behave rationally, they also goad Heemskirk into fits of literally blind rage: 'the sudden desire to annihilate Jasper almost deprived him of his senses by its vehemence. He lost his power of speech, of vision. For a moment he absolutely couldn't see Jasper.'[114] While Jasper is transformed by love, Heemskirk is weakened by his inability to envision Freya as anything other than a potential possession. Blinded by his passionate anger, Heemskirk takes his revenge by wrecking the *Bonito* on the island's dangerous reef. Freya's and Jasper's reason holds no sway. It is Heemskirk's 'savage' reaction, his zealous rage and inability to see reason over passion, that cause the destruction of Jasper's potential as a heroic trader and adventurer. Freya's reason transforms Jasper's impetuous desire into a noble love which controls his baser emotions. Rather than seeing Freya and her island as simply commodities to be controlled, Jasper views both as beautiful and beyond price. Heemskirk's rage, however, stems directly from his commodification of woman/island, viewing both as scarce and valuable resources that can only be won through savage competition. While Jasper rises as a noble adventurer, Heemskirk's choice to react with violent rage instead of rational behaviour turns him into the worst sort of savage and both Freya and the island into mere merchandise.

The loss of the *Bonito* represents the triumph of Heemskirk over Freya/Jasper/Nelson, of savage rage over reason, and of Dutch regulation and commodification over British adventuring and freedom. As the news spreads and men begin to ask Jasper the fate of his brig, he remarks, 'It was an annihilating question.'[115] While Jasper's body remains alive, his spirit is visibly divorced from it, and he wanders the islands 'long enough to become almost one of the sights of the place; long enough to become disregarded at last; long enough for the tale of his haunting visibly to be remembered in the islands to this day'.[116] Despite receiving testimony that proves Jasper's innocence, the courts side with Heemskirk: 'what Dutch court, having once got a hold of an English trader, would accept such an explanation; and, indeed, how, when, where could one hope to find proofs of such a tale?'[117] Jasper's fate is determined by Heemskirk's savage rage but sealed by the rivalry between the Dutch and English traders. After witnessing Jasper in his weakened state, Nelson, who has fared no better, tells the narrator,

> What was the good? Mad! And what sort of husband would he have made, anyhow, for a sensible girl like Freya? Why, even my little property I could not have left them. The Dutch authorities would never have allowed an Englishman to settle there . . . Later on I let it go for a tenth of its value to a Dutch half-caste.[118]

As the news of Jasper's disgrace reaches Freya it sends her into a deep despondency. The rivalry over Freya and the islands has cost Jasper his sanity and Nelson his small island, but also Freya her 'sense'. Consumed by emotion, Freya frets and sickens, saying,

> I've been conceited, headstrong, capricious. I sought my own gratification. I was selfish or afraid . . . Yes; perhaps, when the day came I would not have gone. Perhaps! I don't know . . . Draw the curtain, papa. Shut the sea out. It reproaches me with my folly.[119]

Intriguingly, Elbert argues that this final moment cements Freya's masculine presence:

Whereas the men have appeared as turbulent, irrational, fickle, and fearful, the narrator perversely has Freya articulate these qualities about herself on her deathbed; in the most subversive way, then, he has masculinized her, gotten her involved in male politics, only to make an end of her along with all the other irrational males.[120]

While critics often read Conrad's women as destructive to masculine adventuring, in *Freya* it is the weakness of adventuring, the tawdry savagery of trade, that destroys the only sensible (and ironically 'masculine') character in the text, and by extension renders the 'trade' worthless. Thus the Seven Isles become a place where 'sense' cannot survive, where savagery destroys reason and the commodification of beauty turns all men, and even women, into savage, passionate, fearful, base creatures, consumed by death or madness.

While *Freya of the Seven Isles* has long been dismissed as Conrad's 'lesser' fiction, plagued by awkward phrasing and romantic convention, such criticism ignores its depiction of the Anglo-Dutch relations in the South Seas. The strong anti-Dutch sentiment and the fear portrayed by the Danish 'outsider' Nelson reveal Conrad's interest in and opinions of colonial settlement and trade in the region. Unlike earlier imperial romances, such as the novels of Fredrick Marryat or R. M. Ballantyne, Conrad envisions the islands as unsafe, destroying the lives of those foolish enough both to colonise them and to attempt a system of inter-colonial trade. These negotiations encourage the basest of human emotions and the two Victorian civilising impulses, good sense and a good woman, are not enough to prevent the enterprise's eventual downfall. While Robert Louis Stevenson also saw pitfalls in colonising Pacific islands, Conrad's criticisms are harsher and more definitive. In Conrad's fiction, the islands are a place where traditional boundaries disintegrate, where women are the sole possessors of 'sense' and men are ruled by base passions. The competition over one woman or one island leads only to madness, destruction and death, with irrationality destroying the greatest treasures of the Pacific.

Is the Lady a Tramp? *Because of the Dollars* and Island Economics

In *Freya of the Seven Isles*, Conrad focuses on the destructive potential of the Anglo-Dutch trade rivalry in the Malay Archipelago. In 'Because of the Dollars', Conrad returns to his theme of the destructive influence of trade upon the lives of Europeans in the Pacific. 'Because of the Dollars', however, connects this theme with degeneracy of character, this time showing the effect men's decisions in the Pacific have on the lives of the women and children who follow them to the isles. The result is one of Conrad's clearest indictments of the corruptive force of trade and the destructive potential of Europeans occupying the Archipelago. While Conrad presents Freya as a victim of savage masculinity, in 'Dollars' he introduces women who suffer from the economic realities of Pacific trade.

'Because of the Dollars' opens like *Freya* with a depiction of a Pacific trader. Unlike in his other story, however, Conrad makes clear that this hero, Davidson, is a fair and honourable man. Hollis says of Davidson, 'That's a good man. I don't mean good in the sense of smart or skilful in his trade. I mean a really *good* man.'[121] When asked to explain further, Hollis remarks,

> He's thoroughly humane, and I don't imagine there can be much of any other sort of goodness that counts on this earth. And as he's that with a shade of particular refinement, I may well call him a '*really* good man.'[122]

Davidson makes his lucrative living as a trader by exploring and 'was known to visit in [his ship] places that no one else could find and that hardly anybody had ever heard of'.[123] Although Davidson appears to be the best sort of heroic adventurer in the mid-Victorian style, Conrad quickly establishes that while Davidson may be a good man, it does not necessarily follow he is a strong one. Davidson's ship, the *Sissie*, is owned by a 'portly Chinaman resembling a mandarin in a picture-book'.[124] It is this Chinese counterpart that makes Davidson's heroic explorations and trade possible; bystanders 'couldn't tell if it was Davidson who belonged to the Chinaman or the Chinaman who belonged to Davidson'.[125] Davidson may resemble an early adventure hero, but his dependence on the Chinaman compromises his status as European 'superior'. It is the Chinaman, not Davidson, who suggests that the *Sissie* be used to collect the old dollars that 'had been called in by our Government in exchange for a new issue'.[126] While Davidson is the simplest and least corrupt of Conrad's Pacific characters, his dependence on the Chinaman challenges his position as a heroic coloniser/explorer and, like Nelson's in *Freya*, his masculine heroism is undermined by weakness, in this case his willingness to defer power to a colonised 'Other'.

The plot of 'Because of the Dollars' revolves around Davidson's desire to exchange old dollars for new, a profession that Conrad portrays from the outset as a shadowy business. Hollis explains the process:

> Every trader in the islands was thinking of getting his old dollars sent up here in time, and the demand for empty French wine cases—you know the dozen

of vermouth or claret size—was something unprecedented. The custom was to pack the dollars in little bags of a hundred each. I don't know how many bags each case would hold. A good lot. Pretty tidy sums must have been moving afloat just then.[127]

The fact that traders must hide their dollars in empty wine cases shows the dangerous and unpredictable nature of Pacific trade. The Chinaman suggests to Davidson that 'the *Sissie* would be just the thing to collect them from small traders in the less frequented parts of the Archipelago'.[128] Davidson is clearly no stranger to trade; as Hollis explains early on in the text, 'What with his salary and trading privileges he makes a lot of money.'[129] His decision to exchange the dollars, however, frightens his wife, who 'thought there was some danger on account of the dollars. [Davidson] told her, he said, that there were no Java-sea pirates nowadays except in boy's books.'[130] While piracy would continue throughout the nineteenth century, Davidson's pacifying comments indicate the increased safety of trade ships in the Archipelago.[131] Intriguingly, Davidson places the realities of Pacific trade in a category separate from the dashing adventures of boy's books, implying that the dangers are, at the very least, of a different nature. For Davidson the 'romance' of trade in adventure fiction is quite different from its practice in daily life. To hold a position of power in the Pacific in the late nineteenth century depended less on daring exploits and more on the ability to negotiate complicated trade disputes. While no longer associated with pirates like Bloody Bill, Pacific trade still had numerous perils, largely stemming from growing competition between rival colonial trade interests.

While Davidson represents a new version of the 'adventure hero' as a man facing the dangerous realities of Pacific trade, Davidson's wife also represents a new iteration of the white island woman. The very fact that Davidson *has* a wife and brings her to the islands is an anomaly in the lives of Pacific traders. As Hollis explains,

> Ours, as you remember, was a bachelor crowd; in spirit anyhow, if not absolutely in fact. There might have been a few wives in existence, but if so they were invisible, distant, never alluded to. For what would have been the good? Davidson alone was visibly married.[132]

While wives played an important role in early nineteenth-century Pacific fictions like *The Swiss Family Robinson*, they functioned primarily as mothers instructing children in appropriate behaviour. In the mid-century 'boy's books' to which Davidson refers earlier, women had disappeared almost entirely. By the time of Robert Louis Stevenson's writings, romantic options for men in the Pacific appeared to consist entirely of native women. Conrad and other late Pacific writers, however, categorised the white woman quite differently, avoiding 'the stereotypes of the romance and adventure genre – the noble savage, the villainous degenerate, the simple child-like native, the exotic temptress, [and] the submissive native girl'.[133] This separation corresponded with an ever-increasing cultural emphasis connecting masculinity with imperial expansion in the later nineteenth century. In her work on gender and imperialism, Philippa Levine notes that the British Empire

> celebrated a very particular vision of white maleness as physical, responsible, productive, and hard-working. These were qualities denied to women and to the colonized . . . women's femininity was seen to derive in large part from their lack of physical prowess, their delicacy, and nervousness. This vision of masculinity as that which could transform unproductive spaces profitably was simply not on offer to women or to the colonized. Gender, then, was more than descriptive; it became a hierarchical ordering of quality, skill, and usefulness.[134]

While the Pacific adventure tradition marginalised women, historically 'white women participated with varying degrees of alienation (and enthusiasm) in imperial projects; as teachers, missionaries, nurses, and the help-mates of colonial men'.[135] Conrad's choice to include Davidson's wife as a character in a Pacific story is thus an intriguing and unusual addition as it begins to address the historical realities white women faced living in the Pacific.

While Davidson's wife seems to represent an idyllic addition to the British Pacific world – with 'her sweetness, her gentleness, and her charm', she provides a sense a sense of English decorum and family life for the otherwise rough colonial outpost[136] – she is also immediately treated as a figure of suspicion. Hollis remarks:

> I was perhaps the one who saw most of the Davidsons at home. What I noticed under the superficial aspect of vapid sweetness was her convex, obstinate forehead, and her small, red, pretty, ungenerous mouth. But then I am an observer with strong prejudices. Most of us were fetched by her white, swan-like neck, by that drooping, innocent profile. There was a lot of latent devotion to Davidson's wife hereabouts . . . But my idea was that she repaid it by a profound suspicion of the sort of men we were; a mistrust which extended—I fancied—to her very husband at times. And I thought then she was jealous of him in a way; though there were no women that she could be jealous about. She had no women's society.[137]

Hollis's remarks are reminiscent of the discourse of *Freya of the Seven Isles* which also revolves around an 'outsider' who judges the merits of another man's love interest. In this case, however, it is not Hollis who exhibits the 'savage' and degenerate characteristic of jealousy, but the woman in question. Even before the introduction of any other women to the text, Hollis suspects that Davidson's wife is jealous of his Pacific existence and his connection to the non-domestic adventuring men. She is tainted by her association with the mainland and only serves to weaken the 'noble adventurer' with her jealousy of his necessary trade ventures. While Davidson may be a 'good' man, he is trapped between an external trading sphere and the domestic sphere, both of which threaten his welfare and future.

The seemingly virtuous but highly suspicious character of Davidson's wife is contrasted throughout the text with the other white woman of the story, the ironically named 'Laughing Anne'. Unlike Davidson's wife, Anne does not enjoy the protection of a 'good' man, but is beholden instead to a trader called Pearler Harry. As Hollis records, after taking Anne from Australia, Harry

> dropped her, and she remained knocking about here and there, known to most of us by sight, at any rate. Everybody in the Archipelago had heard of Laughing Anne. She had really a pleasant silvery laugh always at her disposal, so to speak, but it wasn't enough apparently to make her fortune. The poor creature was ready to stick to any half-decent man if he would only let her, but she always got dropped, as it might have been expected.[138]

The exact opposite of Davidson's wife, whose position is so defining she does not apparently merit a name, Laughing Anne is a likable but pathetic figure abandoned to the whims of careless and callous men. In order to safeguard her son, she takes up with trader named Bamtz, a relationship which, Hollis notes

> was coming down pretty low in the world, even from a material point of view. She had always been decent, in her way; whereas Bamtz was, not to mince words, an abject sort of creature. On the other hand, that bearded loafer, who looked much more like a pirate than a bookkeeper, was not a brute. He was gentle—rather—even in his cups.[139]

Anne's inclusion in the story is as unusual as that of Davidson's wife. While prostitution was a reality for many island women throughout the nineteenth century, the typical 'mistress' in the literature of the period was a native woman, as is the case in the works of Robert Louis Stevenson. Conrad's choice to make Anne white attacks the traditional boundaries of adventure fiction, where men protect white women from the seedy nature of the Pacific sex trade. Additionally, while up until this point, trade in the majority of Pacific narratives referred only to material goods, Conrad reminds the reader through Anne's story that the rough men of the Pacific were as eager to trade women as dollars. While earlier stories like Stevenson's commented on the Pacific's ability to corrupt white men, Conrad is one of the first authors to show the Pacific as also corrupting white women.

The corruptive influence of trade is not limited to cast-off women like Laughing Anne. Davidson is not the only trader interested in a cargo of dollars and, as Conrad reveals, the Pacific is not usually populated by 'good' men. The first to hear of Davidson's endeavour is a 'bright creature' named Fector who

> described himself as a journalist as certain kind of women give themselves out as actresses in the dock of a police-court . . . It's a fact that he had been kicked, horsewhipped, imprisoned, and hounded with ignominy out of pretty well every place between Ceylon and Shanghai, for a professional blackmailer.[140]

Fector quickly finds two associates to help him steal Davidson's cargo. The first, Niclaus, is a

> fellow with a Tartar moustache and a yellow complexion, like a Mongolian, only that his eyes were set straight and his face was not so flat. One couldn't tell what breed he was . . . From a certain angle you would think a very bilious white man. And I daresay he was . . . He couldn't, apparently, speak any other European language than English, but he flew the Dutch flag on his prau.[141]

While Fector is simply a liar and a cheat, Niclaus is far more terrifying since his identity slips between Malay, English and Dutch. Here Conrad takes advantage of the myriad possible identities from islander to European present in the Archipelago, and capitalises on fears of racial mixing and masquerade. Fector's other crewman is a 'Frenchman without hands' who was 'always trying to roll cigarettes on his knee with his stumps, telling endless yarns of Polynesia'.[142] Conrad renders this degenerate carcass of a man even more horrifying by adding,

> He was always talking about 'resuming his activities,' some day, whatever they were, if he could only get an intelligent companion. It was evident . . . the sickly woman with her face tied up, who used to look in sometimes through the back door, was no companion for him . . . He looked then like a devil; but a man without hands, unable to load or handle a weapon, can at best go for one only with his teeth.[143]

The Frenchman is the most terrifying of the trio, as he exemplifies both the French threat to British power in Polynesia and fears of the unhealthy desires and degeneration of the masculine body. The three men represent the worst fears of white occupation in the Pacific. While few islanders are represented in Conrad's tale, there is no shortage of savages. Conrad denies these traders any sort of heroic past, noting that 'neither of them was of the bold buccaneer type; and Fector, especially, had never in his adventurous life used other weapons than slander and lies'.[144] With the creation of such characters, Conrad clearly links imperial trade with the worst sorts of monstrosity and villainy.

The conflict over the dollars does not culminate in a fair fight between the 'noble' Davidson and the wretched villains, but instead is triangulated through the poor figure of Laughing Anne. Anne has fallen even further in the world when Davidson revisits her. She appears with

> little more on her than a loose chintz wrapper and straw slippers on her bare feet. Her head was tied up Malay fashion in a red handkerchief, with a mass of loose hair hanging under it behind. Her professional, gay, European feathers had literally dropped off her in the course of these two years, but a long necklace of amber beads hung round her uncovered neck.[145]

Like the villainous Niclaus, Anne has lost part of her European identity to the ravages of the Pacific, becoming almost indistinguishable from the native women. Davidson also learns that her visit is motivated by her son who is dying from a tropical illness while trapped in a house with Bamtz and the villainous traders Fector, Niclaus and the Frenchman. Warned by Anne, Davidson avoids the sneak attacks by the brigands, but in the process of returning to rescue her son, Anne is killed. Anne's death has a profound effect on Davidson who reflects,

> She had died for him. His manhood was as if stunned. For the first time he felt afraid . . . One can hardly picture to oneself Davidson crawling away on all fours from the murdered woman—Davidson unmanned and crushed by the idea that she had died for him in a sense.[146]

The only 'good' man in the Pacific, the last of the great heroes of the adventure tradition, finds himself unmanned by villainous traders and his inability to save a fallen woman. It is Anne, not Davidson, who provides the heroic action of the scene, and her actions save Davidson's life, inverting the usual gender stereotype of adventure fiction. If the only heroic action in the text is provided by a 'fallen' woman, then Conrad shows there can be little hope for the survival of traditional male adventure tradition. Trade, the lure of the dollars, proves the destruction of all men, and possibly all women, in the Pacific.

While destruction seems imminent, Davidson rallies to rescue Anne's son, and then returns to his ship in the hopes of saving his future. Unlike traditional heroes, Davidson is unable to take vengeance on his attackers. It is Anne who fires the shot that kills the Frenchman, and when the other two men simply disappear, 'Davidson did not trouble his head about them.'[147] When he returns to the mainland and tells the Harbour Master his story, there is still no justice: '[The Harbour Master] didn't think . . . that a formal complaint should be made to the Dutch Government. They would probably do nothing in the end, after a lot of trouble and correspondence.'[148] As the robbery was never completed and Anne's murderer is dead, the colonial representative wipes his hands of the mess. While the matter of the dollars costs Davidson his honour and Anne her life, the criminals are never caught nor punished and presumably continue on to profit from further crimes. The villainous traders are successful while Davidson's attempts to trade dollars and Anne's attempts to trade her body are both punished and end in misery.

Davidson is not only disappointed in his faith in the colonial government, but also in his lovely wife, who immediately assumes that the rescued boy is the product of a relationship between Davidson and Anne. In an attempt to make peace, Davidson sends the boy to the 'White Fathers in Malacca' for an education, but even then his wife is not satisfied. As Conrad explains,

> She could not forgive him for not casting the offensive child away utterly. She worked up her sense of her wifely wrongs and of her injured purity to such a pitch that one day . . . she turned on him in a chill passion and told him that his very sight was odious to her. Davidson, with his scrupulous delicacy of feeling, was not the man to assert his rights over a woman who could not bear the sight of him. He bowed his head; and shortly afterwards arranged for her to go back to her parents.[149]

Not only does Davidson lose his wife, but also his little daughter over the affair of the dollars. Davidson's final hope, that Anne's son will have a successful future and perhaps grow up into a fine British boy like those of Ballantyne's *The Coral Island*, is also dashed. Instead, influenced by the Fathers, young Tony 'wants to be a priest; his one dream is to be a missionary. The Fathers assure Davidson that it is a serious vocation. They tell him he has a special disposition for mission work, too.'[150] While missionaries were some of the first heroes and colonisers of the early nineteenth century Pacific, by the time of Conrad's writing the profession was no longer valued as an alternate form of heroic masculinity.[151] Conrad concludes the story on a dark note, commenting,

> So Laughing Anne's boy will lead a saintly life in China somewhere; he may even become a martyr; but poor Davidson is left out in the cold. He will have to go downhill without a single human affection near him because of those old dollars.[152]

Conrad significantly intensifies the destructive nature of trade he first explores in *Freya of the Seven Isles*. At the end of 'Because of the Dollars', trade and the vapid 'froth' of mainland society like Davidson's wife are responsible for the destruction of the last great adventure hero, along with his wife, Laughing Anne and the potential future of colonialism in the Pacific.

While early British narratives championed expansion and settlement in the small islands of the Pacific, their optimism was quickly undermined by the realities of island life. While mid-century scientists first questioned the British role in the development of islands and islanders, by the end of the century even the boldest settlers and adventurers began to have doubts about the British 'civilising mission'. Himself a settler in Samoa, Robert Louis Stevenson worked to negotiate a way for the British and the native islanders to live in harmony but feared the destructive influence that settlers had both on the people and on the landscape of the islands. His contemporary Joseph Conrad took these critiques a step further and argued that any attempt at trade in or settlement on the small Pacific islands was doomed to not only destroy the men involved but also their connection to the women, natives and islands that surrounded them. With so many conflicted British voices, the reading public searched for answers closer to the source, from the islanders themselves. While the British provided their own interpretations of trade and settlement in the Pacific, a parallel narrative from Pacific islanders was also being published and discussed alongside these more popular accounts. In my final chapter, I will be examining these Pacific voices, albeit filtered through the British press, to show an alternate version of British influence in the islands which both confirms and undermines the perspective of British authors.

Notes

1. According to the Stevensons, Vailima meant 'the place of the five rivers'. In actuality, the plantation had only four, but Stevenson liked the sound of 'Vailima' so they simply 'pretended it had five streams'. See Daiches, *Robert Louis Stevenson and His World*, 89.
2. The cause of Stevenson's illness remains mysterious, though tuberculosis and bronchiectasis are possibilities.
3. I have drawn this account of Stevenson's funeral from Ellison, *Tusitala of the South Seas*; Daiches, *Robert Louis Stevenson and His World*.
4. See, for instance, Jolly, *Robert Louis Stevenson in the Pacific*; Colley, 'Robert Louis Stevenson's South Seas Crossings'; Hayes, 'Colonialism in R.L. Stevenson's South Seas Fiction'; Buckton, *Cruising with Robert Louis Stevenson*; Hillier, *The South Seas Fiction of Robert Louis Stevenson*.
5. Gersdorf and Mayer, *Nature in Literary and Cultural Studies*, 51.
6. Scholars like F. R. Leavis, Douglas Hewitt, Albert J. Geurard, and Bernard C. Meyer subsequently lent support to Moser's opinion. For an

in-depth look at Moser's theory, see Moser, *Joseph Conrad: Achievement and Decline.*

7. Pursell, '"People Don't Die Here Sooner Than in Europe"', 113. For a reading of the historical context of Conrad's earlier Malay fiction, see Clemens, 'Conrad's Malaysia'.

8. European explorers named the archipelago for the people group they called 'Malays', but it is now more commonly referred to as Maritime Southeast Asia. It stretches from Southeast Asia to Australia and includes the islands of Brunei, East Timor, Indonesia, Malaysia, the Philippines and Singapore. Geographers continue to debate the island of New Guinea's status as part of the archipelago. Explorers and colonists also referred to the archipelago as the 'East Indies'. For a nineteenth-century perspective available to Conrad, see Wallace, 'On the Physical Geography of the Malay Archipelago'.

9. McGaw, *Stevenson in Hawaii*, 11.

10. Daiches, *Robert Louis Stevenson and His World*, 88–9.

11. Stevenson, *Vailima Letters*, 1, 27.

12. Oliver, *The Pacific Islands*, 62.

13. See my section on William Ellis in Chapter 1.

14. Stevenson, *Vailima Letters*, 1, 33.

15. It is likely Stevenson was referring to 'vao tuitui' or *Mimosa pudica*, a prickly creeper originally native to South America that was introduced to the tropics most likely as an ornamental plant.

16. Stevenson, *Vailima Letters*, 1, 46.

17. Parham, *The Environmental Tradition*, 164.

18. Ibid., 165.

19. Grove, *Green Imperialism*, 9.

20. Ibid., 14.

21. A woody climbing vine that is common in tropical areas.

22. Stevenson, *Vailima Letters*, 1, 42–3.

23. See note 15.

24. Stevenson, *Vailima Letters*, 1, 49.

25. Ibid., 104.

26. Ibid., 106–7.

27. While Stevenson is writing these words a full eight years before Joseph Conrad would publish *Heart of Darkness*, the idea of an impenetrable and haunting foreign landscape as 'the horror' was already growing in British consciousness. See Conrad, *Heart of Darkness*, 68.

28. While Stevenson's other short stories are intriguing for a variety of reasons, the two longer texts best illustrate Stevenson's environmental concerns.

29. Stevenson, *Vailima Letters*, 1, 145.

30. Buckton, *Cruising with Robert Louis Stevenson*, 226.

31. Stevenson, *Vailima Letters*, 1, 159.

32. Dening, *Islands and Beaches*, 32.

33. Stevenson, 'The Beach of Falesá', 3.

34. Colley, 'South Seas Crossings', 877–8.

35. Stevenson, 'The Beach of Falesá', 3, 259, n 3.

36. Ibid., 3.

37. Ibid.
38. Ibid., 4.
39. Levine, *Gender and Empire*, 131.
40. Stevenson, 'The Beach of Falesá', 6.
41. Ibid., 5.
42. Ibid., 10.
43. Ibid., 11. As a side note, when the *Illustrated London News* originally published the story in August 1892, they judged this marriage contract too scandalous and, over Stevenson's objections, excised it. It was not until the story was published in *Island Night's Entertainments* in April 1893 that the corrected version appeared. See Jolly, 'Note on the Texts', xxxiv.
44. Stevenson, 'The Beach of Falesá', 17.
45. Copra was dried coconut used to make oil for candles and soap. With the decline of the whaling industry mid-century, copra had become one of the Pacific's most steadily growing trades. For more on the copra market, see Oliver, *The Pacific Islands*, 62; Dodge, *Islands and Empires*, 187.
46. Wiltshire sees becoming profitable in the South Seas as essential to achieving success in England. Edward Said has famously noted the dependence of Western culture on overseas goods. As he explains, 'There is the hierarchy of spaces by which the metropolitan centre and, gradually, the metropolitan economy are seen as dependent upon an overseas system of territorial control, economic exploitation, and a socio-cultural vision; without these stability and prosperity at home—"home" being a word with extremely potent resonances—would not be possible.' Said, *Culture and Imperialism*, 58–9.
47. Parham, *The Environmental Tradition*, 163.
48. Ibid., 164.
49. Hillier, *The South Seas Fiction of Robert Louis Stevenson*, 165.
50. Buckton, *Cruising with Robert Louis Stevenson*, 161.
51. Ibid., 18.
52. Stevenson, 'The Beach of Falesá', 29.
53. Ibid., 35.
54. Ibid.
55. Ibid., 44.
56. Ibid., 45.
57. Ibid., 51.
58. Hayes, 'Colonialism in R.L. Stevenson's South Seas Fiction', 169.
59. Stevenson, 'The Beach of Falesá', 56.
60. Ibid., 68.
61. This savagery stands in contrast to the actions of the natives who use non-violent methods of control, like taboo.
62. Brantlinger, *Rule of Darkness*, 40.
63. Stevenson, 'The Beach of Falesá', 70.
64. Tulloch, 'Stevenson and Islands, 79.
65. Hillier, *The South Seas Fiction of Robert Louis Stevenson*, 192.
66. Colley, 'South Seas Crossings', 879.
67. Stevenson, 'The Beach of Falesá', 71.
68. Ibid.

69. Jolly, 'South Sea Gothic', 37.
70. Stevenson, *Vailima Letters*, 2, 273.
71. Hillier, *The South Seas Fiction of Robert Louis Stevenson*, 155.
72. Stevenson, *Vailima Letters*, 2, 94.
73. Jolly, 'Introduction', xxx.
74. Garnett was Conrad's publisher, and he encouraged Conrad to continue writing after publishing his first novel, *Almayer's Folly*. For more on Garnett, see Garnett, 'Garnett, Edward William'; Karl and Davies, *The Collected Letters of Joseph Conrad*, 407.
75. Karl and Davies, *The Collected Letters of Joseph Conrad*, 413.
76. Ibid., 417.
77. For more on the publication history of *Freya of the Seven Isles*, see Graver, *Conrad's Short Fiction*.
78. Conrad's choice to approach the islands from a decidedly European point of view is to be expected considering the relatively short time he spent in the Archipelago. As Lloyd Fernando summarises, 'The period Conrad spent in the Malaysian region was a few brief months ... Mostly he learned about his [future characters] from books and newspapers, and from gossip written on or supplied by other expatriates. The Eastern world he portrays really falls within the round of hotels, other expatriate acquaintances, shore gossip, books by other expatriates ... and a skillful seaman's knowledge of certain harbors, bays, rivers, creeks, and shores.' See Fernando, 'Cornad's Eastern Expatriates', 60–1.
79. Graver, *Conrad's Short Fiction*, 163. As Jennifer Turner notes, 'Ironically, although women and the sea belong to the same "popular" literary category, the latter subject is generally thought the more "artistic", with writing about women condemned to the separate, lesser genre of "romance." For Conrad, however, the "pot- boiler", a format evoking few expectations of originality or depth, seems to have allowed greater freedom for experimentation, as his manipulation of the genre creates a sense of awkwardness in the "serious" reader that reflects the awkwardness of the subject matter.' See Turner, '"Petticoats" and "Sea Business"', 143.
80. Elbert, '"Freya of the Seven Isles" and the Heart of Male Darkness', 36.
81. As the narrator informs us, Nelson is not the character's actual name: 'The Englishmen in the Archipelago called him Nelson because it was more convenient, I suppose, and he never protested. It would have been mere pedantry. The true form of his name was Nielsen.' See Conrad, 'Freya of the Seven Isles', 204. For the sake of clarity, I will follow the narrator's example and use the name 'Nelson' throughout this chapter.
82. Ibid.
83. Ibid., 204–5.
84. Ibid., 205.
85. Ibid. Banka, or Bangka, is a real island off the east coast of Sumatra.
86. Larahee notes that Conrad simplifies certain portions of the geography, but the general setting remains identifiable. See Larahee, 'Territorial Vision and Revision in "Freya of the Seven Isles"'.
87. While conflict between the British and the Dutch continued throughout the seventeenth century, culminating in multiple Anglo-Dutch wars, these

events did little to challenge Dutch superiority in the East Indies, which remained largely undisturbed until after the Napoleonic Wars.

88. For a detailed analysis of the Anglo-Dutch conflict in Malaysia see Andaya and Andaya, *A History of Malaysia*; Historical Section of the Foreign Office, *Dutch and British Possessions*; Hyma, *A History of the Dutch in the Far East*; Kennedy, *A History of Malaysia*; Robequain, *Malaya, Indonesia, Borneo, and the Philippines*; Tarling, *Anglo-Dutch Rivalry in the Malay World*.

89. The narrator quickly offers an example of Jasper's style of risk-taking. Sailing to the isles to visit Freya, Jasper takes a dangerous shortcut: 'Instead of standing on for another mile and a half along the shoals and then tacking for the anchorage in a proper and seamanlike manner, he spies a gap between two disgusting old reefs, puts the helm down suddenly, and shoots the brig through, with all her sails shaking and rattling.' See Conrad, 'Freya of the Seven Isles', 208.

90. Ibid., 209.

91. Ibid., 211.

92. Ibid.

93. Ibid., 213.

94. Ibid., 213–14.

95. This is not the first time that Conrad had voiced such an opinion. Earlier in the chapter the narrator says of Nelson, 'It was really pitiable to see the anxious circumspection of his dealing with some official or other, and remember that this man had been known to stroll up to a village of cannibals in New Guinea in a quiet fearless manner (and note that he was always fleshy all his life, and, if I may say so, an appetising morsel) on some matter of barter that did not amount to perhaps fifty pounds in the end.' See ibid., 205. While Nelson is perfectly capable of controlling a group of cannibals, he cowers before the trappings of Dutch authority.

96. Freya also asserts her power to calm down the wild Jasper, stating 'I have tamed him a bit. He's quite a good boy now.' ibid., 215.

97. Joseph Kestner argues the centrality of reason to the masculine script at the end of the nineteenth century in his work on Sherlock Holmes. He notes that Victorians typically conceived masculinity as embodying 'observation, rationalism, factuality, logic, comradeship, daring and pluck'. See Kestner, *Sherlock's Men*, 2. For a more in-depth look at masculinity in the works of Joseph Conrad see Kestner, *Masculinities in British Adventure Fiction*; Roberts, *Conrad and Masculinity*. For a broader discussion of masculinity in the Victorian world, see Mangan and Walvin, *Manliness and Morality*; Roper and Tosh, *Manful Assertions*; Tosh, *A Man's Place*.

98. Elbert, '"Freya of the Seven Isles" and the Heart of Male Darkness', 42.

99. Conrad, 'Freya of the Seven Isles', 224.

100. Ibid.

101. By 1920, the Chinese population in Sumatra far outnumbered the European population; in fact, they were the largest population of non-natives on the island. As one historian contemporary to Conrad states, 'Apart from employment as coolies, the Chinese form a universal class of middlemen, and trade in the islands would be paralysed by their

departure.' See Historical Section of the Foreign Office, *Dutch and British Possessions*, 14, 9. Nelson's comments imply that he feels like a second-class citizen on the island.

102. Freya tells the narrator that she will not leave with Jasper 'before [her] twenty-first birthday; so that there shall be no mistake in people's minds as to me being old enough to know what I am doing'. See Conrad, 'Freya of the Seven Isles', 218.
103. Ibid., 228.
104. Ibid., 233.
105. In a 1921 Presidential Address to the Royal Anthropology Institute, Everard described the European stereotype of Pacific savagery as '"wildness" or "uncontrolledness." In short, these Islanders, when first seen, had developed for themselves a certain degree-in many cases a very high degree-of culture; they were "wild" or "uncontrolled" in that they had not been subjected to the influence of "civilization."' A 'savage' did not lack culture, but control. See Thurn, 'Presidential Address', 15. Travellers, traders and scholars of the late nineteenth and early twentieth century produced multitudes of quasi-anthropological studies of the habits and 'races' of the Malay Archipelago. For some representative examples, see van Alphen, 'Ethnographic Notes on Sumba'; Clifford, 'A Journey through the Malay States of Trengganu and Kelantan'; Furness, 'Glimpses of Borneo'; Morris, 'Race and Custom in the Malay Archipelago'; Skeat, 'Malay Spiritualism'; Skeat, 'The Wild Tribes of the Malay Peninsula'.
106. Conrad, 'Freya of the Seven Isles', 238.
107. Ibid., 238–9.
108. Ibid., 234.
109. Ibid., 240.
110. Ibid., 241.
111. Ibid., 249.
112. Turner, '"Petticoats" and "Sea Business"', 144.
113. Conrad, 'Freya of the Seven Isles', 250.
114. Ibid., 252.
115. Ibid., 261.
116. Ibid.
117. Ibid., 264.
118. Ibid., 268–9.
119. Ibid., 269.
120. Elbert, '"Freya of the Seven Isles" and the Heart of Male Darkness', 43.
121. Conrad, 'Because of the Dollars', 218.
122. Ibid., 219.
123. Ibid., 221.
124. Ibid., 219.
125. Ibid.
126. Ibid., 220. It is rather difficult to discern exactly to which exchange of 'dollars' Conrad is referring as there were a large number of silver dollars in circulation at the turn of the century. In 1895 Britain did, incidentally, mint a new version of silver dollars for trade in the Pacific. For more on the history of Pacific coinage, see Bailey and Bhaopichitr, 'How Important Was Silver?'; Huff, 'Monetization and Financial Development

in Southeast Asia before the Second World War'; St. Clair, 'American Trade Dollars in Nineteenth-Century China'.

127. Conrad, 'Because of the Dollars', 220.
128. Ibid., 221.
129. Ibid., 219.
130. Ibid., 222.
131. In 1848 the British government gave the Philippine government three ships to help capture pirates in the Archipelago, but they achieved limited success. It was not until the 1870s that Britain began to focus on suppressing piracy with any real effectiveness. For more on piracy, see Earl, 'Pirates on the Java Sea'; Robequain, *Malaya, Indonesia, Borneo, and the Philippines*. For more on the connection between piracy and 'Because of the Dollars', see Hampston, '"Because of the Dollars" and the Already Written'.
132. Conrad, 'Because of the Dollars', 222.
133. Baxter and Hand, *Joseph Conrad and the Performing Arts*, 17–18.
134. Levine, *Gender and Empire*, 7.
135. Loomba, *Colonialism/Postcolonialism*, 172.
136. Conrad, 'Because of the Dollars', 222.
137. Ibid., 223.
138. Ibid., 225.
139. Ibid., 225–6.
140. Ibid., 230.
141. Ibid.
142. Ibid., 231.
143. Ibid.
144. Ibid., 232.
145. Ibid., 234–5.
146. Ibid., 244.
147. Ibid., 245.
148. Ibid., 246.
149. Ibid., 247.
150. Ibid., 248.
151. I discuss in detail the role of British missionaries in the Pacific in my first chapter.
152. Conrad, 'Because of the Dollars', 248.

Chapter 5

The Islanders Speak: Pacific Reflections in the British Press

On 20 December 1785 the audience of the Covent Garden theatre was treated to a theatrical performance unlike any they had seen before. A Christmas pantomime, *Omai, or a Trip Round the World* drew its inspiration from the real life Tahitian visitor to England. Only the second Polynesian to visit Europe, Omai was popular with the English social elite and was acquainted with King George III. Presented as an amusing and fantastic story, the story of Omai's life was exceedingly popular with the public, and Omai became the first in a line of Pacific islanders to journey willingly with British explorers and missionaries and one whose remarkable stories would be published and circulated amongst a British audience. While these islanders' stories were filtered through the often unreliable British press, they provide a fascinating glimpse into the Pacific perspective on these visitors to their islands. While multiple book length studies have ignited an interest in Omai, very few Pacific writers have received such treatment.[1] Casting light on largely undiscovered Pacific authors, this chapter seeks to illuminate the British narrative of the Pacific islands by looking at stories circulated by the British press that focus on native islanders. In previous chapters, I have largely provided narratives which focus on how the British interacted with islanders, but in this chapter I show how accounts that focused on the real-life experiences of Pacific natives often challenged these more dominant records. While first-hand accounts from islanders are scarce, the reinterpreted stories and legends of real islanders that filtered into the British consciousness often subvert the prevailing images of Pacific 'savages' living in paradise yet in need of salvation.

Europeans first began recording the impressions of Pacific peoples when they began bringing islanders back on their voyages. Explorer Louis-Antoine de Bougainville brought the first Pacific islander Ahu-toru to Paris in 1768 followed closely by Tobias Furneaux, sailing a companion ship on Captain Cook's second voyage, bringing Omai to England in 1774. These early voyages would not mark the end of Pacific visitors nor would the reading public tire of their stories which continued to be published alongside the narratives of missionaries, traders, scientists and settlers throughout the nineteenth century. This chapter argues that the stories of three Pacific islanders, Lee Boo of Belau, Ta'unga of Rarotonga and Queen Emma of Samoa provide a fresh perspective on the British interactions with Pacific islanders, reinterpreting the viewpoint provided so far only by white authors. The legend of each islander both affirms and subverts the stated mission of the British visitors in the Pacific; while islanders often embraced the customs of the British, they never forgot their heritage, and occasionally used British naiveté to their advantage.

Born in Pelau,[2] Lee Boo travelled to London in 1784 with Captain Wilson of the *Antelope*. On both a mission of trade and exploration, Captain Wilson found himself shipwrecked in Pelau and rescued by the native islanders. His story was popularised after his death from smallpox in 1784 in a children's book called *The History of Prince Lee Boo* and at least twenty editions of the story were published from the 1780s through the 1830s. While the British largely ignored the islanders of Micronesia, preferring the 'milder' and paler-skinned natives of Polynesia, Lee Boo showed the British that islanders could not be categorised by their race or island of origin alone and challenged the British assumption that Pacific islanders must either be 'noble savages' or in need of a 'civilising' force.

While Lee Boo interacted with explorers and traders, Tongan islander Ta'unga befriended the Christian missionaries of the LMS. A convert to Christianity, Ta'unga himself became a missionary to the islands of New Caledonia and published his experiences between 1833 and 1896. His writings provide a glimpse into the ways in which Pacific islanders interpreted British missionary rhetoric as well as the ways that various islanders viewed both the missionaries and each other. While a devout believer in missions, Ta'unga also displays a sense of cultural superiority towards the islands he visits and occupies an intriguing place between influencer and influenced.

Defying boundaries of race, gender and nationality, Emma Forsayth, a Samoan-American woman, in the late nineteenth-century established one of the most powerful trading empires in the Pacific. While 'Queen Emma', as she was nicknamed, had a variety of adventures in the islands, I will be focusing on her life after 1881 when she moved to British New Guinea to establish a trading post with her brother-in-law Richard Parkinson. Her plantations in Kokopo[3] became some of the most successful in New Guinea and she used her vast commercial power to influence both British and German traders and settlers in the area. Queen

Emma's story is unique as she is one of the only Polynesian women to achieve both great financial successes and personal independence. Her story, told and re-told in sensationalised newspaper accounts, provides a counterpoint to the largely male European narratives of the Pacific and shows how the almost invisible group of Polynesian women influenced the Pacific region. Her writings, along with those of her fellow islanders Lee Boo and Ta'unga, presented the British with a Pacific that is was both familiar and new and challenged traditional views presented in the narratives of foreign visitors to the islands.

Onward to England: The Story of Lee Boo

In August of 1783, Captain Wilson of the *Antelope* wrecked his ship on a little-known Pacific island. He had no idea that this misadventure would prove the catalyst for a children's book that would remain popular until the mid-nineteenth century. The book drew its title not from the captain or his ship, but from the brave islander who volunteered to return with them to England. *The History of Prince Lee Boo* provides a fascinating look at British constructions of Pacific islanders during the mid-century.[4] While Daniel J. Peacock has pointed out in *Lee Boo of Belau* that this popular 'history' takes several liberties with the historical record, I argue that *The History of Prince Lee Boo* is still a valuable text for understanding how the British described island thought and custom.[5] The book confirms eighteenth-century ideas of the noble savage free from civilised influence but at the same time shows that Lee Boo acted in a 'civilised' manner and wished to bring the 'best' parts of English culture back to his people in the islands. As Kate Fullagar has argued,

> Lebuu's savagery, when discussed at all, served not, as once with his New World predecessors, to enable discourse about the public world of commerce and social manners but rather to realise discourse about the much more private world of the self. The quieter effect of Lebuu's presence in Britain had less to do with his embodiment of savagery than to a change in the appeal of savagery itself.[6]

While missionaries looked to help the peoples of the islands overcome their innate 'savagery', Lee Boo challenged these presumptions by displaying behaviours interpreted by British readers as both inherently 'civilised' and worthy of emulation.

The British would largely ignore the small islands of Micronesia favouring Polynesia for missionary endeavours and early trade missions.

The History of Prince Lee Boo is surprising then for its continual portrayal of the peoples of Palau as friendly, generous, gracious and equally worthy of British interest. While Captain Wilson and his crew fear abuse at the hands of wild savages, instead 'They found [the islanders] to be a people simple in their manners, delicate in their sentiments, and friendly in their dispositions — a people, in short, who do honour to the human race.'[7] Not only do the islanders not demonstrate any violence towards the shipwrecked crew, the book records that they comport themselves as graciously as any Western people. As *The History* explains, 'The conduct of these people towards the English was, from first to last, uniformly courteous and attentive, accompanied with a politeness which surprised those who were the objects of it.'[8] The islanders are not only kind, they are also polite, indicating a level of civility surprising in people assumed to be savages.

The History, like many early explorer accounts of 'savage' peoples, is quick to explain that while the islanders have a level of civility, they are consistently awed by the British invaders. As the author relates,

> There is every reason to suppose that no European had ever been upon them, before the Antelope, a packet belonging to the East India Company, and commanded by Captain Henry Wilson, was wrecked there in the night between the 9th and 10th of August, 1783.[9]

The British sailors first react to these new peoples by comparing physical characteristics, echoing missionary and trader accounts from the turn of the century, and the text explains 'The natives themselves were of a deep copper-colour, and naked; and the astonishment of those, who first discovered the English, on seeing their colour, plainly shewed that they had never before beheld a white man.'[10] This astonishment at white visitors played directly into British stereotypes of the noble conqueror and appears throughout depictions of exploration. It is the superior technology exhibited by their visitors, however, that truly excites the islanders. As the author remarks, 'Even the grindstone struck them with wonder; and they could not look upon the English but as a superior as well as an uncommon kind of human beings.'[11] British accounts commonly depicted the deification of white visitors and their goods, especially famous explorers such as Captain Cook.[12] So impressed are the islanders by the English, their technology, and their military prowess that the 'the whole country resounded with their praises' and the chief of the island, Abba Thulle, 'within a few days . . . actually gave Captain Wilson the island of Oroolong for the English'.[13] The book continually supports the image of the English as superior islanders helping the natives to victory through military might.

While unabashedly presenting the English as 'superior' to the natives, *The History* still sees echoes of English civilisation in the untutored peoples of the Pacific. As with many accounts of 'noble savages', the book argues that their connection to 'civilisation' is their greatest weakness, explaining,

> All the islands lying in this spot of the globe, and now known to us by the name of the Pelew islands, do not belong to one sovereign; there are several governments or kingdoms, and one of the greatest failings in the characters of the different nations consists in that wherein they are like Europeans — they have wars one with another.[14]

While the text largely connects British superiority with guns and military might, it simultaneously presents the necessity for such actions as a failing of character. While the violent actions of the islanders are seen as a downfall, the cause of the war that Captain Wilson engages in on behalf of Abba Thulle is presented as noble and just. The author notes,

> What was the greatest matter of triumph to the people of Pelew was, their carrying away the stone whereon the king of Artingal used to sit in council; which probably, was with them reckoned as glorious an exploit, as that of Edward the First's bringing to England the stone on which the kings of Scotland used to be crowned, which is now in Westminster Abbey in London.[15]

While on the one hand the book chastises the people for acting like violent Europeans, on the other hand it presents their exploits in battle using traditional stories of British victories. The islanders are presented as noble savages corrupted by European civilisation and yet it is that very corruption that makes them admirable in the European tradition.

Having set up the curious dichotomy of savage/civilised islanders, *The History* introduces its title character, Lee Boo himself, who also exhibits this curious mixture of ideals. As the book relates,

> After due consideration, [Abba Thulle] had come to the resolution of committing his second son, whose name was LEE BOO, to the captain's care, in order that he might enjoy the advantage of improving himself by accompanying the English, and also of learning many things, which, on his return, might prove of essential benefit to his country. He then spoke of his son as a youth of gentle and amiable disposition, sensible, and possessing many good qualities.[16]

The account shows again that the British have awed the islanders to the point that they want to learn even more about these strange visitors to improve their lives. Yet on the other hand, this awe does not overwhelm all common sense about island life. The chief sends his second son, unwilling to part with his eldest who is too important as the heir to the chiefdom. Abba Thulle wishes to take the best parts of European civilisation, but is not willing to sacrifice the daily lives of his people to do so. Thulle also worries that Britain may have a detrimental impact on his son, telling the Captain,

> When Lee Boo got to England, he would have such fine things to see, that he might chance to slip away from him to run after novelty; but that he hoped the captain would keep him as much as he could under his eye, and endeavour to moderate the eagerness of his youth.[17]

Thulle is excited for the chance to send his son to London to learn more of these talented invaders, but he also worries that this land may be full of distractions as well as important discoveries. While the novel presents the islanders as in awe of the British, it also presents Abba Thulle as a wise men who recognises both the promise and potential pitfalls of these visitors.

Although Abba Thulle worries for the steadiness of his son's character, the author of *The History* never seems to be in doubt. Immediately, Lee Boo begins copying 'civilised' behaviours. Despite being bare-chested in his home, the author records that,

> [Lee Boo] felt less and less inconvenience in resuming the use of his jacket and shirt, and the dislike he had to them lost itself in his new taught sense of propriety, which daily increasing, soon became too powerful to suffer him to change his dress in the presence of another person.[18]

As with missionary accounts, Lee Boo proves he is learning standards of propriety by copying English forms of dress. While Lee Boo learns some standards of decorum, others he inherently possesses. *The History* explains, for example:

> Lee Boo was remarkably clean in his person, washing himself several times every day. — There is a saying of great importance and well worthy of attention, that 'cleanliness is next to godliness.' It may not be estimating cleanliness too highly to regard it, as being no less essential to the health of the body, than godliness is to that of the soul. However, no one can pretend not to admire and prefer it to filthiness, which yet so much more prevails, especially amongst the poorer class of people; but, surely, this is the result of a sluggish indolent habit, rather than of necessity, as, though clothed in rags, they may be clean.[19]

These two accounts show Lee Boo occupying a dual role in the narrative as both a noble savage and in need of a civilising influence. Lee Boo inherently understands the need for cleanliness, unlike the 'poorer class of people'. Other lessons, however, such as the need for proper attire he learns through appropriate example.

While *The History* fluctuates between presenting Lee Boo's nobility and civility, it unquestionable asserts Lee Boo's status as an islander by describing a number of his traditional habits. Instead of a pen and ink journal, the text notes that 'It is the custom of the people in the Pelew Islands to make remarks by tying knots in a line, and Lee Boo had brought with him the one he now used for that purpose.'[20] Lee Boo's actions connect to the value of memory and oral tradition in Pacific culture. While he imitated the English style of dress and comportment,

> He wore his hair in the fashion of his own country, was of a middling stature, and had a countenance so strongly marked with sense and good humour, as instantly to prepossess every one in his favour, and moreover enlivened by eyes so quick and intelligent, that they might truly be said to tell his thoughts without the aid of language.[21]

As with depictions of Omai, descriptions of Lee Boo present him as distinctly native but with good taste and cultural acumen.

Lee Boo's status as 'islander' is also confirmed by his continual wonder and amazement at Europeans. These descriptions often present Lee Boo possessing a childish enthusiasm, as when the text records,

> Lee Boo was astonished on seeing the Portuguese ships at Macao: he cried out as he looked at them, *Clow, clow, muc, clow!* that is, *Large, large, very large!* The English had here an opportunity of observing the natural benevolence of his mind.[22]

Other descriptions, however, connect this enthusiasm with a desperate need to understand the workings of new technologies in order to benefit his people on the islands. Given the leisure to explore the construction of a European house, the text notes,

> The upright walls and flat ceilings were still objects of surprise to him: the walls he was continually feeling, as if by that means to acquire some idea of their construction; but the ceilings, self-supported as he imagined, seemed, at that time, quite beyond the reach of his comprehension.[23]

While presenting him as still largely in awe of the forces that operate in European construction, the text emphasises Lee Boo's intelligence in his need to understand them. Early texts by missionaries and traders often described islanders as gawking fools in awe of superior European technology; however, Lee Boo offers an almost scientific inquiry about new experiences. Upon reaching his bedroom in England, for example, the text relates,

> He saw, for the first time, a four-post bed. Scarcely could he conceive what it meant — he jumped in and jumped out again — felt and pulled aside

the curtains — got into bed, and then got out a second time, to admire its outward form. At length, when he was fully acquainted with its use and convenience, he laid himself down to sleep, saying, that *in England there was a house for every thing.*[24]

While displaying his awe and enthusiasm for the new discovery, Lee Boo is also puzzling out the usage of the new object through experimentation. *The History* continually describes Lee Boo as both an ignorant savage but also a clever, rational explorer.

Lee Boo's need to understand the new world of England leads him to request further formal education. This need begins early, as the history records,

> Lee Boo had been but a short time on the voyage, when he requested Captain Wilson to get him a book, and point out to him the letters, that he might learn to read: the Captain kindly embraced every convenient opportunity of gratifying this wish, and had the satisfaction of discovering great readiness of apprehension in his young pupil.[25]

As most island cultures were oral cultures, Europeans, especially missionaries, would largely contribute to the growth of written material on the islands and, in Lee Boo's case, the ability to understand more fully his new circumstances. *The History* uses this curiosity of Lee Boo's as a teachable moment, relating:

> The truant would do well to compare his own opinion of schools with those of Lee Boo, who, regarding them as affording the means of instruetion [sic] and improvement, considered them as highly beneficial, and felt the strongest desire to attend them: whereas, the idler, thinking only of the tasks which he has to learn, sees not the advantages to be reaped there, but looks upon them with disgust, as places of drudgery and punishment, and consequently seeks to avoid them. Let him blush and learn better notions from an untutored native of Pelew.[26]

The savage offers a lesson to the 'civilised' child – the need for an increased education, especially in Western schools. This passage then resonated less with the eighteenth-century idea of the 'noble savage' and more with the mission rhetoric presenting England as a civilising force. Lee Boo would get his wish after landing in England and as the text records, 'After being somewhat habituated to the manners of this country, he went every day to an academy at Rotherhithe, for the purpose of being instructed in reading and writing.'[27] While Lee Boo possesses a natural intelligence and curiosity, the text is clear that a formal education is invaluable to the young islander.

The History is equally clear that Lee Boo's questions and requests are always tied not only to personal interest but also to the goal of improving Pelau. While his remarks are related as charming and naive, the author also notes, 'In all his observations, the grand consideration he seemed to have at heart was, the advantage and improvement of his country.'[28] When Captain Wilson and the crew visit St. Helena, for example, Lee Boo observed,

> that the people . . . had but little wood, yet applied it to a good purpose; whereas his own countrymen were ignorant of the advantages they might enjoy, having a great abundance, but not knowing in what manner to use it. When he went back, he said, he would speak to the king tell him how defective they were, and have men set to work on such bowers as he had seen.[29]

Again, the text asserts Lee Boo's practicality as he uses his new knowledge of the uses of lumber to apply to Pelau's need for an increased military presence. Lee Boo's suggestions often mirror those of early missionaries, for example the text notes,

> Whenever he had an opportunity of viewing gardens, the plants and fruit-trees excited his particular attention: he would make many inquiries concerning them, saying, when he should return home, he would carry with him seeds of such as would grow in Pelew.[30]

Famous missionaries such as William Ellis and John Williams would also comment on the need to improve the variety of crops on Pacific islands by bringing in new seeds.[31] *The History of Prince Lee Boo* encourages the rhetoric developing in the early nineteenth century that the islands needed improvements that only Western civilisation could provide.

Yet while the journey seems to be in the best interests of Lee Boo and the people of Pelau, there are still dangers in an overseas voyage. While Omai travelled extensively, Lee Boo was more sheltered as

> Captain Wilson very prudently avoided taking him to any of the places of public entertainment, for fear of his catching the small-pox, a distemper, for which it was proposed to inoculate him, as soon as he should become sufficiently acquainted with the English language, to be made fully sensible of the necessity of the measure.[32]

Despite the Captain's precautions, Lee Boo did tragically catch small-pox. *The History* records that Lee Boo stated,

> *Good friend, when you go to Pelew, tell Abba Thulle, that* Lee Boo *take much drink to make small-pox go away, but he die — that the Captain and Mother (Mrs. Wilson) very kind — all English very good men — was much sorry he could not speak to the king, the number of fine things the English had got.*[33]

The final words emphasise both Lee Boo's appreciation for England and his regret that he would not be able to bring his discoveries home.

Lee Boo's story due both to its intriguing main character and his tragic ending remained popular with the English readership into the mid-century. While history has largely forgotten Lee Boo, the narrative of his life presents an intriguing look into how British texts represented Pacific islanders in 'non-fiction'. While *The History of Prince Lee Boo* takes a number of liberties and is often less than precise with its record of Lee Boo's statements, it still reveals how the British were interpreting the actions of islanders and navigating the old ideas of the 'noble savage' with the rising emphasis on the need for 'civilising missions'. While scholars and historians may never puzzle out the 'real' Lee Boo, his narrative still deserves consideration as a text which influenced early British thought on the small islands of the Pacific.

The Native Missionary: The Works of Ta'unga

While the real Lee Boo did bravely board a ship and sail far from his home to England, the account of his visit comes largely from British interpretations of his thoughts and feelings. As the century progressed, however, and British missionaries succeeded in their goals of teaching native peoples Western traditions of reading and writing, natives became increasingly able to record in more detail their own experiences. For Tongan missionary Ta'unga, the ability to write allowed him to record his impressions of his missions to other islands. While most accounts of mission efforts in the Pacific come from white missionaries, Ta'unga's letters and reports provide a glimpse into the Polynesian perspective both on the mission projects as well as more generally on Europeans and other islanders.[34] Ta'unga's works have sometimes been dismissed by the scholarly community as simply parroting British missionary rhetoric, but I agree with David Hanlon that there are

> ambiguities and contradictions in Ta'unga's text that reflect a more personal and complicated relationship with the various peoples among whom he worked over the course of his 63-year missionary career. Ta'unga's struggles to incorporate his Rarotongan background, his missionary training, and his experiences in Melanesia and Samoa into an encompassing world view indicate something of the negotiations, tensions and discontinuities involved in local and personal engagements with Christianity.[35]

Ta'unga writes persuasively about his mission to bring the gospel to the other islands of the Pacific. He explains,

> It is my desire that every man should respect [Christ's] blood, that it may become remembered throughout the world. In order for this remembrance to

come about, the word of God must be spread throughout every single island so that every person may reach heaven and sit at the side of Jesus so that there might be boundless joy.[36]

While his mission closely echoes that of his white teachers, Ta'unga focuses on respecting and remembering Christ, two principles which had a particular resonance in Polynesian cultures. Ta'unga argues that it is only when the peoples of the Pacific change their current behaviours that they will be able to please God. As he writes,

> As the number of people who yearn to sanctify his blood increases so God's happiness with those people will increase, and eventually perhaps all men will arrive above in heaven. It is my great wish that all men should do so, that they should be ashamed of their evil ways and return to the good, to abandon wrong and to follow the way of the children of the light so that God might be overjoyed, and all the angels too.[37]

Ta'unga links good behaviour with eternal reward but also with joy. Rather than argue that islanders have a moral duty to follow Christian precepts, Ta'unga argues they should do so because it pleases God.

While Ta'unga is clearly dedicated to his project to bring the gospel to the islands, he relates many of the same fears of visiting foreign islands as white missionaries. Many Pacific cultures viewed outsiders, whether European or islander, as a potential threat and wars between tribal factions were common. Thus when Ta'unga, Aaron Buzzacott of the LMS, and their fellow missionaries attempt to land at Niue they are informed that the local islanders intended to stop them. As Ta'unga records,

> When the boat arrived ashore all the people in it would be killed. They had held a meeting ashore the previous night and had decided they would go aboard the ship and try to persuade them to send a boat ashore. They were going to show false affection in order to deceive us. Then they were going to grab all our belongings.[38]

Ta'unga is concerned for more than just the loss of the missionary's possessions. He continues,

> When we heard the news we departed from that savage land and sailed on, praising God for it was He who forewarned us of the intentions of those wicked people so that we should not be dealt with as John Williams [Wiliamu] had been.[39]

Ta'unga clearly fears for his life, as well as the lives of his companions. His fears are well founded, as historians R. G. and Marjorie Crocombe explain, 'With the exception of Ta'unga, almost all the Polynesian teachers who had ventured into the New Caledonia area had either been eaten by cannibals or died of disease.'[40] While Ta'unga is committed to his mission he is not unaware of the dangers he and his fellow missionaries face.

While early missionaries often blamed the natives' fearful and violent reactions on foolish superstitions or 'uncivilised' savagery, Ta'unga points to very real causes for their dislike of visitors. Overwhelmingly, the islands Ta'unga visits have been stricken with illness and both the chiefs and the people are looking for answers for their distress. He records, for example,

> On 24 August a canoe arrived from the Isle of Pines and informed us that the chief of that island had driven the teachers away. When we asked why, they said it was because the people were all dying and the chief had been asking why they died. We said, 'It is because you have not received the Word of God.'[41]

Despite Ta'unga's attempts to connect salvation with healing, the islanders continue to ban or kill missionaries believing them to be the cause of their suffering. He understands, however, that this violent retribution was largely a part of Polynesian tradition. As he explains,

> That was why wars were so frequent, because of disease. If all the priests said that a particular priest had caused the disease, the people would kill him. When they said it was caused by a particular household, all members of that household would be killed . . . That was how many of our mission teachers died and that means were sought to us. Great was our affliction from this very cause, for many epidemics occurred while we were there and we were blamed for them.[42]

Pacific disease theory often connected illness with behaviour, especially spiritual deviance. As Raeburn Lange explains,

> Illness was regarded to some extent as punishment for behaviour that threatened social harmony, and fear of illness acted as a means of maintaining social control. Sickness indicated, then, not merely a disordered physiological system but also a spiritual derangement and a disruption of social relationships.[43]

While not understating the principles of infectious disease, the islanders recognised that killing the suspected source of the disease could eliminate illness and thus death and epidemic quickly became linked – much to the detriment of the mission efforts.

Ta'unga quickly learns that along with cultural tradition which placed the blame for disease on specific groups or individuals, other Europeans were perpetuating the idea that missionaries were responsible for the spread of illness. At the Isle of Pines, Ta'unga learns that a European ship had arrived before them and

> The crew had asked, 'Why do you suffer those fellows from Samoa and Rarotonga to remain among you? The God of Samoa and Rarotonga is killing you and you will be consumed.' Then we said, 'These people from the ships are deceivers, why did you listen to them?' They answered that as soon as the chief heard what had been said he was very angry with the teachers and drove them away on board one of the ships.[44]

Ta'unga asks the chief for clarification as to why they believe the Europeans and is told,

> the chief was angry because the teachers had declared that there was but one God, Jehovah, who was the God of all the earth, but when those ships arrived, the foreigners told them, 'Jehovah is not our God but only the God of Samoa and Rarotonga and this God is angry with you. That is why you die in such numbers.'[45]

Traders and whalers quickly figured out that by blaming disease on missionaries, who visited the Pacific in smaller numbers, they could trade with the people without interference. Ta'unga explains that the people of the Isle of Pines

> came to us saying, 'The people of the Isle of Pines have died through you, for you prayed to your God to kill every one of us.' Twenty-one ships have visited us and they have asked us, 'Why do you treat those Samoans and Rarotongans so well? Why don't you chase them away? They are the cause of your death. As for us Europeans, we do not die because we do not have Jehovah.'[46]

Not only do other Europeans blame disease on the interference of missionaries and their God, but they also target the native missionaries specifically. At Lifu, Ta'unga learns,

> that a ship's captain had told the high chief . . . 'It is Jehovah who has killed you. All the islands are consumed by deaths wrought by Jehovah. But in Samoa, and it is really from there that this illness comes, the white men are consumed by death! Likewise when the ships which travel about reach Samoa, the crews dare not go inland for fear of that sickness. Jehovah is a man-eating god. It is only in the white men's land that nobody dies. That is because the white men have no god. If only you people would live without gods like the Europeans do, you would not die.'[47]

The islanders are faced with two opposing viewpoints: that not believing in Jehovah causes disease and that Jehovah is the god of rival islanders not of the successful Europeans. With so many more of the latter accounts provided by traders and other sailors, native missionaries had an especially difficult challenge in converting other islanders.

While Ta'unga's accounts continually relay the difficulty in converting the islanders of New Caledonia to Christianity, he continues in his larger mission which is to understand these often isolated people groups. R. G. and Marjorie Crocombe explain,

> It was generally accepted by the missionaries at that time that the role of 'native brethren' was to make initial contacts, establish peace, learn the language and obtain at least nominal acceptance of Christianity and thus to venture their lives in order to, as Pitman phrased it, 'prepare the way for more efficient labourers from privileged Britain.'[48]

To this end, Ta'unga's accounts, like William Ellis's, also supplement his experiences with local culture and custom, providing an islander's perspective on Pacific traditions usually only recorded from the European viewpoint.

As with many other observers of Pacific life, Ta'unga's spends several lengthy passages discussing the practice of cannibalism. Many exist to clarify the practice and methodology of cannibalism. He explains:

> When an enemy is taken, they grab him and chop him up in pieces and give him to the womenfolk who carry him back to their houses. The thighs particularly are cut up small. Then they light their earth ovens and cover them up, and when the bodies are cooked they meet together to eat. The men each take an arm and consecrate it before placing it on the grave of their dead parents. These are then eaten by the priests. If it is a chief who has been killed they divide his body out to each and every man, woman, and child, so that all may partake of it.[49]

Along with these clinical descriptions, which portray cannibalism almost as impartially as any other cultural practice, Ta'unga gives far more detailed and personal recollections. Unlike most missionaries who only record second-hand evidence, Ta'unga witnesses cannibalism at Mare. He relates that humans

> are like fish to them . . . the flesh of man is really dark when it is cooked. You have probably seen the sea-cucumbers on the reef, well, it is just like that. The aroma it gives forth is exactly like that of goat's meat. It does not smell like pork. They despise pork and chicken, but they will not leave off human flesh.[50]

He also warns that the practice is widespread in the islands, noting, 'Perhaps you will want to ask, "Is there only one island where they do these things?" I am telling you that it is done in all these islands, not one is different.'[51] According to Ta'unga, cannibalism was an important practice for the islanders of New Caledonia and one he witnessed first-hand.

Ta'unga attempts only to record cannibalism to educate fellow missionaries, yet he also finds himself involved in the practice during his work in the islands. At Mare, his Samoan hosts inform him that they have recently murdered some Europeans who visited the islands. He asks,

> 'What did you do with the Europeans who were killed? Did you eat them?' [The Samoan] replied that they were eaten and that shares were sent to all the clans. One chief caught a European and took him home alive. He did not kill him straight way. He lit the oven first, and then placed a covering on the ground. Next he led the European to the oven so he could see it. Then he was killed, cooked, and eaten.[52]

Ta'unga is unhappy, though seemingly unsurprised, to learn that these islanders have cooked and eaten Europeans. As an islander, he makes sure to distance himself as a Tongan and a Christian from the practice so often associated with all Pacific islanders. At Yate or Adi, Ta'unga is attacked by two islanders who are then caught by the local villagers and prepared as a feast. Ta'unga records,

> They were very happy and the ovens were burning and it was nearly time to kill the second man. Then I called out saying, 'Share out our man. Give me my share for I must go . . . Divide them. Give me my share.' So they brought me one of the arms and I called out, 'I won't accept that. Give me the live man. That is my share—let that be your gift to me.'[53]

Ta'unga makes it clear that he does not support the practice of cannibalism by saving his enemy's life. Later, in New Caledonia, Ta'unga is treated to a sacrificed man and records,

> The flesh was dark like sea-cucumber, the fat was yellow like beef fat, and it smelled like cooked birds, like pigeon or chicken. The share of the chief was the right hand and the right foot. Part of the chief's portion was brought for me, as for the priest, but I returned it.[54]

Again, Ta'unga distances himself from the actual practice of cannibalism but continues to describe it in familiar terms, drawing on images of foods acceptable to Europeans. As William Arens notes, 'Rather than a special ritual event . . . the consumption of human flesh was a matter of course as a result of the desire for meat.'[55] Ta'unga's description of cannibalism expresses a delicate balance between showing an understanding of the importance of cannibalism to Pacific culture and denouncing the practice as barbaric and against Christian teachings.

Ta'unga's works never achieved that status and popularity in England as stories about earlier islanders like Lee Boo and Omai. They were, however, highly influential in providing information to missionaries like

William Wyatt Gill, who often published books and articles about the Pacific that were circulated in England and added to the general knowledge about Pacific peoples. Ta'unga also left quite a legacy in the Pacific, helping complete a Rarotongan translation of the bible and becoming a figure of legend in the islands. His letters and journals are some of the few works written by a Polynesian islander that reflect a new and original perspective both on mission efforts in the islands but also on how islanders viewed each other and their various customs.

A Queen of New Guinea:
Emma Forsayth as a New Breed of Islander

While texts written by Pacific islanders are difficult to find, texts by Polynesian women are all but non-existent. Yet women seem ubiquitous to the British South Seas narrative: from their early descriptions as dutiful mothers and daughters to their roles as mistresses or temptresses, women often appear as secondary characters in fictional and non-fictional accounts of the islands. To presume that the British only saw women in these subservient positions does a disservice both to the historical record and to the nineteenth-century men and women of the Pacific. The story of 'Queen Emma' of New Guinea, for example, describes a half-Samoan, half-American woman not as plaything for traders or a convert for missionaries, but as a fiercely clever and independent businesswoman. Records of Queen Emma are spotty and often contradictory but all confirm the impression that she was a powerful woman and a popular figure in the late nineteenth century, especially in the Australian press. By exploring the legends that sprung up around this real-life Polynesian/American, I argue that we can gain a more accurate picture of the power island women wielded in the nineteenth-century Pacific.

In her 1913 obituary, the *Sydney Morning Herald* claimed '"Queen Emma," as she was affectionately called throughout the Western Pacific, was one of the most notable figures in South Sea circles.'[56] Legends of her vast trade empire, her lavish parties, her disregard for social niceties and her variety of relationships rippled through Pacific society and Australian newspapers published stories of her life and legacy through the 1950s. By the 1970s her life had provided inspiration for a novel and a biography and in 1988 a television miniseries.[57] While Emma[58] was a veritable Pacific celebrity and a powerful figure in German and Australian politics in the late nineteenth and early twentieth centuries, she is all but invisible in historical and literary criticism.

Stories of Emma's early years highlight both her beauty and her education. Sidney Baker argues that despite having six sisters, 'The pick of the bunch was Emma. Even when she was very small the oldest inhabitants agreed that she was the prettiest creature who ever lived in Samoa.'[59] She received her education in America before returning to Samoa 'aged 15, a most sophisticated young creature'.[60] Her beauty and education made her popular with the men of Samoa and George Blakie's account remarks,

> Mr. Coe [her father] was forced to sit up at nights armed with a large waddy to whack at over-ardent swains. Every male from 15 to 80 wanted to marry Emma. Wealthier individuals were prepared to give Mr Coe as many as a dozen cows and a couple of hundred coconuts in return for his fair daughter. Penniless citizens were eager to kidnap her.[61]

Later reporters of Emma's story, like Baker, emphasise her role as a femme fatale even from a young age.

Emma's first marriage was to a British trader/adventurer named William Forsayth but was reportedly unhappy, though stories differ as to the cause of the disharmony. Baker blames the failure of the marriage on Emma's selfish nature, arguing

> [Emma] sought little more than gratification of her personal whims and pleas-ures. Which probably explains why Emma Forsayth tired of her husband after a year or two of marriage and ran away with an ex-New Zealand miner named Thomas Farrell, who owned an Apia hotel.[62]

Blakie's account, in contrast, highlights Emma's desire for excitement and writes,

> [The marriage] was a very satisfactory arrangement for Mr. Forsayth, but as far as Emma was concerned, it was a poor show. Mr. Forsayth was horribly respectable, and dull. Worse, he was very jealous, and Emma was the type of lass to keep such a gentleman on his toes. The marriage quickly became wobbly. You can gauge something of the situation, perhaps by the fact that Mr. Forsayth took to fishing as a hobby.[63]

While more traditional colonial attitudes interpreted Emma's actions as selfish, flaky and indicative of poor character, those who embrace the 'free spirit' often championed in Pacific adventure fiction saw Emma's actions as playful, daring and exciting.

Emma and her new lover Farrell left Samoa for the Duke of York islands, part of the Bismarck Archipelago between New Britain and New Ireland in Eastern Papua New Guinea. Emma wasted no time in purchasing a steamer and setting up a trading post 'long before the establishment of any settled Government, being, in fact, the pioneer of planting in the Western Pacific'.[64] Papers record her rise to power with an almost reverent awe. Blakie writes that 'the natives bowed before her and Mr. Farrell wasn't far behind' and a letter to the editor of *The Brisbane Courier* in 1911 explained

> She came to one of the islands . . . with a few followers and a revolver in her belt, where she began operations by trading with the natives in European goods, such as Manchester prints and Sheffield knives. With tact, bravery, and conspicuous business talent, inherited probably from her American father, she gradually, though not without dangerous experiences, won the confidence of the savages.[65]

While newspaper accounts read like nineteenth-century adventure fiction, the dangers to Emma were undeniable. In his biography of Emma, R. W. Robson notes,

> The jungles of the New Britain mainland swarmed with a Melanesian people rated then among the most ferocious and treacherous cannibals known. If the stranger escaped the axes, spears, clubs, and cooking-fires of the prowling natives, he inevitably collected one or the other of the virulent local diseases—malaria, or the dysentery, or well-nigh incurable tropical ulcers.[66]

While dramatised for effect, nineteenth-century explorers as early as Cook documented the fierceness of the Melanesians and, as noted in Ta'unga's narrative, disease was an ever present fear. Of course, a great deal of the islanders' anger towards Europeans developed out of poor trade relations. As anthropologist Peter Lomas notes, the hostility often exhibited by the peoples of New Guinea stemmed from

> the bad relations between islanders and Europeans generated by early contacts in connection with the labor trade . . . Even before vessels seeking workers for plantations in other parts of the South Pacific arrived, there was general dislike and suspicion of Whites as a result of contacts with whalers to South America, and possibly sandalwood traders, often rough and violent towards the local population, who had also put ashore on occasion from the 1850s on for food and water.[67]

While Emma feared the 'savagery' of the local population it was trading posts like hers that inspired such distrust to begin with.

While Farrell assisted Emma in her earliest endeavours, all the accounts remark on Emma's independence and foresight in developing her fledgling empire. Robson explains,

> [Emma] attacked the problems of organizing a household, a trading station, a supply of fresh food, and security. Emma found no difficulty in directing trading operations; but her Coe vision reached far beyond the raw little trading-station, to the exciting possibilities in those wide fertile plains around

Blanche Bay, over there on the Gazelle Peninsula. She knew why the Germans had planted coconuts in Samoa.[68]

Emma employed the Danish scientist and early anthropologist Richard Parkinson to help develop her dreams of a vast plantation. As the introduction to his memoir *Thirty Years in the South Seas* explains:

> The main items sought by trade with the islanders were coconuts for processing into copra. At that time the trade depended heavily on village people being willing to collect and process the coconuts. This did not provide as regular or reliable a supply as the traders needed, and it became obvious to Emma and Farrell that the best way to develop the business was to establish their own coconut plantations, along the lines of those in Samoa. Accordingly, they set up the Western Pacific Plantation and Trading Company, which was registered in Sydney.[69]

Emma consolidated her power over the islands by buying islands from local chiefs for nominal sums and meticulously recording these transactions through contractual agreements. The actual sum differs by report with the *The Farmer and the Settler* recording,

> Land in those days was exceedingly cheap, and was sold by the acre for pipes of tobacco. Queen Emma bought a big stretch of country not far from where Rabaul now is situated for a box of trade goods, probably not larger than she could carry under an arm. The Mortlock Islands, she bought, it is said, for five pounds of trade tobacco, representing a cash value of half a sovereign.[70]

The Argus in Melbourne adds that 'Soon afterwards the native chiefs of the French Islands sold the group to "Queen" Emma for £50.'[71] These transactions cemented Emma's power in the islands of Western New Guinea and her reputation as a savvy businesswoman.

Descriptions of Emma's plantations usually portray her as benevolent, if temperamental, which is unusual considering Emma's connections with the unscrupulous Melanesian labour trade. Baker notes that

> Emma was something of a colonial pioneer in another way. She opposed German tactics of ill-treating the natives. She became their protector, an arrogant, tempestuous protector at times, but opposed to physical cruelty. It was the first big step on the way to her apotheosis as a queen.[72]

In a letter to an editor, another author writes

> A power to be reckoned with by the Administration, a kindly mistress to her many European employees, a protective deity to the ignorant nation, this lady . . . was kindness and hospitality itself . . . No one could fail to admire the wisdom and philanthropy of her conduct towards those upon whose labour the success of her enterprise depended. Queen Emma employs 1200 Kanakas on her estates, who never go on strike.[73]

Yet for all her recorded benevolence, Emma's plantations did employ the labour trade which notoriously indentured islanders into service without consent.[74] As Robson records,

> Farrell was deep in this 'labour recruiting trade', and Emma shared in its profits, but she always insisted that Farrell and Company's' 'recruiting' was orderly, and that the 'repatriation' clauses of the 'contracts' were scrupulously observed. Nonetheless, the overseas labour trade traffic stank; and the records indicate that Emma hated her association with it.[75]

Thirty Years in the South Seas offers a slightly different picture noting 'Farrell could not get a recruiting licence in Sydney, and so Emma wanted to transfer the registration of her ship *Bella Brandon* to Parkinson, under the German flag.'[76] While Emma may not have liked the trade, she was certainly willing to concede its necessity and endeavour to develop it. The labour trade became largely unpopular with the British colonies as early as mid-century. As Jane Samson notes, 'Once designated "slavery," the labor trade inherited the political importance of Britain's African antislavery campaign and its images of international moral guardianship.'[77] British authorities in Queensland passed 'An Act to Regulate and Control the Introduction and Treatment of Polynesian Labourers' in 1858 and antislavery groups in Britain lobbied for the Pacific Islanders Protection Bill which was passed in 1872. Although the early labour trade gained willing recruits among the islanders by honouring business contracts, the increasing need for workers at the end of the century meant that the German government put pressure on plantations to both get and keep Pacific labourers under contract, with or without the islanders' consent. Emma may have treated her workers well according to nineteenth-century standards, but her plantation empire capitalised on the labour of Polynesians imported from across Melanesia.

The narrative of Emma's success in New Guinea takes an interesting turn as she found her plantation at the centre of a heated debate over colonisation at the turn of the century. Germany had been slowly gaining power at the end of the nineteenth century and began exercising its colonial interests by consolidating power in the South Seas. As Robson records,

> Official Britain, similarly [to Germany], was indifferent. But not the British colonies in Australia. They were vociferously opposed to the establishment of any 'foreign' colony in the great archipelagos north and northeast of Queensland. A British Navy officer, Captain Moresby, in 1873, after discovering and naming Port Moresby, had annexed all of eastern New Guinea. But his enterprise was officially repudiated by Whitehall.[78]

With public opinion in Australia united against German annexation

> Queensland finally sent magistrate H.M. Chester across from Thursday
> Island to Port Moresby, to formally annex, on April 4, 1883, on behalf of the
> British Crown, all of New Guinea eastward of the 141 meridian, and all the
> unclaimed islands adjacent thereto. But once more the British Government,
> to the fury of the Australian colonies, would not confirm or support
> Queensland's action.[79]

Recognising the lack of support from the British mainland and eager to
gain a strategic foothold in the Eastern Pacific, Germany quickly stepped
in and 'to the consternation of Whitehall, and the near-hysterical
anger of the Australian colonies, but with no surprise in New Britain,
Germany formally annexed northeast New Guinea and the islands adja-
cent thereto, by declarations at Mioko on November 3, 1884; and at all
points in New Britain, New Ireland, and New Guinea, in the ensuing
fortnight. The British had been completely out-manoeuvred.[80] For
Emma, this change was not wholly unwelcome as she

> disliked the English, and if she had to choose between them, would have
> preferred the Germans to the English as landlords in New Guinea. 'I like the
> colonial English,' she said, 'and the Australians and New Zealanders. But the
> English, no. They think they are the elect of God, and they do not like my
> breeding or my ways.'[81]

For Emma, the British did not signify a 'civilising' force or even a potentially valuable trade ally, but instead a stuffy and restrictive social order.

The annexation of New Guinea by Germany, even if preferred by
Emma, raised serious challenges to her status as 'Queen'. The German
government was quick to challenge Emma's rights to her purchased
islands. Thanks to her forethought in gathering written contracts from
local chiefs, Emma was able to maintain her claims and keep her empire,
despite the pressures of the new government. It was not politics that
ended Emma's reign but passion. Emma fell in love with an ex-army
officer from Germany, Paul Koble, who she eventually married in
1895.[82] Either persuaded by her love for him, or fearing the escalating
tensions between Germany and the other European powers, especially
Britain, she sold her commercial enterprise to a German syndicate for a
fortune.[83]

While Emma's relationships certainly added to her legend as a notorious beauty and femme fatale, most accounts are impressed more by her
business acumen then her affairs of the heart. Robson records Australian
Senator Staniforth Smith as stating,

> Queen Emma is certainly the most remarkable business woman I have
> ever met. She has a thousand employees, a huge plantation of 3,000 acres,

a number of trading and recruiting vessels, wholesale and retail stores, etc. She arrives at the office early in a rickshaw, and ... directs the whole ramifications of this vast business with consummate skill.[84]

When her granddaughter got engaged in 1920, the announcement proclaimed,

> Miss Forsayth's grandmother was the remarkable American Samoan identity of the islands known as Queen Emma. Her business attainments in New Britain built her a fortune, and gained her the respect and admiration of all the hard-headed business firms of New Guinea.[85]

A 1916 article proclaimed,

> Amongst the most successful traders of an early period were the German South Sea skipper Hernsheim and Mrs Forsayth, commonly known as 'Queen Emma.' Starting in a small way, they gradually widened their nets of operation scattering traders over a considerable part of the Archipelago, and founding respectively the now so important trading concerns 'Hernsheim and Co.' and 'Forsayth and Co.,' both of which in a material degree have contributed to the development of German New Guinea. Hernsheim as well as Queen Emma accumulated immense wealth, while the latter, in addition, gained fame.[86]

By the end of the nineteenth century, Queen Emma's reputation as a titan of trade in New Guinea was well established and her title unchallenged.

Most British accounts of Pacific women record them as secondary characters, useful largely in their role as potential wives or, more likely, mistresses. Yet the real women of Polynesia held active roles both in tribal societies and in the developing global world of the late nineteenth century. The legend of Queen Emma challenged the presumed authority of British men, by building an alternate empire largely without the need for white colonial men. The vast popularity of her story shows that Britain had lost confidence in the perfect domination of a masculine empire and that the islanders had ideas of their own.

By looking at accounts of Pacific islanders like Lee Boo, Ta'unga and Queen Emma, we can continue to see the deconstruction of the idyllic paradise first envisioned by British explorers to the Pacific. *The History of Prince Lee Boo*, while lacking historical accuracy, presents the islanders as complex individuals unable to be categorised simply as 'noble savages' or in need of a superior civilising force. Instead, Lee Boo shows islanders as having agency and willing and able to improve their own societies. Ta'unga's writings, notable for their very existence, provide a very different perspective on missionary enterprises from those written by the first visitors to the Pacific. While Ta'unga agrees with the Christian missions, his account shows the tensions between understanding and respecting Polynesian traditions and his desire to spread the gospel. Finally the legend of Queen Emma undermines the British narrative of white male colonial superiority over the islands. With her mixed heritage as well as her gender, Emma flaunted tradition and presented a new vision of agency in the islands.

Though the earliest island stories of *The Swiss Family Robinson* and British missionaries indicated that islands would prove a paradise, where white men and the gospel would transform heathen spaces into productive outposts of empire, over a hundred years of settlement this hopeful narrative proved unsustainable. Mid-century adventure novelists like Marryat and Ballantyne worked to show the islands as the glories of empire, where boys became men and 'civilised' savages. It was not adventure, however, but the promise of new discoveries that drew Victorian naturalists to the islands and the theories they developed on islands so far from their own would shake Britain's inherent belief in its own religious and cultural supremacy to its core. As other European powers began gaining influence over the small islands of the Pacific and horrible stories of villainous traders and regressively evolving settlers began flooding novels and periodicals, Victorians began to re-evaluate their initial optimism. After moving to Samoa, Robert Louis Stevenson began casting the whites as well as the islanders as traitorous destroyers of paradise. Joseph Conrad indicted European Pacific trade as destroying the best qualities of British men and women and perverting them into 'savages'. These 'savages' were not silent participants but instead their stories contradicted assumed theories of the 'noble savage' or the 'violent islander' in need of outside help and instead portrayed strong and independent peoples of the islands. By the turn of the century, British authors painted a very different portrait of Pacific life from those early stories of stalwart castaways. Instead of heroic adventurers on valiant missions, these tales were dark and disturbing, with the islands acting as highly destructive to the 'civilised' society so prized by British authors. While the early nineteenth century adventurers, explorers and missionaries could not wait to get to the islands, by the early twentieth all they wanted to do was abandon the nightmare they had found – or perhaps created – instead.

The legacy of the dark side of Pacific fiction, which explored the 'savage' nature of island life at the turn of the century, can be seen throughout the twentieth century and beyond in texts as diverse as James A. Michener's *Tales of the South Pacific* (1948), William Golding's *Lord of the Flies* (1954), Scott O'Dell's *Island of the Blue Dolphins* (1960), J. Maarten Troost's *The Sex Lives of Cannibals: Adrift in the Equatorial Pacific* (2004), and even ABC's hit television series *Lost* (2004–10).

Having come a long way from the idyllic colonial paradise typified by *The Swiss Family Robinson* and *Gascoyne*, the Pacific islands continue to hold a place in the Western imagination as places of wonderful but terrible beauty that inspire both admiration and trepidation.

Notes

1. Book length studies of Omai include Alexander, *Omai, Noble Savage*; Clark, *Omai, First Polynesian Ambassador to England*; Connaughton, *Omai: The Prince Who Never Was*; Hetherington, *Cook & Omai: The Cult of the South Seas*; McCormick, *Omai: Pacific Envoy*.
2. The Republic of Palau in the Western Pacific has also been spelled Belau and Pelew.
3. Kokopo, also called Herbertshöhe during the German colonial period, is the capital of East New Britain.
4. *The History* drew largely on Keate's account of Wilson's tale but interpreted the events for an audience of children. For the original account, see Keate, *The Voyage of Captain Henry Wilson*.
5. Peacock, *Lee Boo of Belau*.
6. Fullagar, '"Savages That Are Come Among Us"', 225.
7. *The History of Prince Lee Boo*, 4.
8. Ibid., 26. 'Politeness' had a particular resonance in eighteenth-century society and while a great deal of slippage occurred when using the term, the fact that *The History* applied to the islanders is worthy of note. For more, see Fitzmaurice, 'Changes in the Meanings of Politeness in Eighteenth-Century England'; Klein, 'Politeness and the Interpretation of the British Eighteenth Century'; Langford, 'The Uses of Eighteenth-Century Politeness'; Sweet, 'Topographies of Politeness'; Watts, 'Language and Politeness in Early Eighteenth Century Britain'.
9. *The History of Prince Lee Boo*, 3–4.
10. Ibid., 6.
11. Ibid., 8.
12. Whether or not such deification actually occurred, of course, is a whole other debate perhaps most famously argued in Pacific studies between Marshall Sahlins and Gananath Obeyesekere over Cook's legacy. See Sahlins, *How 'Natives' Think*; Obeyesekere, *The Apotheosis of Captain Cook*.
13. *The History of Prince Lee Boo*, 14. Oroolong is now usually spelled Ulong.
14. Ibid., 10.
15. Ibid., 17.
16. Ibid., 32.
17. Ibid., 38.
18. Ibid., 50.
19. Ibid., 51–2.
20. Ibid., 52–3.
21. Ibid., 77.
22. Ibid., 54.

23. Ibid., 58.
24. Ibid., 76.
25. Ibid., 71.
26. Ibid., 72.
27. Ibid., 84.
28. Ibid., 67.
29. Ibid., 73.
30. Ibid., 95.
31. I discuss in greater detail the missionaries' connection to Pacific agriculture in Chapter 1.
32. *The History of Prince Lee Boo*, 80.
33. Ibid., 98. The italics are in the original text.
34. Ta'unga wrote his accounts in a form of Rarotongan developed by European teachers to represent the oral language phonetically. While his writings are filtered through this system, and by necessity through translation into English, they still offer one of the closest glimpses into Polynesian thought in the nineteenth century. In Rarotongan, Ta'unga meant 'a skilled craftsman or teacher'. See Davis, 'Rarotonga Today'.
35. Hanlon, 'Converting Pasts and Presents', 149.
36. Crocombe and Crocombe, *The Works of Ta'unga*, 6.
37. Ibid., 7.
38. Ibid., 15.
39. Ibid., 16. The original text uses the brackets to indicate alternate spellings.
40. Ibid., 118.
41. Ibid., 37.
42. Ibid., 59.
43. Lange, 'Changes in Rarotongan Attitudes toward Health and Disease', 32.
44. Crocombe and Crocombe, *The Works of Ta'unga*, 37–8.
45. Ibid., 38.
46. Ibid., 63.
47. Ibid., 81.
48. Ibid., 118.
49. Ibid., 90.
50. Ibid.
51. Ibid.
52. Ibid., 78.
53. Ibid., 58.
54. Ibid., 92.
55. Arens, *The Man-Eating Myth*, 32. While Arens is sceptical of the validity of Ta'unga's depictions of cannibalism, Patrick Brantlinger notes that the potential for exaggeration in native accounts does not discredit them as evidence. See Brantlinger, 'Missionaries and Cannibals in Nineteenth-century Fiji', 24–5.
56. 'South Sea Pioneers: Deaths of Mr. and Mrs. Kolbe'. Slightly altered versions of the obituary ran in several Australian papers including 'New Ireland Echo: Death of Mrs. Kolbe'; 'Personal'.
57. See Dutton, *Queen Emma of the South Seas*; Robson, *Queen Emma: The Samoan-American Girl Who Founded an Empire in 19th Century New Guinea*. Robson's account, while more historical, relies on a largely

anecdotal style and unfortunately rarely includes citations of source material. For the miniseries, see Banas, 'Emma: Queen of the South Seas'.

58. Sources record Emma's last name as Coe, Forsayth, Farrell and Kolbe depending on which of her husbands or lovers they choose to highlight. I have chosen to follow in the tradition of previous writers and refer to her by her first name for the purpose of clarity.
59. Baker, 'Queen of the Islands', 7.
60. Blakie, 'Poor Queen Emma', *Western Mail*, 10. This account was also reprinted in other papers, see for example Blakie, 'Poor Queen Emma', *The Mail*.
61. Blakie, 'Poor Queen Emma', 10.
62. Baker, 'Queen of the Islands', 7.
63. Blakie, 'Poor Queen Emma', 10.
64. Baker, 'Queen of the Islands', 7.
65. O'Connor, 'Queen Emma: To the Editor', 19.
66. Robson, *Queen Emma*, 96.
67. Lomas, 'The Early Contact Period in Northern New Ireland (Papua New Guinea)', 3.
68. Robson, *Queen Emma*, 98.
69. Parkinson, *Thirty Years in the South Seas*, xvi.
70. 'Land-Grabbing: Land Laws and Land Owners in German New Guinea', 3.
71. Reid, '"Queen" Emma of Rabaul', 2. These numbers are repeated in Baker's accounts. Robson varies the numbers slightly, recording, 'The chief of the Mortlocks . . . sold her those islands for four axes and ten pounds of tobacco; and it was reported—and never denied—that she acquired the French Islands . . . for £50.' Robson, *Queen Emma*, 123.
72. Baker, 'Queen of the Islands', 7.
73. 'Queen Emma.'
74. For a more detailed description of the Pacific labour trade see Scarr, 'Recruits and Recruiters'; Firth, 'Transformation of the Labour Trade'.
75. Robson, *Queen Emma*, 128.
76. Parkinson, *Thirty Years in the South Seas*, xvi.
77. Samson, *Imperial Benevolence*, 126.
78. Robson, *Queen Emma*, 131.
79. Ibid.
80. Ibid., 135.
81. Ibid., 132. The source of Robson's quotation is not specified.
82. Her previous partner, Tom Farrell, died in 1890.
83. Baker records a sum of £175,000 and places Emma's net worth at £500,000. Similar sums are recorded in Blakie's and Reid's accounts.
84. Robson, *Queen Emma*, 153.
85. 'Engagements', 11.
86. 'Queen Emma', *The Land*, 10. The same account appeared in other papers including 'Queen Emma', *Chronicle and North Coast Advertiser*, 6.

Bibliography

'Engagements'. *Sunday Times*, 9 May 1920.

The History of Prince Lee Boo: Son of Abba Thulle, King of the Pelew Islands: Brought to England by Captain Wilson, Commander of the Antelope, East India Packet, Which Was Wrecked off These Islands, on Her Passage, from China, on the 9th, of August, 1783: With an Account of Lee Boo's Death: And He Was Buried in Rotherhithe Church-Yard, Where a Tomb is Erected in His Memory. London: Plummer and Brewls, 1823.

'Land-Grabbing: Land Laws and Land Owners in German New Guinea'. *The Farmer and the Settler*, 13 February 1920.

'New Ireland Echo: Death of Mrs. Kolbe'. *Northern Star*, 30 July 1913.

'Personal'. *Clarence and Richmond Examiner*, 29 July 1913.

'Queen Emma'. *The Land*, 20 October 1916.

'Queen Emma'. *Chronicle and North Coast Advertiser*, 6 October 1916.

'South Sea Pioneers: Deaths of Mr. and Mrs. Kolbe'. *Sydney Morning Herald*, 26 July 1913, 16.

Alexander, Michael. *Omai, Noble Savage.* London: Harvill Press, 1977.

Alphen, J. J. van. 'Ethnographic Notes on Sumba'. In *The Indonesia Reader*, ed. Tineke Hellwig and Eric Tagliacozzo. 211–13. Durham, NC: Duke University Press, 2009.

Andaya, Barbara Watson and Leonard Y. Andaya. *A History of Malaysia.* London: The Macmillan Press, 1982.

Aravamudan, Srinivas. *Tropicopolitans.* Durham: Durham University Press, 1999.

Arens, William. *The Man-Eating Myth: Anthropology and Anthropophagy.* Oxford: Oxford University Press, 1980.

Asker, D. B. D. 'H.G. Wells and Regressive Evolution'. *Dutch Quarterly Review of Anglo-American Letters* 12, no. 1 (1982): 15–20.

Bailey, Warren and Kirida Bhaopichitr. 'How Important Was Silver? Some Evidence on Exchange Rate Fluctuations and Stock Returns in Colonial-Era Asia'. *The Journal of Business* 77, no. 1 (2004): 137–73.

Baker, Sidney J. 'Queen of the Islands'. *The Sydney Morning Herald*, 19 September 1953.

Ballantyne, R. M. *The Coral Island.* London: Penguin Books, 1995.

——. *Gascoyne, the Sandal-wood Trader.* San Antonio: The Vision Forum, 2009.

——. *The Island Queen: Dethroned by Fire and Water.* San Antonio: The Vision Forum, 2009.

Banas, John. 'Emma: Queen of the South Seas'. Anro Productions, 1988.

Barker, Francis, Peter Hulme and Margaret Iversen. *Cannibalism and the Colonial World*. Cambridge: Cambridge University Press, 1998.

Baxter, Katherine Isobel and Richard J. Hand, ed. *Joseph Conrad and the Performing Arts*. Farnham: Ashgate, 2009.

Beaglehole, J. C. *The Exploration of the Pacific*. 3rd edn Stanford: Stanford University Press, 1966.

Beer, Gillian and George Levine. *Darwin's Plots: Evolutionary Narrative in Darwin, George Eliot and Nineteenth-Century Fiction*. Cambridge: Cambridge University Press, 2000.

Blakie, George. 'Poor Queen Emma'. *The Mail*, 23 October 1954, 10–11.

——. 'Poor Queen Emma'. *Western Mail*, 21 October 1954, 10–11.

Bolyanatz, Alexander H. *Pacific Romanticism: Tahiti and the European Imagination*. Westport: Praeger, 2004.

Bradley, Ian. *The Call to Seriousness: The Evangelical Impact on the Victorians*. New York: Macmillan, 1976.

Brantlinger, Patrick. *Dark Vanishings: Discourse on the Extinction of Primitive Races, 1800–1930*. Ithaca: Cornell University Press, 2003.

——. 'Missionaries and Cannibals in Nineteenth-century Fiji'. *History & Anthropology* 17, no. 1 (2006): 21–38.

——. *Rule of Darkness: British Literature and Imperialism, 1830–1914*. Ithaca: Cornell University Press, 1988.

Bristow, Joseph. *Empire Boys: Adventures in a Man's World*. London: Harper Collins Academic, 1991.

Brown, J. Macmillan. 'Melanesia'. In *Peoples and Problems of the Pacific*. 1–87. London: Unwin, 1927.

——. 'The Solomon Islands as They Are'. In *Peoples and Problems of the Pacific*. 9–16. London: Unwin, 1927.

Buckton, Oliver S. *Cruising with Robert Louis Stevenson: Travel, Narrative, and the Colonial Body*. Athens: Ohio University Press, 2007.

Campbell, I. C. *A History of the Pacific Islands*. Berkeley: University of California Press, 1989.

Campbell, John. *Maritime Discovery and Christian Missions, Considered in their Mutual Relations*. London: John Snow, 1840.

Carlyle, Thomas. *Thomas Carlyle: Selected Writings*. London: Penguin Books, 1986.

Christensen, Allan C. 'Textual Voyages of Self-Formation and Liberation: Darwin's "The Voyage of the Beagle" and Dana's "Two Years before the Mast"'. *Papers on Language and Literature: A Journal for Scholars and Critics of Language and Literature* 46, no. 3 (2010): 243–90.

Clark, Blake. *Omai, First Polynesian Ambassador to England; The True Story of his Voyage There in 1774 with Captain Cook; Of how he was Feted by Fanny Burney, Approved by Samuel Johnson, Entertained by Mrs. Thrale & Lord Sandwich, and Painted by Sir Joshua Reynolds*. Honolulu: University of Hawaii Press, 1969.

Clark, Timothy. *The Cambridge Introduction to Literature and the Environment*. Cambridge: Cambridge University Press, 2011.

Clemens, Florence. 'Conrad's Malaysia'. *College English* 2, no. 4 (1941): 338–46.

Clifford, Hugh. 'A Journey through the Malay States of Trengganu and Kelantan'. *The Geographical Journal* 9, no. 1 (1897): 1–37.

Colley, Ann C. 'Robert Louis Stevenson's South Seas Crossings'. *Studies in English Literature, 1500–1900* 48, no. 4 (2008): 871–84.
Connaughton, R. M. *Omai: The Prince Who Never Was*. London: Timewell Press, 2005.
Conrad, Joseph. 'Because of the Dollars'. In *The Complete Short Fiction of Joseph Conrad*, ed. Samuel Hynes. Hopewell, NJ: Ecco Press, 1992.
——. 'Freya of the Seven Isles: A Story of Shallow Waters'. In *The Complete Short Fiction of Joseph Conrad*, ed. Samuel Hynes. 204–70. Hopewell, NJ: Ecco Press, 1992.
——. *Heart of Darkness*. 3rd edn New York: W.W. Norton & Company, 1988.
Cook, James. *The Journals*, ed. Philip Edwards. London: Penguin Books, 2003.
Cousins, George. *The Story of the South Seas: Written for Young People*. London: John Snow, 1894.
Craib, John L. 'Micronesian Prehistory: An Archeological Overview'. *Science* 219, no. 4587 (1983): 922–7.
Crane, Kylie. *Myths of Wilderness in Contemporary Narratives: Environmental Postcolonialism in Australia and Canada*. New York: Palgrave Macmillan, 2012.
Crawfurd, John. 'On Cannibalism in Relation to Ethnology'. *Transactions of the Ethnological Society of London* 4 (1866): 105–24.
Crocombe, R. G. and Marjorie Crocombe. *The Works of Ta'unga: Records of a Polynesian Traveller in the South Seas, 1833–1896*. Honolulu: University of Hawaii Press, 1968.
Daiches, David. *Robert Louis Stevenson and His World*. London: Thames and Hudson, 1973.
Darton, F. J. Harvey. *Children's Books in England*. 3rd edn Cambridge: Cambridge University Press, 1982.
Darwin, Charles. *The Descent of Man and Selection in Relation to Sex*. New York: P.F. Collier, 1901.
——. *The Voyage of the Beagle*. New York: P.F. Collier & Son, 1909.
——. *On the Origin of the Species*. London: Penguin Books, 2009.
Davis, T. R. A. 'Rarotonga Today'. *The Journal of the Polynesian Society* 56, no. 2 (1947): 197–218.
Dawson, Graham. 'The Imperial Adventure Hero and British Masculinity: The Imagining of Sir Henry Havelock'. In *Gender and Colonialism*, ed. Timothy P. Foley, Lionel Pilkington, Sean Ryder, and Elizabeth Tilley. 45–59. Galway: Galway University Press, 1995.
Defoe, Daniel. *Robinson Crusoe and the Further Adventures of Robinson Crusoe*. London: Bloomsbury, 2015.
Dening, Greg. *Islands and Beaches: Discourse on a Silent Land, Marquesas 1774–1880*. Honolulu: The University of Hawaii Press, 1980.
Diderot, Denis. *Ramaeu's Nephew and Other Works*. Trans. Jacques Barzun and Ralph H. Bowen. Indianapolis: Hackett, 2001.
Dodge, Ernest S. *Islands and Empires: Western Impact on the Pacific and East Asia*. Minneapolis: Minnesota University Press, 1976.
Dutheil, Martine Hennard. 'The Representation of the Cannibal in Ballantyne's "The Coral Island": Colonial Anxieties in Victorian Popular Fiction'. *College Literature* 28, no. 1 (2001): 105–22.
Dutton, Geoffrey. *Queen Emma of the South Seas: A Novel*. New York: St. Martin's Press, 1997.

Earl, George. 'Pirates on the Java Sea'. In *The Indonesia Reader*, ed. Tineke Hellwig and Eric Tagliacozzo. 173–6. Durham, NC: Duke University Press, 2009.

Ebbatson, Roger and Ann Donahue. *An Imaginary England: Nation, Landscape and Literature, 1840–1920*. Aldershot: Ashgate, 2005.

Edmond, Rod. *Representing the South Pacific: Colonial Discourse from Cook to Gauguin*. Cambridge: Cambridge University Press, 1997.

Elbert, Monika M. '"Freya of the Seven Isles" and the Heart of Male Darkness'. *Conradiana: A Journal of Joseph Conrad* 26, no. 1 (1994): 35–55.

Ellis, William. *Polynesian Researches: During a Residence of Nearly Six Years in the South Sea Islands; Including Descriptions of the Natural History and Scenery of the Islands—with Remarks on the History, Mythology, Traditions, Government, Arts, Manners, and Customs of the Inhabitants*. 2 vols, vol. 1. London: Dawsons of Pall Mall, 1967.

——. *Polynesian Researches: During a Residence of Nearly Six Years in the South Sea Islands; Including Descriptions of the Natural History and Scenery of the Islands—with Remarks on the History, Mythology, Traditions, Government, Arts, Manners, and Customs of the Inhabitants*. 2 vols, vol. 2. London: Dawsons of Pall Mall, 1967.

Ellison, Joseph W. *Tusitala of the South Seas: The Story of Robert Louis Stevenson's Life in the South Pacific*. New York: Hastings House, 1953.

Etherington, Norman. 'Ellis, William (1794–1872)'. In *Oxford Dictionary of National Biography*, ed. Lawrence Goldman. Oxford: Oxford University Press, 2004.

Fernando, Lloyd. 'Cornad's Eastern Expatriates: A New Version of His Outcasts'. In *Joseph Conrad: Third World Perspectives*, ed. Robert D. Hamner. 59–78. Washington, DC: Three Continents Press, 1990.

Firth, Stewart. 'The Transformation of the Labour Trade in German New Guinea, 1899–1914'. *The Journal of Pacific History* 11, no. 1 (1976): 51–65.

Fitzmaurice, Susan. 'Changes in the Meanings of Politeness in Eighteenth-Century England: Discourse Analysis and Historical Evidence'. In *Historical (Im)Politeness*, ed. Jonathan Culpeper, Dániel Z. Kádár and Jim O'Driscoll. 87–115. Bern, Switzerland: Peter Lang, 2010.

Friedlaender, Jonathan S., ed. *Genes, Language, & Culture History in the Southwest Pacific*. Oxford: Oxford University Press, 2007.

Fulford, Tim and Peter J. Kitson, eds. *Romanticism and Colonialism: Writing and Empire, 1780–1830*. Cambridge: Cambridge University Press, 1998.

Fullagar, Kate. '"Savages that are come among us": Mai, Bennelong, and British Imperial Culture, 1774–1795'. *The Eighteenth Century* 49, no. 3 (2008): 211–37.

Furness, William Henry, 3rd. 'Glimpses of Borneo'. *Proceedings of the American Philosophical Society* 35, no. 153 (1896): 309–20.

Garnett, Richard D. C. 'Garnett, Edward William (1868–1937)'. In *Oxford Dictionary of National Biography*, ed. H. C. G. Matthew and Brian Harrison. Oxford: Oxford University Press, 2004.

Gersdorf, Catrin and Sylvia Mayer, eds. *Nature in Literary and Cultural Studies: Transatlantic Conversations on Ecocriticism*. Amsterdam: Rodopi, 2006.

Girouard, Mark. *The Return to Camelot: Chivalry and the English Gentleman*. New Haven: Yale University Press, 1981.

Glendening, John. '"Green Confusion": Evolution and Entanglement in H.G. Wells's *The Island of Dr. Moreau*'. *Victorian Literature and Culture* 30, no. 2 (2002): 571–97.

Grafton Elliot, Smith. 'The Place of Thomas Henry Huxley in Anthropology'. *The Journal of the Royal Anthropological Institute of Great Britain and Ireland* 65 (1935): 199–204.

Graver, Lawrence. *Conrad's Short Fiction*. Berkeley: University of California Press, 1969.

Green, Martin. *The Robinson Crusoe Story*. University Park: The Pennsylvania State University Press, 1990.

Grove, Richard H. *Green Imperialism: Colonial Expansion, Tropical Island Edens and the Origins of Environmentalism, 1600–1860*. Cambridge: Cambridge University Press, 1995.

Guest, Harriet. *Empire, Barbarism, and Civilization: Captain Cook, William Hodges, and the Return to the Pacific*. Cambridge: Cambridge University Press, 2007.

Gunson, Neil. *Messengers of Grace: Evangelical Missionaries in the South Seas 1797–1860*. Melbourne: Oxford University Press, 1978.

Hampston, Robert. '"Because of the Dollars" and the Already Written'. *Conradiana: A Journal of Joseph Conrad Studies* 34, no. 1–2 (2002): 95–106.

Hanlon, David. 'Converting Pasts and Presents: Reflections on Histories of Missionary Enterprises in the Pacific'. In *Pacific Lives, Pacific Places: Bursting Boundaries in Pacific History*, ed. Brij V. Lal and Peter Hempenstall. 143–54. Canberra: Coombs Academic Publishing, 2001.

Hannabuss, Stuart. 'Ballantyne's Message of Empire'. In *Imperialism and Juvenile Literature*, ed. Jeffrey Richards. Manchester: Manchester University Press, 1989.

——. 'Islands as Metaphors'. *Universities Quarterly* 38, no. 1 (1983–4): 70–82.

Hayes, Timothy S. 'Colonialism in R.L. Stevenson's South Seas Fiction: "Child's Play" in the Pacific'. *English Literature in Transition (1880–1920)* 52, no. 2 (2009): 160–81.

Haynes, R. D. 'The Unholy Alliance of Science in *The Island of Doctor Moreau*'. *The Wellsian: The Journal of the H. G. Wells Society* 11 (1988): 13–24.

Hetherington, Michelle. *Cook & Omai: The Cult of the South Seas*. Canberra: National Library of Australia, 2001.

Hillier, Robert. *The South Seas Fiction of Robert Louis Stevenson*. New York: P. Lang, 1989.

Historical Section of the Foreign Office. *Dutch and British Possessions*. Peace Handbooks. Vol. 14, London: H.M. Stationary Office, 1973.

Horsman, Alan. *The Victorian Novel*. Oxford: Clarendon Press, 1990.

Howe, K. R. *Where the Waves Fall: A New South Sea Islands History from First Settlement to Colonial Rule*. Pacific Island Monograph Series. Honolulu: University of Hawaii Press, 1984.

Howse, Derek, ed. *The Background to Discovery: Pacific Exploration from Dampier to Cook*. Cambridge: Cambridge University Press, 1990.

Huff, W. G. 'Monetization and Financial Development in Southeast Asia before the Second World War'. *The Economic History Review* 56, no. 2 (2003): 300–45.

Huggan, Graham. *Australian Literature: Postcolonialism, Racism, Transnationalism*. Oxford: Oxford University Press, 2007.

Huxley, Julian, ed. *T. H. Huxley's Diary of the Voyage of H.M.S. Rattlesnake.* Garden City, NY: Doubleday, 1936.

Huxley, T. H. *Science and Christian Tradition.* New York: D. Appleton and Company, 1913.

Hyma, Albert. *A History of the Dutch in the Far East.* Ann Arbor: George Wahr Publishing, 1953.

Jackson, Kimberley. 'Vivisected Language in H. G. Wells' *The Island of Doctor Moreau*'. *Wellsian: The Journal of the H. G. Wells Society* 29 (2006): 20–36.

Johnston, Anna. *Missionary Writing and Empire, 1800–1860.* Cambridge: Cambridge University Press, 2003.

Jolly, Roslyn. 'Introduction'. In *South Sea Tales.* Oxford: Oxford University Press, 2008.

——. 'Note on the Texts'. In *South Sea Tales.* xxxiv. Oxford: Oxford University Press, 1996.

——. *Robert Louis Stevenson in the Pacific: Travel, Empire, and the Author's Profession.* Farnham: Ashgate, 2009.

——. 'South Sea Gothic: Pierre Loti and Robert Louis Stevenson'. *English Literature in Transition (1880–1920)* 47, no. 1 (2004): 28–49.

Karl, Fredrick R. and Laurence Davies, eds. *The Collected Letters of Joseph Conrad.* Vol. 4. Cambridge: Cambridge University Press, 1996.

Keate, George. *The Voyage of Captain Henry Wilson, Principally Relating to His Shipwreck on the Pelew Island Including the History of Prince Lee Boo* [in English]. Windsor, VT: Charles Spear, 1808.

Kemp, Peter. *H.G. Wells and the Culminating Ape: Biological Themes and Imaginative Obsessions.* London: The Macmillan Press, 1982.

Kennedy, J. *A History of Malaysia: A.D. 1400–1959.* New York: St. Martin's Press, 1962.

Keown, Michelle. *Pacific Islands Writing: The Postcolonial Literatures of Aotearoa/New Zealand and Oceania.* Oxford: Oxford University Press, 2007.

Kestner, Joseph. *Masculinities in British Adventure Fiction, 1880–1915.* Burlington, VT: Ashgate, 2010.

——. *Sherlock's Men: Masculinity, Conan Doyle, and Cultural History.* Aldershot: Ashgate, 1997.

Kirch, P. V. and M. I. Weisler. 'Archaeology in the Pacific Islands: An Appraisal of Recent Research'. *Journal of Archaeological Research* 2, no. 4 (1994): 285–328.

Kirch, Patrick V. 'Peopling of the Pacific: A Holistic Anthropological Perspective'. *Annual Review of Anthropology* 39 (2010): 131–48.

Kirch, Patrick V. and Jennifer G. Kahn. 'Advances in Polynesian Prehistory: A Review and Assessment of the Past Decade (1993–2004)'. *Journal of Archaeological Research* 15, no. 3 (2007): 191–238.

Kirch, Patrick Vinton, ed. *Island Societies: Archaeological Approaches to Evolution and Transformation.* Cambridge: Cambridge University Press, 2009.

Klein, Lawrence E. 'Politeness and the Interpretation of the British Eighteenth Century'. *The Historical Journal* 45, no. 4 (2002): 869–98.

Krieger, Michael J. *Conversations with the Cannibals: The End of the Old South Pacific.* Hopewell, NJ: Ecco Press, 1994.

Kutzer, M. Daphne. *Empire's Children: Empire and Imperialism in Classic British Children's Books.* New York: Garland Publishing, Inc, 2000.

Lamb, Jonathan. *Preserving the Self in the South Seas*. London: Chicago University Press, 2001.

Lange, Raeburn. 'Changes in Rarotongan Attitudes toward Health and Disease: Historical Factors in the Development of a Mid-Twentieth-Century Understanding'. *Pacific Studies* 10, no. 1 (1986): 29–53.

Langford, Paul. 'The Uses of Eighteenth-Century Politeness'. *Transactions of the Royal Historical Society* 12 (2002): 311–31.

Lansbury, Coral. *The Old Brown Dog: Women, Workers, and Vivisection in Edwardian England*. Madison: University of Wisconsin Press, 1985.

Lansdown, Richard, ed. *Strangers in the South Seas: The Idea of the Pacific in Western Thought*. Honolulu: University of Hawaii Press, 2006.

Larahee, Mark D. 'Territorial Vision and Revision in "Freya of the Seven Isles"'. In *Joseph Conrad: The Short Fiction*, ed. Daphna Erdinast-Vulcan, Allan H. Simmons and J. H. Stape. 96–110. Amsterdam: Rodopi, 2004.

Lee, Michael Parrish. 'Reading Meat in H. G. Wells'. *Studies in the Novel* 42, no. 3 (2010): 249–68.

Lestringant, Frank. *Cannibals: The Discovery and Representation of the Cannibal from Columbus to Jules Verne*. Berkeley: The University of California Press, 1997.

Levine, George. 'Reflections on Darwin and Darwinizing'. *Victorian Studies* 51, no. 2 (2009): 223–45.

Levine, Philippa, ed. *Gender and Empire*. Oxford: Oxford University Press, 2004.

Lilley, Ian, ed. *Archaeology of Oceania: Australia and the Pacific Islands*. Malden, MA: Blackwell Publishing, 2006.

Lincoln, Margaret, ed. *Science and Exploration: European Voyages to the Southern Oceans in the 18th Century*. Woodbridge: Boydell Press, 2001.

Lomas, Peter. 'The Early Contact Period in Northern New Ireland (Papua New Guinea): From Wild Frontier to Plantation Economy'. *Ethnohistory* 28, no. 1 (1981): 1–21.

Loomba, Ania. *Colonialism/Postcolonialism*. London: Routledge, 1998.

Loxley, Diana. *Problematic Shores: The Literature of Islands*. New York: St. Martin's Press, 1990.

M, W. J. 'Cannibalism in Queensland'. *Science* 10, no. 240 (1899): 155–6.

MacKenzie, John M. *Propaganda and Empire: The Manipulation of British Public Opinion, 1880–1960*. Manchester: Manchester University Press, 1984.

Maher, Susan Naramore. 'Recasting Crusoe: Fredrick Marryat, R.M. Ballantyne and the Nineteenth-Century Robinsonade'. *Children's Literature Association Quarterly* 13, no. 4 (1988): 169–75.

Mangan, J. A. and James Walvin, eds. *Manliness and Morality: Middle-class Masculinity in Britain and America*. New York: St. Martin's Press, 1987.

Marryat, Fredrick. *Masterman Ready*. London: Bloomsbury Books, 1994.

Matisoo-Smith, E., J. H. Robins and R. C. Green. 'Origins and Dispersals of Pacific Peoples: Evidence from mtDNA Phylogenies of the Pacific Rat'. *Proceedings of the National Academy of Sciences of the United States of America* 101, no. 24 (2004): 9167–72.

Maude, H. E. 'Beachcombers and Castaways'. *The Journal of the Polynesian Society* 73, no. 3 (1964): 254–93.

McCormick, E. H. *Omai: Pacific Envoy*. Auckland: Auckland University Press and Oxford University Press, 1977.

McCulloch, Fiona. '"The Broken Telescope": Misrepresentation in "The Coral Island"'. *Children's Literature Association Quarterly* 25, no. 3 (2000): 137–45.
McCusker, Maeve and Anthony Soares, eds. *Islanded Identities: Constructions of Postcolonial Cultural Insularity*. Amsterdam: Rodopi, 2011.
McGaw, Martha Mary. *Stevenson in Hawaii*. Honolulu: University of Hawaii Press, 1995.
McLean, Steven. 'Animals, Language and Degeneration in "The Island of Dr. Moreau"'. In *H.G. Wells: Interdisciplinary Essays*. 25–33. Aldershot: Cambridge Scholars, 2008.
Michel-Michot, Paulette. 'The Myth of Innocence: Robinson Crusoe, "The Coral Island," and "Lord of the Flies"'. In *William Golding: The Sound of Silence*. 35–44. Liége: University of Liége, 1991.
Miller, J. Hillis. 'Reading "The Swiss Family Robinson" as Virtual Reality'. In *Children's Literature: New Approaches*. 78–92. Basingstoke: Palgrave Macmillan, 2004.
Molineux, Catherine. *Faces of Perfect Ebony: Encountering Atlantic Slavery in Imperial Britain*. Cambridge, MA: Harvard University Press, 2012.
Moore, Clive. *New Guinea: Crossing Boundaries and History*. Honolulu: University of Hawaii Press, 2003.
Morris, Margaretta. 'Race and Custom in the Malay Archipelago'. *Journal of the American Oriental Society* 27 (1906): 195–216.
Morton, Peter. *Vital Science: Biology and the Literary Imagination 1860–1900*. Boston: Unwin, 1984.
Moser, Thomas C. *Joseph Conrad: Achievement and Decline*. Cambridge, MA: Harvard University Press, 1957.
Munich, Adrienne Auslander. 'Queen Victoria, Empire, and Excess'. *Tulsa Studies in Women's Literature* 6, no. 2 (1987): 265–81.
Nunn, Patrick D. *Climate, Environment, and Society in the Pacific during the Last Millennium*. Amsterdam: Elsevier Science, 2007.
Nussbaum, Felicity A. *Torrid Zones: Maternity, Sexuality, and Empire in Eighteenth-Century English Narratives*. Baltimore: Johns Hopkins University Press, 1995.
Obeyesekere, Gananath. *The Apotheosis of Captain Cook: European Mythmaking in the Pacific*. Princeton: Princeton University Press, 1992.
——. *Cannibal Talk: The Man-Eating Myth and Human Sacrifice in the South Seas*. Berkeley: California University Press, 2005.
O'Connor, D. 'Queen Emma: To the Editor'. *The Brisbane Courier*, 16 August 1911.
Oliver, Douglas L. *Oceania: The Native Cultures of Australia and the Pacific Islands*. 2 vols, vol. 1. Honolulu: University of Hawaii Press, 1989.
——. *The Pacific Islands*. Honolulu: University of Hawaii Press, 1989.
Parham, John, ed. *The Environmental Tradition in Literature*. Aldershot: Ashgate, 2002.
Parkinson, Richard. *Thirty Years in the South Seas: Land and People, Customs and Traditions in the Bismarck Archipelago and on the German Solomon Islands*. Trans. K. John Dennison. Ed. J. Peter White. Sydney: Sydney University Press, 2010.
Peacock, Daniel J. *Lee Boo of Belau*. Honolulu: University of Hawaii Press, 1987.
Philmus, Robert M. 'The Satiric Ambivalence of "The Island of Doctor Moreau"'. *Science Fiction Studies* 8, no. 1 (1981): 2–11.

Pratt, Mary Louise. *Imperial Eyes: Travel Writing and Transculturation*. New York: Routledge, 2008.

Prendergast, Christopher. 'The World Republic of Letters'. In *Debating World Literature*, ed. Christopher Prendergast. 1–25. London: Verso, 2004.

Prout, Ebenezer. *Memoirs of the Life of the Rev. John Williams: Missionary to Polynesia*. New York: Allen, Morrill & Wardwell, 1843.

Pursell, Andrew. '"People Don't Die Here Sooner Than in Europe": Conrad, Australia and Contexts of Race and Place in "The Planter of Malata"'. *Review of English Studies* 62, no. 253 (2011): 113–25.

Quayle, Eric. *Ballantyne the Brave: A Victorian Writer and His Family*. Chester Springs: Dufour Editions, 1967.

Ravenscroft, Alison. *The Postcolonial Eye: White Australian Desire and the Visual Field of Race*. Farnham: Ashgate, 2013.

Redfern, Nick. 'Abjection and Evolution in *The Island of Dr. Moreau*'. *Wellsian: The Journal of the H.G. Wells Society* 27 (2004): 37–47.

Reed, John R. *The Natural History of H.G. Wells*. Athens: Ohio University Press, 1982.

Reid, Frank. '"Queen" Emma of Rabaul'. *The Argus*, 4 April 1931.

Rennie, Neil. 'The Palm-Tree Shall Grow'. In *Far-Fetched Facts: The Literature of Travel and the Idea of the South Seas*. 198–222. Oxford: Clarendon Press, 1995.

Robequain, Charles. *Malaya, Indonesia, Borneo, and the Philippines*. London: Longmans, 1958.

Roberts, Andrew Michael. *Conrad and Masculinity*. New York: Palgrave, 2000.

Robson, R. W. *Queen Emma: The Samoan-American Girl Who Founded an Empire in 19th Century New Guinea*. Sydney: Pacific Publications, 1979.

Roper, Michael and John Tosh, eds. *Manful Assertions: Masculinities in Britain since 1800*. London: Routledge, 1991.

Rose, Jacqueline. *The Case of Peter Pan or the Impossibility of Children's Fiction*. London: Macmillan, 1984.

Ruskin, John. 'Lilies: Of Queens' Gardens'. In *Essays, English and American*, ed. Charles W. Eliot. New York: P. F. Collier & Son 1910.

Sahlins, Marshall. 'Cannibalism: An Exchange'. *New York Review of Books* 26, no. 4 (1979): 47.

——. *How 'Natives' Think: About Captain Cook, For Example*. Chicago: University of Chicago Press, 1995.

Said, Edward W. *Culture and Imperialism*. New York: Alfred A. Knopf, 1993.

Salmond, Anne. *The Trial of the Cannibal Dog: The Remarkable Story of Captain Cook's Encounters in the South Seas*. New Haven: Yale University Press, 2003.

Samson, Jane. *British Imperial Strategies in the Pacific, 1750–1900*. The Pacific World. Vol. 8, Aldershot: Ashgate, 2003.

——. *Imperial Benevolence: Making British Authority in the Pacific Islands*. Honolulu: University of Hawaii Press, 1998.

Scarr, Deryck. *A History of the Pacific Islands: Passages through Tropical Time*. Richmond: Curzon Press, 2001.

——. 'Recruits and Recruiters: A Portrait of the Pacific Islands Labour Trade'. *The Journal of Pacific History* 2 (1967): 5–24.

Seeyle, John. 'Introduction'. In *The Swiss Family Robinson*. vii–xxi. London: Penguin, 2007.

Siegl, Karin. *The Robinsonade Tradition in Robert Michael Ballantyne's 'The Coral Island' and William Golding's 'The Lord of the Flies'*. Salzburg University Studies. Lewiston, NY: E. Mellen Press, 1996.

Sivasundaram, Sujit. *Nature and the Godly Empire: Science and Evangelical Mission in the Pacific, 1795–1850*. Cambridge: Cambridge University Press, 2005.

Skeat, W. W. 'The Wild Tribes of the Malay Peninsula'. *The Journal of the Anthropological Institute of Great Britain and Ireland* 32 (1902): 124–41.

Skeat, Walter. 'Malay Spiritualism'. *Folklore* 13, no. 2 (1902): 134–65.

Smith, Vanessa. *Literary Culture and the Pacific: Nineteenth-Century Textual Encounters*. Cambridge: Cambridge University Press, 2005.

——. *Intimate Strangers: Friendship, Exchange, and Pacific Encounters*. Cambridge: Cambridge University Press, 2010.

St. Clair, David J. 'American Trade Dollars in Nineteenth-Century China'. In *Pacific Centuries: Pacific and Pacific Rim History Since the Sixteenth Century*, ed. Dennis Owen Flynn, Lionel Frost and A. J. H. Latham. 152–70. London: Routledge, 1999.

Stevens, Laura. *The Poor Indians: British Missionaries, Native Americans, and Colonial Sensibility*. Philadelphia: University of Pennsylvania Press, 2004.

Stevenson, Robert Louis. 'The Beach of Falesá'. In *South Sea Tales*, ed. Roslyn Jolly. Oxford: Oxford University Press, 2008.

——. *Vailima Letters: Being Correspondence Addressed by Robert Louis Stevenson to Sidney Colvin*. 2 vols, vol. 2. New York: Greenwood Press, 1969.

——. *Vailima Letters: Being Correspondence Addressed by Robert Louis Stevenson to Sidney Colvin*. 2 vols, vol. 1. New York: Greenwood Press, 1969.

Stewart, Paul D. *Galapagos: The Islands that Changed the World*. New Haven: Yale University Press, 2007.

Sulloway, Frank J. 'Darwin's Conversion: The Beagle Voyage and Its Aftermath'. *Journal of the History of Biology* 15, no. 3 (1982): 325–96.

Sunderland, J. P and A. Buzzacott. *Mission Life in the Islands of the Pacific: Being a Narrative of the Life and Labours of the Rev. A. Buzzacott*. London: John Snow, 1866.

Sussman, Herbert. *Masculine Identities: The History and Meanings of Manliness*. Santa Barbara: Praeger, 2012.

Sweet, R. H. 'Topographies of Politeness'. *Transactions of the Royal Historical Society* 12 (2002): 355–74.

Tallmadge, John. 'From Chronicle to Quest: The Shaping of Darwin's "Voyage of the Beagle"'. *Victorian Studies* 23, no. 3 (1980): 325–45.

Tarling, Nicholas. *Anglo-Dutch Rivalry in the Malay World: 1780–1824*. Cambridge: Cambridge University Press, 1962.

Thomas, Frank R. 'The Precontact Period'. In *The Pacific Islands: Environment & Society*, ed. Moshe Rapaport. 121–33. Honolulu: Bess Press, 1999.

Thomas, Nicholas. *Islanders: The Pacific in the Age of Empire*. New Haven: Yale University Press, 2010.

Thurn, Everard F. 'Presidential Address. On the Thoughts of South Sea Islanders'. *The Journal of the Royal Anthropological Institute of Great Britain and Ireland* 51 (1921): 12–24.

Tosh, John. *A Man's Place: Masculinity and the Middle-Class Home in Victorian England*. New Haven: Yale University Press, 1999.

Tulloch, Graham. 'Stevenson and Islands: Scotland and the South Pacific'. In *Robert Louis Stevenson Reconsidered: New Critical Perspectives*, ed. William B. Jones, Jr. Jefferson, NC: McFarland, 2003.

Turner, Jennifer. '"Petticoats" and "Sea Business": Women Characters in Conrad's Edwardian Short Stories'. In *Joseph Conrad: The Short Fiction*, ed. Daphna Erdinast-Vulcan, Allan H. Simmons and J. H. Stape. 142–56. Amsterdam: Rodopi, 2004.

Vason, George and James Orange. *Life of the Late George Vason of Nottingham: One of the Troop of Missionaries First Sent to the South Sea Islands by the London Missionary Society in the Ship Duff, Captain Wilson, 1796: with a Preliminary Essay on the South Sea Islands*. London: John Snow, 1840.

Vint, Sherryl. 'Animals and Animality from the Island of Moreau to the Uplift Universe'. *The Yearbook of English Studies* 37, no. 2 (2007): 85–102.

Wallace, Alfred Russell. 'On the Physical Geography of the Malay Archipelago'. *Journal of the Royal Geographical Society of London* 33 (1863): 217–34.

Ward, John M. *British Policy in the South Pacific*. Westport: Greenwood Press, 1976.

Watt, W. 'Cannibalism as Practised on Tanna, New Hebrides'. *The Journal of the Polynesian Society* 4, no. 4 (1895): 226–30.

Watts, Richard J. 'Language and Politeness in Early Eighteenth Century Britain'. *Pragmatics: Quarterly Publication of the International Pragmatics Association* 9, no. 1 (1999): 5–20.

Webb, Jessica. 'Corrupting Boyhood in Didactic Children's Literature: Marryat, Ballantyne and Kingsley'. *Atenea* 27, no. 2 (2007): 81–93.

Webster, Anthony. *Gentleman Capitalists: British Imperialism in Southeast Asia 1770–1890* London: Tauris Academic Studies, 1998.

Wells, H. G. 'Biographical Note'. In *The Island of Dr. Moreau*, ed. Patrick Parrinder. vii–xii. London: Penguin Books, 2005.

——. *The Island of Doctor Moreau*. London: Penguin Books, 2005.

——. 'Zoological Retrogression'. In *The Fin de Siècle: A Reader in Cultural History, c.1880–1900*, ed. Sally Ledger and Roger Luckhurst. 5–12. Oxford: Oxford University Press, 2000.

Williams, John. *A Narrative of Missionary Enterprises in the South Seas: With Remarks upon the Natural History of the Islands, Origin, Languages, Traditions, and Usages of the Inhabitants*. London: John Snow, 1837.

Wilson, Kathleen. *The Island Race: Englishness, Empire and Gender in the Eighteenth Century*. London: Routledge, 2003.

Wyss, Hilary E. *Writing Indians: Literacy, Christianity, and Native Community in Early America*. Amherst: University of Massachusetts Press, 2000.

Wyss, Johann. *The Swiss Family Robinson*. Trans. Mary Godwin. Ed. John Seeyle. London: Penguin Books, 2007.

——. *The Swiss Family Robinson*. Trans. William H. G. Kingston. Ed. John Scieska. London: Penguin Books, 2009.